D1565076

STUBBORN CHILD

STUBBORN CHILD

Mark Devlin

ATHENEUM

New York

1985

Library of Congress Cataloging in Publication Data

Devlin, Mark.
    Stubborn child.

    1. Devlin, Mark.   2. Juvenile delinquents—United
States—Biography. 3. Problem children—United States—
Biography.   I. Title.
HV9104.D39   1985   365'.6'0924 [B]   84-45053
ISBN 0-689-11476-1

Published simultaneously in Canada by McClelland and Stewart Ltd.
Composition by Westchester Book Composition, Inc.,
Yorktown Heights, New York
Manufactured by Fairfield Graphics, Fairfield, Pennsylvania
Designed by Kathleen Carey
First Printing April 1985
Second Printing August 1985

This book is dedicated to Mark Zanger. It is also dedicated to my children. But most of all, I want to dedicate this book to Stubborn Children and to stubbornness, to those who absolutely refuse to give in to those things they do not believe in.

When I wish to cry, I cannot.
Sometimes I cry without wanting to.

REUBÉN DARÍO

Contents

Prologue

IN THE YEAR OF OUR LORD 1654, on the twenty-second of August, an act was passed by the House of Deputies of the Massachusetts Bay in New England. It provided for the punishment of Stubborn Children by "corporall punishment by whipping or otherwise" if "it appears by too much experience that divers children and servants doe behave themselves too disrespectfully, disobediently, and disorderly toward their parents, masters and gouvenours."

The next reference to Stubborn Children is found in the Provision Statute, 1699–1700, which permitted the courts to commit offenders to houses of correction. The law stated "Stubborn Children, runaways, common nightwalkers, both male and female, common railers and brawlers, persons who with disorderly act or language accost or annoy persons of the opposite sex, lewd and lascivious persons in speech or behaviour, idle and disorderly persons, prostitutes, disturbers of the peace, keepers of noisy and disorderly houses, and persons guilty of indecent exposure, may be punished by imprisonment in a jail or House of Correction for not more than six months, a fine, or by both such fine and imprisonment."

When the Constitution of Massachusetts was adopted in 1780, it provided, and continued to provide, that "All such laws which have heretofore been adopted, used and approved, in the prov-

3

ince, colony, or State of Massachusetts Bay, and usually practiced on in the courts of law, shall still remain and be in full force until altered or repealed by the legislators; such part only excepted as are repugnant to the rights and liberties contained in this Constitution."

In the year of our Lord 1956, it was still a crime to be a Stubborn Child, and in that year, at age seven, I was charged with that crime.

Home Investigation

HOME INVESTIGATION

BOYS DIVISION   DATE: 3/16/56

NAME:	NUMBER:	DATE OF BIRTH:	NATIONALITY:	COLOR:
Mark Devlin	3944BR	April 16, 1948	American	White

ADDRESS: **TELEPHONE:**
275 Chestnut Street, Jamaica Plain, Massachusetts   JA 4-1767

COURT APPEARANCE: **OFFENSE:**
West Roxbury, MA.   Stubborn Child

SCHOOL GRADE:	SCHOLARSHIP:	CONDUCT:	ATTENDANCE:
Second	Fair	Poor	Poor

RELIGION:
Catholic (Baptism—Our Lady of Lourdes, attends)

SOURCES OF INFORMATION:
West Roxbury Court—Juvenile Probation Office Schools
Christine Devlin—Mother
Massachusetts Society for the Prevention of Cruelty to Children
New England Home for Little Wanderers

Description of Offense
Boy appeared in West Roxbury Court on Stubborn Child complaint
brought by mother who stated that boy had been a constant source of

trouble to her, and claimed that she could not control boy's actions in the home. He has been urinating in the oil burner and defecating in the bathroom sink. He disrupts the whole house, gets the other children up early and throws cereal, etc., all over the floor, and in general makes a great mess all over the house. Mother claims boy is accident prone and is never without a black eye or bruise. Late last summer he broke into Roxbury's Boy's Club and did a great deal of damage there. However, because the Club authorities liked the boy so much, charges were not filed and he was allowed to work off the damages. Destructive patterns persisted, however, and in January arrangements were made to have the boy studied at the New England Home for Little Wanderers (report attached). Mother was simultaneously advised to take out a Stubborn Child's complaint against boy, in order for him to be placed through the Court.

School History
This boy began his school career attending the Endicott School 9–14–54, in the kindergarten. He continued at the Endicott School in the first grade and transferred to the Jefferson School 3–1–55, where it was reported that boy was absent about twenty days, truant two days, and tardy once. He received a C average in conduct, a B average in classwork. At the Jefferson School his teacher reported he was a classroom behavior problem and would only do what he wanted, was disrespectful, but was intelligent and bright and that his talents were being wasted. He was running away from home and school frequently, and it was noted at the Jefferson School that many times the boy came to school without adequate clothing and without lunch. Oftentimes other children and teacher would share lunch with boy. He transferred to the St. Francis De Sales School, Roxbury 9–2–55 in the second grade. He attended twenty-six days and was absent seven and one-half days. It was reported that boy was discharged from St. Francis De Sales School for "lying, contempt of authority, and disobedience." He transferred to the Dillaway School, Roxbury, 11–22–55 in grade two and records show attendance of two and four-tenths weeks, and absent thirty-two days. He transferred to the Bowditch School when family moved to Jamaica Plain, but Mark was placed at the Home for Little Wanderers (January 26, 1956—March 2, 1956) so no school record was available at the Bowditch School.

Home and Neighborhood
Mark, his mother, and five siblings occupy a third floor six room apartment of a three family dwelling in a residential area, a short distance

from the Jamaica Plain business district, for which they pay $45.00 per month. Although the apartment for the most part appeared clean at the time of visit, the furnishings were in a state of complete disrepair, with the exception of the T.V. set. Mother stated that she has only one bed and one crib for the children, and that Mark sleeps on a couch.

Parents
FATHER—Bud Devlin married Christine Devlin 8/17/46. He is employed at the Haartz-Mason Manufacturing Company in Watertown as a laborer and earns $57.00 per week. They are legally separated and mother stated that divorce proceedings are now under way. Mother described him as a poor provider for family needs, as a heavy drinker and as an extremely cruel and abusive parent, particularly with Mark. He has been contributing $27.00 per week for maintenance of the children.
MOTHER—Christine Devlin is a short woman about thirty-one years old, extremely pretty and talkative. Many times during interview she expressed a great deal of concern regarding the welfare of her children, particularly Mark. However, this is in direct contrast to statements made by the Society for the Prevention of Cruelty to Children (see Report below) whose Agent states that after an initial contact with Mrs. Devlin that he is very much of the opinion that she is a neglectful parent who is in the habit of leaving her children to look after themselves while she would go out. It is noted above that Mother receives $27.00 per week from Father and also has been receiving $120.00 per month in the form of Aid to Dependent Children from the Public Welfare offices.

Interview
Mother stated that from the very start she had an extremely difficult time with Mr. Devlin. She described him as being a drunkard and added that either last August or September he spent one month at Deer Island, after being involved in an assault and battery charge, and presently is under one year probation. Mother feels that father is totally to blame for Mark's misbehavior and described at length the numerous beatings that the boy has suffered at the hands of his father. She described how he has on occasion beaten Mark as though Mark were an adult and told how the boy would be smashed against the wall and thrown under beds, etc., and that the boy has suffered this treatment since he was an infant. According to the mother, Mark suffers from asthma because of these beatings and is presently enuretic for perhaps these same reasons.

She stated that many of Mark's expressions of misbehavior are a direct

9

imitation of what he has seen his father perform. For example, urinating and defecating in the kitchen sink, on the floor, etc. In this respect mother also stated that Mark had a feeding problem when he was about two years old and a doctor told her that it was because the boy was suffering from insufficient love and attention. She described the boy as having a wild imagination, constantly telling stories that involve murder and bloodshed. Oftentimes during his sleep, according to his mother, Mark will scream and shout. She stated that Mark has a voracious appetite and will eat all the time but seldom with the rest of the family. She described that he will usually take his food, climb atop a shelf and have his meal there. However, he has very good relations with his siblings.

Mother then returned to the subject of her husband and commented that Mr. Devlin was always in the habit of leaving her, or deserting her, about the time of each child's birth, and then sometime later would return to the home and plead with her to take him back. Mother stated that she always took her husband back "for the sake of the children" but she is now convinced that she should divorce him. Mother admitted that she is keeping company with a fellow she called "Bill." She added that all the children, including Mark, like Bill a great deal and get along with him.

At this point mother expressed concern over the fact that other neighborhood children have been in considerable trouble and are presently at the Detention Center in Roslindale and that she is afraid that Mark may come into contact with these boys and "that their bad behavior will rub off on him." She conceded that she has tried to discipline Mark by spanking him, but found that did not prove successful and now punishes him by denying him such privileges as going out, etc. She stated that her first wish is that Mark be returned home but is convinced that she has her doubts and feels that he will continue to get into further trouble. She further states that although Mark has promised her that he will be a better boy she feels incapable of handling him at home, and although she is reluctant to swear out a Stubborn Child complaint she believes that Mark needs help and therefore taking out the complaint was in Mark's best interests.

Report of the Massachusetts Society for the Prevention of Cruelty to Children:
The SPCC was in contact with the family in July of 1955 when a neighbor complained that the children were not being fed, nor properly cared for. After an investigation by a SPCC Agent, it was found that the children

were being fed but that they could receive better supervision from their mother. It was also found that there were inadequate furnishings in the house, and especially, the sleeping arrangements were very poor. The three boys slept in one single bed. Blankets were found to be dirty and there was no bed linen. The SPCC is keeping in contact with the family, and at the present time is making periodic checks.

Summary of Report from New England Home for Little Wanderers Medical Report: Mark is a fair-sized youngster for his age of seven point eight years. Hyperactive. Electroencephalograph was performed and although at the summary of the test a negative or normal classification was reported, certain activity of the E.E.G. patterns reveal an area which could be further explored.

School Report: He is at a third grade level. He was at school for two weeks. He was disruptive and refused to work within this setting when the work became demanding. He was removed from the school setting.

House Staff Report: He was spunky, restive, showed interest in sex. He was obscene in remarks and gestures. Calls girls "puffy" and "not puffy." Resisted taking naps as prescribed by others. Difficult at mealtimes. Gives evidence of good intelligence. Will steal if given the chance.

Psychological Report: Showed a superior score. Resisted Thematic Aperception Test. Said his father hated him and that he [Mark] loved his mother best. Revealed strong underlying anxiety.

Psychiatric Report: Appeared to like the Home. Is good when not having a mad fit. Called his father "a drunken bum." He was removed from Parochial school. He paws at girls and women and doesn't realize that this is wrong. Father has a reputation for cruelty and abusive language.

Recommendations:
After a period of training, boy should be returned to his home, with mother, if at that time another home investigation shows considerable improvement in the physical condition of the home, and in the attitude of the mother.

Respectfully submitted,
William T. Michaels, Visitor

Disposition:
Continued to April 6, 1956. Temporary Disposition of Mark Devlin to the Roslindale Detention Center, Division of Youth Service, for further study.

Observation

ROSLINDALE DETENTION CENTER
FOR BOYS

MARCH - APRIL 1956

$\mathfrak{Division}$ $\mathfrak{of}$ $\mathfrak{Youth}$ $\mathfrak{Service}$

DETENTION CENTER FOR BOYS

REPORT OF CLINICAL STUDY

CASE NUMBER: 2325   **DATE OF ADMISSION:** 3/16/56

NAME: Mark D. Devlin   **BIRTHDATE:** 4/16/48

ADDRESS: 275 Chestnut Avenue, Jamaica Plain, Massachusetts

FATHER: Hugh Robert Devlin   **MOTHER:** Christine Devlin

CASE HISTORY

Mark Devlin was admitted to the Roslindale Detention Center for Boys on March 16 at the request of the West Roxbury Court on that date charged with Being a Delinquent By Reason of Stubbornness. His case was continued to April 6, and he was sent to the Detention Center for Observation. Wechsler Intelligence Scale for Children administered on March 18, and boy showed a Verbal Scale 11; Performance Scale I.Q., 124; Full Scale I.Q. 111. Result of preliminary examination by Dr. Cone is reported as follows:

Report of Dr. Cone:
Mark is unable to sit still in his chair for even a second; he is constantly shifting about with his hands and feet, and practically his entire body is in constant motion. He also has very marked facial tics, particularly on the right side. On the surface he has a very charming and winning smile, but this is only a thin veneer and does not last long when he is frustrated. He reacts to frustration with marked aggressive behavior, impulsiveness

15

and severe temper tantrums. His attitudes are very anti-social in line with his background history, and he even boasts of having a criminal record. He reads very well for his age, and is of superior intelligence. He is an anxious boy, who finds it difficult to discuss his relationships with his family easily.

Psychological Evaluation:
Mark showed no overt tension or apprehension during the testing. He was hyperactive throughout the interview. He seemed completely uninhibited and consequently went outside the prescribed boundaries set by the test. His concentration was poor and he seemed not to keep his concerted interest on the task at hand. He brought up many points which were irrelevant to the testing, moved about a good deal, and frequently asked questions which were out of context, and often went off on "Flight of Ideas" verbalization. He was extremely friendly and cooperative and it was felt that good rapport was established within the limits set by the boy's poor concentration, hyperactivity, and lack of inhibition. The boy's test results place him in the Bright Normal category and are considered an accurate index of the boy's functional intelligence at the present time. Optimally, however, there is little doubt that the boy could achieve an I.Q. in the Superior classification.

Interview:
Mark's behavior was similar to that during the testing. Lack of inhibition and distractibility characterized his behavior. He dismissed things with little attempt at evasion, but some rationalizing and minimizing was [sic] evident when certain weighted areas were discussed. For example, when speaking of his mother's angry prolonged tirades the boy found it difficult to impossible to admit that he was the object of these outbursts. He impressed us as an uninhibited, but likeable boy.

This boy is the product of an extremely punitive, rejecting and sordid environment. The boy stated that his father "hates me more than anyone." The mother has also been rejecting to the boy. This boy has found little in the way of love and support in the home.

Mark is an immature and uninhibited young man who has never experienced anything but abuse and rejection in the home. It is quite surprising that he has achieved the level of ego development that he has in view of the emotional impoverishment of his background. He seems to have developed considerable ego strength. His lack of inhibition has

16

caused difficulty in school but the boy shows interest in scholastic matters and it is felt that he could do well academically if properly motivated. He is an attractive and likeable youngster who forms relationships easily, both with his peers and adults.

Mark is in need of a placement which will offer him the love and acceptance and stability he has never had. Understanding and accepting figures for identification purposes in a stable setting are indicated. The boy has a great deal of potential which should be exploited and it is believed he would respond well to the proper handling. The boy should definitely not be returned to his home and after a period of training in a group setting, a foster home should be found for this boy.

L.D., Psychologist

Excerpt from Social Worker's Report:
Boy's teacher stated that he was very daring. He disrupts the class by calling to the teacher, "Drop dead! You stinkin' bum!" She states that he wants to know that he is right all the time. In taking a test, for example, instructor reported he might ask if a certain thing is right, and if it was not, he would be likely to tear up his test paper and smash a pencil or book on the floor. Boy showed an I.Q. of 83 (low-average) on the California Test of Mental Ability, which School feels is not a true one, as he will never complete tests. At times he was profane and obscene in his language. He will steal and lie. For example, his lying: One minute he will tell the teacher that his father is a drunken bum and in the next, he will invent some lie about something wonderful that his father has done for him. But Mother has stated that the father never cared for the boy. Suffice it to say that from the time of his birth to the present, Mark Devlin's home environment has conspired to deprive him of all of the basic elements necessary for proper emotional development. Father in all respects is a totally inadequate role-model. Mother, too, is unsupportive and unequipped for understanding the boy's problems.

R.F., Social Worker

Psychiatric Evaluation:
Mark is a seven-year-old boy of superior intelligence who has a great many conflicts that are the result of the unhappy family life to which he has been subjected. He has picked up many anti-social traits and has in many ways identified with his father. He is also in constant rebellion with his mother as evidenced by the constant turmoil he creates at home. It is unlikely there will be any improvement in his emotional problems

17

so long as he remains in the home. A stable, controlled, supervised placement where he can remain for the next eight years or so until adolescence is recommended.

In view of the lack of family funds to place him in a private boarding school, it is probably necessary for him to be committed to the Youth Service Board and placed at one of their facilities. It is the utmost importance that a stable type of placement be found for Mark, where he can remain for many years. Otherwise the prognosis is very poor. It is possible that various tranquilizing drugs may be of some help in relieving his hyperactivity.

T.R., Assistant Superintendent

Disposition:
As a result of the aforementioned studies, a conference was held on April 6, 1956 between Judge Spisak and said psychologists, teachers, counselors, and social workers, and each gave a summary of their contact with Mark. They felt that both the mother and the father were psychopathetic personalities. Boy is normal physically, otherwise very active. It was therefore recommended and subsequently agreed to by the Court and Parole Board that Mark Devlin be Adjudicated Delinquent By Reason of Stubbornness and remanded to the Youth Service Board's John Augustus Hall.

BOOK I

John Augustus Hall

APRIL 6, 1956

1.

March 16, 1956

A STRANGE MAN CAME to my house. He and my mother took me to a place where a black-robed man sat at a large desk in front of me. He asked my mother and several others who were already in the room many questions about me. He gave me a rather stern look as he got up from his desk and left through a side door. My mother, with tears in her eyes, came to tell me that I would have to go away again. She had promised I'd never have to go away again like I did in January, when she put me in the Home for Little Wanderers. I had been back home for only two weeks, and so the thought of being taken from my mother again caused me to have a real screaming fit. When I came out of it, she was gone. The stranger came to take me with him. Although I pleaded with him not to, he didn't listen. He put me into his car and drove away.

After a time we arrived at a long, flat brick building. It was the Roslindale Detention Center. Once inside, I was placed in a cage and told to have a seat. I sat there for a very long time as I watched strange adults come in and go out of the back door where earlier I'd been brought in. They looked at me with surprise, remarking among themselves how tiny and young I looked. One of the adults asked me how old I was, and when I told him seven, he whistled. He asked a man sitting in a glass-enclosed booth what I was in for. The man in the booth answered, "Stubborn

21

Child." I was wondering about all this when a man came and took me with him. He took me down a hall and up a flight of stairs. He handed me a pair of dungarees, a polo shirt, a pair of sneakers, and underwear. He also gave me a pair of pajamas, a towel, and a toothbrush. I was given a shower and, because it was now early evening, told to change into my pajamas. I thought how wonderful my new clothes smelled. The man said nothing as he walked me to a steel door in the corridor. He opened it and told me to get inside. He slammed it, and as I heard the click of the lock, a wave of terror came over me. The room was pitch-black because it was already dark outside. I screamed and kicked at the door and cried for my mother. When I heard the jingle of keys coming closer, I felt joy in my heart and smiled; I knew my mother had come to take me. Instead, I saw a mean face looking in through a small opening in the window. The face was looking at me and said, "Shut up, you little cocksucker, or I'll kick you so far up the ass you'll be shittin' shoe leather. Now get in the fuckin' sack because your mother ain't going to be seeing you for a long time." I walked a few feet over to the window that would not open. I pressed my burning face to the cool pane and looked out into the blackness, remembering....

I watched the rain fall hard on the street below and saw a large white moth in a corner under the lintel pull its wings tighter about itself. It was a savage rain. I wanted to run out, run into its eye. I could only press my face closer to the windowpane and watch the gray wind whip and lash the trees. This wind also made the windows shake and bang. A draft sneaked in and around the jamb, where poor construction and time-worn spaces had allowed its intrusion. Like the moth, I pulled my wings tighter about me. It was useless; the chill was already in my bones. It was an aching chill that made me tremble. Suddenly the rain stopped. Outside, that early September hurricane had washed the earth clean. It had left in its wake an eerie calm in which the leaves on the trees now appeared silvery against a purple-blue sky. I slipped out against my mother's earlier warning. On the street I found large puddles, broken twigs and branches, large brown chestnuts, and leaves scattered in disarray, forming an uneven, rich tapestry about me.

I was six in that fall of 1954, a time when I began to sense my presence in the world. Like the sparrows that hopped and flitted and gorged themselves with earthworms, I had life. Like the chestnuts, I had form. And like the leaves, I had color and beauty.

Although the rain had gone, it had left me small oceans upon which to sail ships and emulate my father, whom I knew only to be at sea. I stooped to pick up a thick twig at my foot. Finding another, longer and thinner, I skewered a large, damp leaf to it and fashioned a sailboat. As I navigated it through the green spiked chestnut jackets that lay in the water like mines, I giggled when I saw my distorted reflection where stray, marauding winds sent ripples across the puddle.

I went over to the thick bottom limb of a chestnut tree that hung down across the sidewalk and half into the gutter. The leafy branches, like long, tensed fingers, seemed to be reaching up in an attempt to grab the space they had been ripped away from. I straddled a branch and felt its rough skin against my legs. Inching my way along and upward, I felt it quiver. My weight was too great; we fell to the ground, where the branch shuddered and its leaves shook in a final spasm. Embarrassed, I looked about me. I saw only the flesh-colored blurs of tiny faces against fogged windowpanes. My mother called to me, and when I was back inside, she beat me, just as she had many times during that summer, the first I remembered.

Other times, when the horizon was fuchsia and high, thin wisps of cirrus clouds floated randomly and lazily like cigarette smoke in a pale blue sky, I was already at play in the woods of Franklin Park, having sneaked out earlier when it was still dark. I played alone until the golfers came to play on the public course. I ran out onto the fairway from my secret places to greet them. They were my friends; they liked my adventurous spirit and the fact that I would find their lost golf balls, for which they would pay me a nickel for each one I retrieved. With a few nickels in my pocket, I would run over to the zoo area of the park to buy peanuts for the elephants and watch the antics of the monkeys or to talk to the Jewish elders who lined the benches at the entrance of the park and engaged in animated conversations. When dusk descended and darkness came, it was only then that I realized I would have to go home to the beating I knew I would get. Yet each morning, when my mother and siblings were asleep, I would be back there.

I lived with my mother, three sisters, and two brothers. Cheryl, the oldest, was seven, I was six, Kevin was four, Hugh was three, Patrice was two, and Donna was an infant. We occupied a welfare flat on Michigan Avenue in Dorchester, Massachusetts. It was a run-down brick-and-wood structure, where chunks of plaster had fallen away exposing the studs and lath like veins and bones. Large, fat cockroaches and silverfish crawled in and out of these wounds, from which a dank mustiness saturated the air.

I did not think about my father; he was not living with us. He was always, it seemed, at sea. I felt awe for sailors; I saw them as brave and strong, and so this is what I imagined my father to be. The first time I remember his coming home was on a Sunday in the spring of 1954. He helped my mother make dinner as he whistled to himself. I watched them from the chair to which he had ordered me to sit and be still. He frightened me. He was always trying to beat me up, and he succeeded often. I tried to avoid him while he was home, and when he returned to sea, I was happy. Sometime during that summer, though, I heard that he had stolen my mother's welfare check. It was a story I heard more than once. This made my mother cry, and it pained me when she did because I worshiped her.

Despite my father's beatings and my mother's occasional strappings, I was a happy, curious child, always moving on to the next thing. I loved my Jewish neighborhood with its tree-lined streets, neat houses, and friendly people. On days that I did not wander out to Franklin Park, I would go from house to house, store to store, spending time with anyone who would talk to me. I knew that when I grew up, I would be a mailman.

My favorite adult neighborhood friend was a man named Nathan, the owner of the local variety store. He was always glad to see me and talk to me, as were his older retired friends, who would stop by in the afternoon to sit on boxes and hold conversations. When I did not come around for days or when I came in the late afternoon, they would ask me where I'd been because they had been waiting for me.

One afternoon Nathan asked me to his house for dinner. I knew Jewish people ate different food from Catholics, and so I asked him what he was having. When he told me that it was chicken, I told him I didn't want to eat chicken because it would make me Jewish. Nathan and his friends laughed uproariously as I stood there with a sheepish grin. Assured that I would not turn Jewish, I went to Nathan's house for Sabbath dinner. I ate the chicken, and much to my surprise, my appearance did not change.

Our Jewish neighbors, who knew I was given to wandering and exploring, often told my mother that I was a born leader, and many of them told me they wished that I were their son. I was the darling of the neighborhood, but I was not my mother's darling, for if I was not wandering alone, I was leading my younger siblings on adventures.

Once, during the summer of 1954, I had taken Kevin and Hugh—Hugh was still wearing diapers—to Franklin Field, which was quite a bit farther from Franklin Park and about a mile from where we lived. There was a community pool there and swings and slides as well as lawn bowling for the older citizens. Hugh, Kevin, and I played and swam until sunset. On our way home the police stopped us and put us in a cruiser. They yelled at my mother to watch me more carefully; it was not the first time they had been called to find me.

Another time, not long after, I convinced all the children, except Donna, that there were lions and tigers roaming the woods of Franklin Park and I knew where they were. Soon all five of us were deep in the woods of Franklin Park; it was late afternoon. By nightfall we were lost and frightened. Although I was just as frightened as they were, I felt responsible and pushed them on until at last we reached the main highway. We scrambled down a stone wall that bordered the park and into the hands of the waiting police. When we arrived home, my mother was livid. She would have beaten me right then and there had it not been for the cops, who warned her that it was her fault for not watching me more carefully. Later, in my bed on the couch, I believed my mother was angry because I had not found lions and tigers and because I had also gotten lost. I slept well, having escaped what I knew would have been a severe beating. It was the first summer I remembered; I liked summer.

When fall came, I was placed in kindergarten at the local elementary school. I liked school, too, but what I didn't like was the way my classmates teased me about my shabby clothes, tattered shoes, and my never having a lunch to bring. For this reason I often played hooky and wandered the woods of Franklin Park. I knew about when school would let out for the day, so I would hang around some nearby doorway until the children came out, and I would blend in with them. If my mother were watching from the window, it would appear as if I had been in school all day. My teacher did not always ask for notes from me because my mother would often keep me out of school for many days at a time whenever I had no clothes or shoes. It seemed that my sister Cheryl always had nice clothes and new shoes and a lunch. I guessed it was more important for girls to have these things.

In the late spring of 1955, just after my seventh birthday, my mother kept Cheryl and me out of school. She told us that she was going to move into a new apartment with a real shower and wallpaper. When we saw the apartment, it was so nice that I thought it meant I would also get new clothes and shoes and bag lunches for school.

But when the school term was over, we moved again, this time to a ramshackle apartment in a poor neighborhood with treeless streets. We lived on the top floor of a dilapidated three-decker wooden house that was bordered on either side by empty lots littered with old tires, trash, and broken bottles. At first I really hated this new place, but I was soon filled with the hope of new adventures and discoveries, and so I once more took up my wandering ways.

The area close to my new home in Roxbury bustled with activity since it was located near the main downtown section of the city. In the center of downtown Roxbury, on Dudley Street, was a busy bus and train station. From the upper platform one could take the el train to the North End of Boston or southwest to Jamaica Plain. All around the station were thriving shops that offered "E-Z" credit and layaway plans, a five-and-dime, and bars and movie theaters. Halfway between Dudley Street and the street I lived on was the Roxbury Boy's Club. It was a great place for young boys, so for a modest price my mother enrolled me. It offered many activities like baseball, basketball, swimming, and Ping-Pong; there was a library, too, and storytelling hours throughout the day. I liked to read and to hear stories, but the librarian, Mr. Morrone scared me; I guess it was because of his closely cropped hair, pinkish eyes, and thick glasses. One day my mother brought me in to see him to show him how well I read. Mr. Morrone listened to me and then told me that he would like to make me his assistant. I declined; I liked running and jumping around better and exploring best of all.

My mother no longer had to worry about my wandering too far from home since there was more than enough in the neighborhood to keep me occupied. I spent most of my time at the club. I was learning how to swim. Swimming became my favorite activity. The pool we swam in was very long and had a diving board. When I saw the older boys diving off it and making great splashes into the water, I wanted to do this, too. However, I was told that only the older boys and those who could swim really well were allowed to use it, and so I set about the task of transforming myself from tadpole to frog. I spent hours hanging onto the edge of the pool and kicking my feet until my legs grew strong and coordinated; by the summer's end I had surpassed the swimmers in my group and was allowed to use the diving board. For my achievement I was given an award by the director, Mr. Jackson. I liked him, and we soon became friendly. I would often stop by his office in the daytime to talk to him.

I loved the Boy's Club, but it was closed on weekends. On Saturdays, if my mother had money, she would give Cheryl and me each a quarter to go to the local theater. Admission was only fifteen cents, leaving us money to buy candy or popcorn. With our empty candy boxes we could make little horns. The show started at nine in the morning and let out at four. We would watch cartoons like *Casper the Friendly Ghost* and then a serial or two, like *Hopalong Cassidy*. Finally there would be two or three full-length films like *The Werewolf*, or *The Creature from the Black Lagoon*. At the end of the show we flattened our popcorn boxes and sailed them up onto the stage to show our delight. When we emerged from the darkened theater, we had to squint our eyes at the light.

Some Saturdays my mother did not have the money to send us. I would fall in with the other neighborhood kids whose mothers also didn't have any money and go in search of tonic bottles. The twelve-ounce bottles fetched two cents apiece; the quart bottles five cents, but only if they were all squeaky clean. Because there were so many kids scouring the empty lots and alleys for these treasures, they were not always easy to find. Usually I had no problem. If we were unable to find the money for admission, our friends would try to sneak us in through the side exit doors. This did not always work. I sometimes missed the movies and would walk the deserted streets, waiting to hear what my friends had seen.

My mother had taken up with a new man she had met at a local bar called the Roxbury Grille. His name was Bill, and I didn't like him; he reminded me of my father. He was always drunk and mean. I don't know if he was living with us, but it seemed he was there every night. Because of this, I would stay out as late as I could. Once my mother had gone to meet him at the Roxbury Grille. I was home watching the other children. I was leaning out the window, yelling down to a couple of the kids I knew on the street below, when Bill and my mother came in. My mother screamed for Bill to get me out of the window. He came over and threw me hard against the wall on the other side of the room. I did not know whom I hated or feared more, Bill or my father.

My father came once a week to bring my mother money. They were separated now, but if I knew he was coming, I would hide because he would always ask for me in a drunken voice and try to beat me up. One evening I was home when my father came over, and I was left to watch my sister Donna, who was asleep in her crib, while my father and mother went out. They said they would be back very soon. When they did not return for what seemed to me a long time, I became hungry. I found a can of Franco-American spaghetti in the pantry. After opening it, I put it in a pan on the stove to heat. Just then I heard my father's voice on the stairs; I could tell that he was very drunk. Frightened, I ran to hide behind the stove. When they walked into the kitchen, I heard my mother say to him that the spaghetti was all the food she had in the house. She called for me, and when I did not answer, she told my father to "get me." My father said that if I did not come out right away, I would get a beating. Thinking he wouldn't beat me, I slunk out from my hiding place only to look into his glaring eyes and at his folded leather belt. He began to whip me about my legs, arms, back, and anywhere else he could strike. The stinging, searing pain drove me into Donna's room and under her crib. I pressed my belly against the wall, but it was not enough out of his reach. He began to strap my back as hard as he could. Through my labored gasps I heard my mother call to him to stop.

I awoke in the Boston City Hospital. I began to have asthma

attacks. My back was covered with bruises and cuts. The cuts healed, but my asthma attacks remained, and I began to have nightmares as well as daydreams of blood and terror and other violent things.

When I had recovered from my wounds, I went back to the Boy's Club. Mr. Jackson and Mr. Morrone knew I had been ill and were extra nice to me.

Other than these minor scrapes I had not gotten into any really serious trouble until just a few weeks before school was to begin. The movie *Davy Crockett* was to be played at the Roxy that weekend. This was truly a big event; Davy Crockett was every little boy's hero. It was all we boys talked about, and I was sure my mother would give me the money. But when Saturday came, she said that she didn't have it. I tried to tell her how important this was and that if I didn't go, I would be teased by all the boys in the neighborhood. She wouldn't give in. I went on a mad scramble for bottles; there were none to be found. Then I remembered Mr. Jackson had money in a big safe in his office. I went down behind the club, found a good stone, and heaved it through a window. I climbed in to find myself standing in the library. I felt kind of silly and almost sneaked back out, but I just had to see Davy Crockett. I found my way to Mr. Jackson's office and tried to open the door of his big safe, but it wouldn't budge. I next tried the round thing with numbers on it, as I had seen Mr. Jackson do. Still, it would not open. This had been my last hope. Dejected, I got another idea; I would play alone inside the club, and even better, I would first go swimming. I ran down the long, dark stairway to the basement where the pool was located. Once there, I could not get the door open. I climbed back up the stairs and went into the large recreation room, where I turned on the TV set to watch cartoons. I grew bored and tried to play a game of Ping-Pong against myself, running to each side as I hit the ball. After a time I decided that playing alone wasn't much fun, so I left through the window.

On Monday, when I went to the Boy's Club, I saw a lot of

30

commotion at the library. Mr. Morrone, Mr. Jackson, and a policeman were looking at the broken window and scratching their heads. I gulped and slipped away.

The next Saturday, when I did not have money to go to the show, I again decided to break into the Boy's Club because the streets were so lonely. I thought maybe the pool door would be open this time. I threw a rock against the window and scampered in. I was going to have fun. I wasn't there long before I heard voices at the front door. I looked and saw the police. Someone must have seen me break in. I got scared and ran down to the pool door. There was a little landing there, and I curled up into a ball in a corner. It was very dark, so I felt safe. Soon I heard two men coming down the stairs; as their voices got closer, my heart pounded, and I was sure they could hear it. They reached the bottom of the landing, and I could barely make out the foot of one of them only a few inches from my face. They checked the pool door and found it locked. As they turned to go back up the stairs, one of them brushed me. He jumped up in the air because he told his friend he had felt a rat. Little did they know that I was that little rat. They turned on a flashlight and found me.

The two men were policemen, and they took me to the station, called my mother, and bought me ice cream. While they waited for my mother to come get me, they sat me on a desk and talked to me about breaking the law. When my mother arrived, she began to talk angrily at me, but the police talked angrily at her, saying they thought I was a nice boy. I was afraid that when my mother got me home, she would beat me badly; she did not but made me stay in my room for the rest of the weekend. On Monday she took me to the Boy's Club, where Mr. Jackson and Mr. Morrone screwed up their faces and furled their eyebrows at me. My punishment was that I had to work for Mr. Morrone for one month until the damages had been paid off. Although I did not look forward to working for Mr. Morrone, I managed to perform my tasks and even got to like him.

In September of that year, 1955, I was enrolled at what we kids called Sister School, which was a Catholic school where all the teachers were nuns. Most of us dreaded Sister School because we knew nuns to be mean and humorless. Once I had settled in and had gotten used to it, I didn't mind. Best of all, we children all wore the same uniforms, and I always had lunch. As a result, perhaps, I became the best reader in my class. My mother was very proud of me. Then, just before Thanksgiving, tragedy struck; I was accused of carving my initials into my desk. I'm not sure if I did it, but I think someone else did it to get me in trouble. The nun gave me the rattan across my hands and tried to get me to confess; I wouldn't. I was taken to the principal's office, and my mother was called to come get me. I was expelled. My mother was very upset with me. I got a beating when I got home and was made to stay in my room without any TV for three days. After my punishment was over, she took me to a regular school that I didn't like. I wasn't there very long when my mother moved back to Jamaica Plain and I was placed in the New England Home for Little Wanderers in January 1956.

My mother brought me there and told me that I would have to stay for a while. I tried to be brave, but I ran after her and begged her not to leave me there all alone. She said that I had to stay and that she would see me soon. By the day's end I loved the home; I was treated kindly. There were other children there, too. During the day we attended classes, where we painted and colored and learned how to read and write and to do arithmetic. Sometimes during the day adults would take me out of class and into their office, where they would give me little tests or ask me questions about my mother or father. In the evenings we were free to watch TV. Most of the kids at the home were about my age, but there was one older girl who was twelve and who was always grabbing me and calling me cutie pie. When she hugged me, I liked it. One evening she and I were watching TV when she turned to ask me if I knew how to have sex. I told her I didn't. She lay on a couch and told me to get on top of her. I did, and she held me. It was such a nice feeling I wanted to stay there, but we heard footsteps and understood that a counselor was coming, and she pushed me off her. Later I wanted to do it again, but she said no.

On the weekends we sometimes went to the Children's Museum or tobogganing behind our building. Sometimes we went on little trips to town where, if we had money, we could buy candy. I liked the trips, but I never had any money. During the entire time I was there, six weeks, I didn't see my mother or siblings. I often thought about them, and I couldn't wait to go home, even though I would miss my warm, clean bed at the home and the nurse who would kiss me good-night and come down later to wake me and change my wet sheets.

Finally the day arrived for me to leave. I was given a shopping bag full of toys from the staff at the home. They all came to see me off. When I got home, I hugged my brothers and sisters and shared my toys with them. I hoped that I would never have to go away again. . . .

I remained at the window, crying as quietly as I could, while thoughts crowded in my mind and tiny fissures opened in my skull and cheekbones. Exhausted, I turned to get into bed. I saw that it was a bunk bed and there was another little boy asleep in the bottom bed. I climbed up into my bed, pulled the covers over me, and cried myself to sleep.

Children's voices and the warm March sun on my face awakened me. The banging of cell doors made me realize that I wasn't home. I wondered where I was and why I was there. The boy on the bottom bunk introduced himself. Outside in the corridor other young boys milled around my cell door. They wondered who I was and what crime I had committed. I said that I hadn't committed any crime, and they said I had to have; otherwise I wouldn't be at Roslindale. Although I found this confusing, at least I no longer had to wonder where I was, or why. I thought that perhaps I was there because I had broken up my mother and father; I had heard my father say this to my mother as I lay in bed one night. I was convinced that was the reason.

The boys all welcomed me. Heartened, I dressed and was shown where to wash up and go to the bathroom. After we all had washed, we were taken downstairs to the cafeteria for breakfast. I was not used to having more than cereal for breakfast, and we had toast and eggs and milk; I liked this. After breakfast we were placed in a large brick- and glass-enclosed rec room, which had a long table for cards and benches to sit on and a TV set on a shelf suspended high above on the wall. Most of us had to sit on the floor with our backs to the wall while guards watched us from a desk separated from us by a sheet of glass. I sat and studied my surroundings and the new people I was with. I didn't like this place: The grownups were very mean, and the boys were older than I and seemed tough and scary.

At about 8:00 A.M. a master came into the rec room and told certain boys, whose names he read from a paper, to line up for court. When they were gone, the rest of the boys were sent to classrooms. I was left alone with another boy, who was also new, to await our places. A master turned on cartoons for us. I could not pay attention. I felt funny all over, and I wanted to run away, but I couldn't because the masters could see me, and also the windows had iron things across them so they couldn't be opened. I didn't know how far from my home I was but thought I must be very far away.

After a time, at midday, I was taken to a man's office. He asked me lots of questions the way they did at the home. After lunch I was made to take a nap with the very few other small boys at Roslindale. I was awakened from my nap and taken to a classroom. I enjoyed learning things, so at least for a while I was able to forget where I was until somebody came to take me to a room and made me take tests, something I hated doing.

Each day there were more questions and new tests. But evenings and weekends we were taken out to a yard with a high fence to play. Sometimes we were taken to the gymnasium to watch basketball or boxing matches. I joined in the boxing a couple of times. I did okay, and the masters said I was a "little scrapper."

On Sunday we were allowed to have family visits. Each week my mother came to see me, and often she brought Cheryl. Each time I believed she was going to take me home. But each time she told me that I had to stay. I could not understand why. When visiting hours were over, fear gripped me like a vise. I would cling to my mother and plead with her to take me home. The guard would always have to wrench me away. While the guard held me, I would watch my mother and Cheryl walk away through tear-filled eyes. When they were out of earshot and sight, the guard would usually give me a whack and say something like "You're never gettin' outta here. You little cocksucker."

On April 6, 1956, ten days before my eighth birthday I was taken to see the man in the black robe again. When I saw my mother, I was sure that this meant she was taking me home, and my little heart gladdened. When I was made to stand between two men and not near my mother, I knew something was wrong. I looked around at the small sea of impassive faces in hopes of finding some answer.

The black-robed man came in, sat down, and, without looking at me, fixed his glasses and read from something on his desk. When he was done, different people read to him from papers about me. Now and then he'd look from them to me; once or twice he smiled, and I thought it meant that I was going home. Mostly he gave me hard looks, which made me slink down. He didn't ask me any questions.

When it was over, and after another tear-filled fit, I was taken back to the detention center. Almost upon my return I was taken before the parole board, a small body of individuals who determined to which one of the several institutions of the Division of Youth Service an offender would be sent and also when the offender would be paroled home.

I was taken into a room where four or five adults sat at a long table. I was placed facing them in a chair several feet away. A

35

big, fat man with a cigar, whose name was Mr. Gaspar, introduced himself as the head of the board. He talked to me about the country and about pigs and cows. I told him that although I had never seen a real pig or a cow before, I liked them. He told me that I was going to go to a camp where there were many pigs and cows. I couldn't believe my ears, and I could hardly wait.

2.

Some people shake; they call them a Quaker,
but I'd rather call myself a troublemaker.

Mark Devlin, age eight
JOHN AUGUSTUS HALL

MY MOTHER WAS NOT THERE when I arrived, though I assumed she would be. Neither were there any pigs or cows. I met a man with silver hair, who told me that she had called, that she knew where I was, and that she would see me on visiting day. The man with the silver hair had twinkling Santa Claus eyes, a soft, raspy voice, and a gentle smile. He told me his name was Thomas Costello. When he said that he had heard a lot about me and was happy to have me there, I relaxed. He introduced me to his secretary, who started hugging me and telling me how cute I was. When she finished, Mr. Costello took me through a door into a dining room, through a hall he told me was called the Great Hall, and led me down a flight of stairs into the basement.

36

There I was greeted by stares from the many young boys who sat on benches. Several feet in front of the boys sat a fat man behind a desk. As I was escorted to the desk, the boys began to whisper. The fat man hushed them. Mr. Costello turned me over to this man, who introduced himself as Mr. Potter. He, in turn, took me into a room off to the side, where he introduced me to Mr. Martin, who was in charge of the clothing room. He issued me the same sort of standard institution wear I'd received at the detention center. After showering myself, I asked for a comb. Mr. Martin laughed and told me not to worry, I wouldn't have my mop of hair much longer. I gulped because I had noticed that all of the other boys were skinheads—their hair was about an eighth of an inch long—and I thought they looked really goofy. Mr. Potter also assigned me to a locker; I placed my towel and toothbrush in it and took my seat on the bench. Some of the boys came over to say hi and to ask me questions: What was my name? What was I in for? I was glad to see other little boys there.

It was now close to suppertime, and the master lined us up, smallest in front. It turned out that I was the smallest, and I took my place at the head of the line. We were marched up the stairs and into the dining room. After going through the serving line, we were seated four to a table, on which there was a large pitcher of milk. The masters and staff sat at a long table facing us. We were allowed a half hour in which to eat, and no talking was permitted. When we arrived back in the locker room, I saw through a passageway another locker room where taller and older boys were lined up to take their turn at eating. I found out that this was called the Big Dorm, while ours was known as the Little Dorm. The boys ranged in age from about ten to thirteen years. I think there were only one or two boys my age; all told, there were about forty of us at the hall.

That evening a new master came on duty. He called me to the desk and told me his name was Mr. Milici. Like most of the staff, he was middle-aged and wore a crew cut, in the style of the day. I spent that first evening with the other boys playing card games

37

like fish, war, and old maid. Some boys had plastic model airplanes or cars they'd received from home to work on, while other boys read funny books. Around eight the other boys showered, and we were each given pajamas and slippers to wear to bed. At about eight-thirty we were lined up and taken to our top-floor dormitory, above the Great Hall. I was assigned the third cot in the first of three rows of neatly made beds.

I was exhausted from all the day's events and fell asleep to the whispering of the other boys. When I awoke, the sun was not yet up. I looked around me and took in my new surroundings. For once, I had not wet my bed. The dry bed, new sheets, and clean pajamas felt wonderful. I lay there wondering what was happening. I wondered if I was being punished for my parents always fighting with each other; it seemed my father was always beating me because of that reason. I wondered, now that I was not home, if they were back together; I hoped so. I imagined that someday soon I would walk between them, each one smiling down at me.

That day I was taken to a large schoolroom off the Great Hall. There I met the teacher, Mrs. Shaner. She taught the first four grades and was a wonderful, sprightly lady who wore her gray-streaked hair in a bun behind her round face. She was an excellent teacher, and I did well in her classes.

My mother wrote to me once or twice a week, as did my two grandmothers. My mother also came to see me every week without fail. Once in a while she'd bring my nana or my siblings, and on rare occasions, my father. He would always be very clean and well dressed and sober, a surprise to me. I didn't think I had ever seen him that way. But I didn't like it when he came because he always asked me why I was so bad, and he would keep poking me with his finger and sprayed me with saliva as he talked. But seeing my parents together gave me new hope. Once I asked my mother and father to hold hands. When they wouldn't, I knew I would be staying at John Augustus Hall longer.

Although I tried to be brave and to hope, some nights I felt so empty and lonely I cried myself to sleep. If any of us wanted to cry, we had to wait until the boys on either side of us were asleep.

One morning, soon after my arrival, I met Jim, the night watchman. As I lay awake in the predawn light, he pulled up a chair beside my bed and asked me if I liked cowboy stories. I nodded. He told me that he had been a cowboy. His thick, curly hair, squinty eyes, large jowls, and leather belt and boots made me a believer. I called Jim "Curley" because in all the cowboy shows I'd seen there was always a curly-haired guy named Curley. He told me that he had ridden saddle with Wyatt Earp and Doc Holliday and that he'd shot it out with Jesse James and the Dalton boys as well as other desperadoes. I lay there entranced. He made me promise never to tell anyone that he and I were "pardners" or that I had heard cowboy stories from him. I kept my promise until one morning Jim brought in a newspaper that said the *Tombstone Gazette* and showed a picture of him fighting it out with a gang near a bank. When I saw this, my eyes bugged out. I had to tell the other kids that Jim was a cowboy and that he was my special friend. None of them would believe me, but later in the day I was taken to see Mr. Costello. He told me that Jim was lying. I tried to defend him through my tears. Mr. Costello would not listen, and after that I never saw Curley again.

Ten days after my arrival I celebrated my birthday with cards and a model airplane from home. I also had my hair shorn. Then began the task of waiting until my hair was long enough to start applying a pink wax from a tube called Butch Stick to it and trying to brush it up and back, at least to give the appearance of having some hair, only to have it shorn again the next month. If there was anything that we kids didn't like, it was these haircuts.

Once a week in the evening the Catholic boys were gathered together and taken by bus to Clinton, a town a few miles away, for catechism studies. Our instructor was named Father D'Angelo. He was a strong-looking man with a chiseled face and loving eyes.

School, playtime, and religious studies filled our weekdays.

39

With the approach of summer, and its longer daylight hours, we would be taken out to play on a field behind the institution. We would run and jump in all directions like baby kangaroos. While the older boys played baseball, the younger ones like myself went to play in the dirt and to look at the different insects. The play field itself was not really very big, but within the perimeters of the grounds I saw woodchucks and chipmunks dashing about, and rows of pines around a sparkling blue reservoir beyond, and hazy hills as far as the eye could see. At the north end was a chicken coop no longer in use, and behind it were bushes of wild berries. To the east was an embankment that led up to a smaller field called the Little Field; it was about a third the size of the Big Field. All across the rest of the eastern front from north to south the view was cut by a stretch of hill covered with tall, strawlike grass.

When summer finally arrived and school was let out, we spent our days and evenings playing on the Big Field. Sometimes in the evenings we would have a cookout in the courtyard of the hall. Tables would be brought out, and we would eat hot dogs, hamburgers, and coleslaw and would drink bug juice, a sweet colored beverage that the bugs liked. Some evenings we'd hold talent contests in the gymnasium. I'd always get up and sing— actually, yell more than sing—but I had fun. On Saturdays we were taken by school bus to a lake in a nearby town where we would spend the whole day. The outside people, as we called them, would frequently stare at us in an odd way. We were told not to mix with their children, an instruction I did not understand. On the way back from the lake we would often sing songs like "I've Been Working on the Railroad." If Mr. Milici were on the bus, he would lead us in song:

"The first marine went over the wall," he'd sing, to which we would sing, "Parlay-voo."

"The second marine went over the wall."

"Parlay-voo."

"The third marine went over the wall, got shot in the ass with a cannonball."

"Hinky dinky, parlay-voo."

On Sunday we went to church in Clinton. Father D'Angelo always served the mass. When I saw him up on the altar, I began to want to be a priest. I liked church, but I didn't like the way the outside people always looked at us funny. On Sunday afternoon our families came to see us until it was time for supper. Sunday evenings we would watch movies like *Robin Hood*. It was something we all looked forward to.

I liked summers at the hall because the rules and regulations relaxed. Once in a while Mr. Potter or Mr. Milici would take us on hikes through the surrounding woods and explain to us the kinds of flora and fauna. Once—but only once—Mr. Milici, who was a real sportsman, took us down to the reservoir to fish. A few of the boys caught sunfish. I didn't catch anything, but I loved fishing, and I wished we would go again.

There was only one master whom we hated and were scared of. His name was Mr. Pauley, and he was about fifty and had extra-large ears and a mouth that turned down at the corners. He hated little kids; he even told us so. Some nights he would make us sit in front of our lockers for hours, picking on us and calling us shitheads and other names. One evening he was really upset because his friend the gym teacher had died of a heart attack. He yelled at us and said that it was our fault. He singled out six boys for punishment. He made them stand in a line facing him and then gave each one a hard slap across the face. By the time he got to the last boy he was really lathered up. The boy's name was Stiller, and he was about ten. Mr. Pauley slapped him with such force that Stiller's head hit the concrete floor and split open. We all screamed like banshees. Mr. Milici, who was in the Big Dorm, came running in and, seeing Stiller, cursed and yelled at Mr. Pauley. We all cheered; Stiller was taken to the hospital, and Pauley was never seen by us again.

Weary of summer, I eagerly looked forward to going back to school and to seeing Mrs. Shaner again. I had become fond of her, and she of me. During that new school year Mr. Costello also began to show a special interest in me. He often met me when I came out of class at the end of the day to ask me how things were going. Sometimes, during lunch, he would look at me with soft eyes and the hint of a smile, which would make me squirm and wriggle; that, in turn, would make him chuckle out loud, and I would get all flushed.

In her letters my mother would always remind me to be good so that I could get out on parole. I wrote her that I was being good, but I would leave out the parts about my having fits; I was trying so hard to be perfect. When I wasn't and I broke one of the rules, such as talking in the dining room, I would become so ashamed and angry at myself that I would have terrible temper tantrums like a two-year-old. I was not the only boy who had fits, yet mine were the most frequent and violent. I even managed to earn the nickname of Fit-taker. Whenever I committed some infraction, I would have to sit in front of my locker and be subjected to the "silent treatment," during which the other boys playing around me could not speak to me, nor I to them. For some reason this kind of punishment made me panic and caused me to cry uncontrollably, to start hitting and kicking my locker or bench, and to plead angrily and submissively by turns with the master not to do this to me. Usually these fits were accompanied by severe bed-wetting episodes. I hated having these fits, and I hated wetting the bed. This earned me the nickname Bed-wetter. I often got into fistfights over these nicknames and found to my surprise that I was a pretty good fighter. Although fighting was a major infraction, the masters, if they were bored, would often let us go at it.

Mr. Costello would become angry with me when I had fits, and he wouldn't talk to me or look at me for days at a time. Nonetheless, our relationship grew. On Sundays, before we went to church, we were each given a quarter to put into the poor box when the basket was passed along the pews. Mr. Costello always had me sit next to him. When it was time to put money into the box, Mr. Costello would hand me a dollar to put in. Once in a while he would take me into the vestry, where Father D'Angelo changed his clothing. From the first time I went in I felt more sure than ever that I wanted to be a priest. I told the father this, and he helped me in my catechism studies by giving me closer instruction. In the spring of 1957 I turned nine and made my first communion. In the church audience I saw my mother, Cheryl, and my nana.

My second summer at the hall was much different from my first. I was so close to Mr. Costello that I no longer had to go to the Big Field in the evenings. He would call for me, and I would sit with him on the big front porch overlooking the reservoir. There we would talk, or I would sing songs and watch the ducks fly as the sun set and as the sky became crimson. Some evenings Mr. Costello's nephew Joseph would come to sit with us. Other times, under Mr. Costello's watchful eye, Joseph and I would play tag or wrestle on the thick green front lawn. I always felt very special, but I felt equally odd that I was being permitted to play with an outside kid.

When the boys went to the lake, I often preferred to stay behind if Mr. Costello was at the hall. He would let me wander the grounds while he worked in his office. Wandering and exploring were still what I loved best. When I wasn't exploring, I would pick blueberries or black raspberries and bring them back to the kitchen. There the cook would help me wash them. I would put some into a bowl and sprinkle them with sugar and a bit of milk and share them with Mr. Costello. Some of the masters complained to Mr. Costello that he was taking their power to control me away from them and that they didn't think I should be given special treatment; they even said as much to me. But how they felt didn't seem to matter to Mr. Costello. He was the boss, and he knew it.

During the summer months Mr. Martin was in charge of the grounds keeping, and along with this duty he kept a small vegetable garden. Mr. Costello arranged to let me help Mr. Martin around the grounds. Mr. Martin liked me, too, and said to me that I didn't belong at the hall. I liked being a farmer and helping

43

Mr. Martin hoe and weed his vegetable garden. He taught me how to turn the soil and how to plant furrows; after a while I felt that I knew enough to start my own garden. I was allowed to purchase some tomato seeds. I then selected a spot I thought would be perfect. I set about turning the soil, planting the seeds, and weeding my garden. Two weeks went by, and I saw no sprouts. I decided that my garden needed fertilizer, and when I came upon a dead woodchuck, I decided it needed a decent burial. So I buried it in the middle of my garden, where I said a high mass and a small prayer to the God of Tomato Sprouts and crossed my fingers. Another week went by, and still I saw no sprouts. Disappointed, I went in shame to tell Mr. Martin my problem. He went with me to my garden to see what the trouble was. He took one look at my plot, and he began tittering: I had built my garden in a grove of crab apple trees where the ground got little sun. I had known this, but I was afraid my little friends would get burned as they grew. I gave up my life of farming and went back to helping Mr. Martin in his garden.

That summer, in the middle of August 1957, I went before the board. I was so proud. I scrubbed myself well that morning in preparation for my parole hearing. I had learned from other boys that going before the parole board did not always mean parole. And so I wanted to be as convincing as I could about how I'd be a good boy if they sent me home. I waited in a chair upstairs with other boys near the room where the parole hearings were being held. When it was my turn, I felt myself begin to perspire. I went in and took my seat in front of the board members. Mr. Gaspar was there; so were Mr. Costello and a couple of other persons. Mr. Gaspar said how glad he was to see me. He thought that I had grown a bit and that I looked well. He went on to explain that he had heard many good things about me. He said that he was proud of my behavior over the past few months. He also told me that Mrs. Shaner thought I was a fine student. Because of these reports, I was to be paroled at the end of the month. I promised that I would be a good boy for my mother. He went on to explain that there were conditions of parole. One was a curfew, and another was that I could not associate with known criminals. I did not understand this. When I asked him who these criminals were and how I would know them, he explained these criminals were the boys I had been in with at John Augustus Hall. As I got up to leave, the board members and Mr. Costello congratulated me. For the next ten days until my parole I went through cycles of incredible joy and deep depression; I could not understand why. The day before my release seemed endless; the night, even longer. Finally, on August 25, 1957, I was paroled. My mother came to get me, and when I went to the car, I saw her boyfriend Bill. The staff came to say good-bye, along with Mr. Costello; they all made me promise not to return. I promised that I never would. Mr. Costello hugged me and held me for a moment as we looked into each other's eyes. I could not believe that I was going home.

My new home, in which my mother had now lived for a time, was in a brick tenement building. It was on the main street, and the el ran right by our living room window. Each time a train would go by I could feel the building rumble and the television picture would go haywire. Yet I was so happy to be home, and I was excited, too, by the sounds and smells of the city.

Inside the apartment I had the sensation of feeling big and tall because it was so tiny and John Augustus Hall had been so big. It took several days for me to get used to it. My brothers and sisters surrounded me as though I were a hero returning from some foreign war. Their eyes were full of wonder as we hugged and kissed each other. They tried to ask me some questions about "camp." I said it was fun, but I didn't want to talk about it much.

I discovered that we did not live far from Franklin Park, and my first instinct was to run up there. I stayed awhile, but things did not feel the same; I didn't know any of the new golfers. Where I once would have easily made friends with them, I now felt shy and withdrawn. I felt different from outside people. I hated that feeling. I even felt it around my siblings and friends. It seemed as though I had forgotten how to make friends or at least I didn't deserve to have outside kids as friends.

My sister Cheryl was not living at home. She was staying with the LeClairs, the parents of Cheryl's best friend, Casey. I did not know why. Sometimes Cheryl would come over to baby-sit with us, and sometimes Cheryl would have to clean the house. It seemed that my mother was interested only in Bill at the time. Cheryl and my mother would get into loud arguments, and Cheryl would stomp out the door. I wondered why Cheryl did not get sent away.

For the first few days I was treated as special by my mother. But soon I was being yelled at for the slightest wrongdoing and being watched more closely than my siblings were. And I was always reminded that my parole officer was only a phone call away and that I could go back. That fear was always inside me so that I was sometimes afraid to even move. Yet it seemed the other children got away with murder. I was at home, and still I felt so separate. But mostly I felt confused.

Bill was now openly living with my mother. When he returned home from work, he was always drunk. My mother would make him a nice supper, after which they would retire to the parlor, where they would sit and drink highballs. After a time they would usually start arguing, and it would get worse and worse. Sometimes it seemed every other word was a swearword. We children would lie in bed, fearing for our mother. Patrice, who slept in the next room with Donna, often crept into bed with Hugh, Kevin, and me because she was so frightened. Once in a while Bill would hit my mother, and we would begin to cry. On Bill's command she would come in and through her tears threaten to strap us if we didn't quiet down. Occasionally Bill would run out the door, and we would crawl into bed with our mother to comfort her and ourselves. It felt wonderful to fall asleep together in her big, soft bed.

Bill did not care for us children. He cared least of all for me. On those rare evenings when the children were allowed into the parlor to watch TV, I was not. On other occasions, usually his payday, he would bring home pizza and ginger ale and give my siblings a few pennies with which to play penny ante. As usual I was not invited to join in the fun but had to lie in my wet bed and listen to them. Sometimes my mother would sneak me a piece of pizza and a little ginger ale. I wanted to ask her what was so wrong with me.

Some nights, if I had given my mother trouble during the day or even for no reason at all, he would call me to come out of my bed and to come into the parlor or have my mother wake me to go to him. He would make me stand in front of him, and in his gruff, adult voice, he would call me a creep, asshole, punk, or jailbird, sometimes making threatening moves toward me. Or sometimes he would just stare at me through his beady dark eyes.

In the fall of 1957, I was placed in the fourth grade at the Margaret Fuller School. I did not do well from the start. I felt really anxious about being in such close contact with outside kids. And again, as often as not, I had tattered clothes and no lunch. Older now, I hated lunchtime and sometimes spent my mornings dreading it. When the bell rang, I would drop down in my seat. I watched the giggling children pull out sandwiches, fruit, and desserts from their lunchboxes. I tried not to look up, for I knew that some of them were looking at me and smirking. The teacher would offer me lunch from her box. I would sit up and say as loudly as I could that I never ate lunch. All the while hunger gnawed at my stomach.

Through it all I was happy to be home. Every month, when my mother got her welfare check, she put out a feast because for a few days before she received her check, all we had to eat was cereal, and we felt lucky if there was milk for it. Even the rats were hungry or bold enough to come into the kitchen as we ate.

After a time, as I began to see that I was treated more harshly than my brothers and sisters, I began to resent them and to become jealous that they were outside kids and had friends. I wanted friends, too. I took money from my mother's purse and bought milk shakes for a few of the neighborhood kids. I thought this

47

would make me their friend. I was caught and strapped. This, and the problems I was having at school, prompted my mother to call Mr. Wachtel, my parole officer.

One day, when I returned from school, he was sitting in the parlor. A wave of horror came over me. What was going on? Mr. Wachtel told me that I was a failure at home and at school and that he was taking me back to John Augustus Hall. I wished I could have died right there, so great was my misery. I had been home only six weeks. I felt as if everyone were ganging up on me, and now Mr. Costello would hate me. I felt like two different people, living two different lives, in two different worlds.

When we arrived, I was taken to see Mr. Costello. He looked at me with accusing eyes. I wanted to tell him that my siblings could do anything they wanted to do but I could not. It wasn't fair. But I believed that because I had been returned, I must be a very bad person. Mr. Costello told me he was ashamed of me. I broke down and had a terrible fit; I had loved my mother and had also really loved Mr. Costello, and now I had lost him, too.

When I was brought down to the Little Dorm, I was greeted with genuine affection and with good-natured taunts from those who knew me about my coming back. I endured my shame for a few days, but soon it all was forgotten.

I was placed in the fourth grade, and I was really happy to see Mrs. Shaner again. I did not hear from or see my mother for some time, and when I did, she was still angry with me. Mr. Costello did not pay any attention to me or smile at me in the dining room, although I tried to look at him and hoped he would. Around Christmas my mother began to write and to see me again. And Mr. Costello and I became close once more.

When I saw Father D'Angelo again, I told him how I was a bad boy and that must make me a sinner. He told me to have faith. He told me God worked in strange ways. He told me that God loved sinners and that the meek would inherit the earth. He told me that many martyrs and even Jesus Himself had endured many struggles; I wondered if I was suffering for some divine plan.

48

Every Saturday we went to our catechism class. I learned that some of the older boys were studying for their confirmations, the time when they would be confirmed into God's Army. I wanted to enlist, but Father D'Angelo told me that I was too young, that perhaps in a couple of years I would be ready. But I wasn't to be denied; I wanted to join God's Army and become closer to the priesthood. I began to ask the older boys at the hall to let me read the books they were studying for their confirmations, and although they thought the request funny, they let me borrow them. All winter I studied whenever I could, and I asked questions of those who were in confirmation class until I knew more than most of them.

In the spring of 1958, just after my tenth birthday, I was moved to the Big Dorm. It was only a week or so before confirmation. I approached Father D'Angelo with my desire to be confirmed. He seemed amused until I asked him to question me. The harder his questions, the more exact were my answers. Finally it was agreed: I would be confirmed. There was no boy happier than I. Proudly I wrote to my mother to tell her that I was going to be confirmed. I was sure that my surprise would prove to her that I was a good Catholic and, therefore, a good boy. Surely I would now be accepted by her as part of the family. I wrote and asked her to be at the church. She wrote and said that she would be there. It all made sense now; how could a good Catholic be a bad boy?

I received my cardinal red confirmation gown, donned it, and stepped onto the bus with the other boys. I thought we made a festive-looking army. Mr. Costello chose to sit on the bus beside me. On the way to the church he asked me what confirmation name I had chosen. I said that I didn't know I was supposed to choose one. He and I laughed because for all my study, I had missed this. I thought about it, and when we arrived at the church, I told Mr. Costello that I wanted to choose Peter, after Peter the Fisherman, whose life story I had read several times. During the ceremony I looked out into the sea of suits, pastel-colored dresses, and holy faces but did not see my mother. I tugged at Mr. Cos-

49

tello's suit and whispered that she had not come. He assured me that she would be there.

I was confirmed Mark Peter Dennis Devlin; I had joined God's Army. When it was over and families moved to embrace their newly confirmed sons, I ran in and around them. With bright eyes I searched for my mother's face. I looked for a long time; she was not there. I bowed my head and wept; even Mr. Costello could not console me. I got a letter from her shortly after saying that she had had car trouble. I immediately believed her, but something in the back of my mind wasn't sure; I think I was beginning to distrust her.

During the summer of 1958 I was still not old enough or big enough to play on the Little League team at the hall, so Mr. Costello arranged with the coach to allow me to be the bat boy whenever the team went to the town park to play an outside team. But as much as I looked forward to these outings, whenever we went to the town park I hated the way we were stared at by both the kids and the grownups.

I still spent my evenings on the porch with Mr. Costello, watching the ducks fly around the reservoir. These were the happiest times for me; everything seemed right, and I felt I was a truly good boy. On one hot July afternoon, as I was playing on the Big Field, I was called to see Mr. Costello. When I arrived at his office, he took me out onto the front lawn to show me something. What I saw was a small pool dug into the lawn and surrounded by a chicken wire fence. Inside it were a small house and three bright yellow baby ducks waddling about. Mr. Costello told me they were mine to name and take care of. I immediately called them Huey, Dewey, and Louie in honor of Donald Duck's three little nephews. This gave Mr. Costello a great big belly laugh; I could always make him laugh.

The next morning I set about the task of cleaning the ducks' pen and their pool as well as giving them drinking water and food. At first they ran away from me, quacking and running in all directions with their tiny wings flapping helplessly. After a time they got to know me and would run up to me when they saw me. I spent a great deal of my time with them, but soon I missed my friends and playing on the field with them. It was near the end of August, and I hadn't gone to see the ducks for a few days. Feeling badly, I caught some frogs to feed to them. I ran down to their pool, but as I got near, I stopped dead in my tracks: The pool and the ducks were gone. I ran into Mr. Costello's office, crying. He told me that officials higher up had told him that the ducks could not stay. For days I didn't know what to do with myself.

In late summer construction began on a long, rectangular brick building against the north side of the hall and extended alongside the Big Field stretching up toward the chicken house. We learned it was to be a new dormitory. As it began to take shape, I came to hate it; it looked like the detention center at Roslindale, and it blocked the view of the pines, the reservoir, and the woodchucks and chipmunks. We had now lost the Big Field and had only the Little Field on which to play, but it was too small for all of us, and it had no baseball diamond. To make matters worse, Mr. Costello called for me less and less. I really missed him, and when I would see him, I would hug him and hold him and ask him why they had to build that ugly building and why he didn't see me more. He said the hall needed more space, and because of this, he was busier now. None of this I understood. But I was glad that we were going back to school and staying indoors all evening because I didn't have to see the building I hated.

I turned eleven the following spring, and in July I was put on parole again. My mother was still living on the same tenement block as the first time I was paroled; things had not changed really. Again I was treated nicely during those first few days, and then again I was more closely watched. This time I felt much shyer and more self-conscious than I had my first time at home. Not only did I have problems relating to outside kids, but I also now had to try to relate to girls since my mother insisted that my sister Cheryl take me to the local dance at St. Peter's. My sister knew most of the young teen-agers there; I knew no one. My sister introduced me to a couple of people, then was gone for the rest of the night, dancing and talking with her friends. There was a piano in the dance hall, and I spent the whole evening standing next to it with my hands folded. After the dance Cheryl came to take me home and laughed at me when she saw me in the same position she had left me in a couple of hours before. On our way home she confided to me that her friends thought I was weird. She asked me why I hadn't joined in, and I told her I didn't know.

Once again I took money from my mother's purse to buy frappes for kids, and once again I was caught. I would probably have been sent back, but my brothers, older now, were sneaking cigarettes and pilfering from the five-and-dime, so I guessed that stealing from my mother's purse didn't seem as bad. But it got me a good strapping and a warning.

One Sunday, two weeks after I was returned home, I opened our back door to find two small dogs sitting there. Each of them had a pained, starved look on his face. I understood; I knew how they felt. Their mangy skin was pressed hard against their ribs, and I thought surely the skin would rip. I took some hamburger meat from my mother's refrigerator and fed them. Monday morning I was in Mr. Wachtel's car on my way back to John Augustus Hall.

In the two weeks I had been at home the boys had moved up to an empty field with foot-high grass and lots of purple clover. There wasn't any room to play baseball or to play any other sports either, and so we spent our time playing tag or catching bees and pulling their stingers out.

Father D'Angelo had been transferred, and Mr. Costello no longer called for me. Feeling that I had no one left in the world, I decided to run away and to live in the woods with the animals. I thought about it for a week or so and told a couple of the other kids about my plans, but no one wanted to go with me. After supper one evening in late August, when we were taken to the

52

field, I inched my way to a short stone wall that bordered a cow pasture. Thinking that no one saw me, I jumped over the wall and right into the waiting arms of two of the teen-aged masters' aides; they beat me, split my lip, bloodied my nose, and ripped my clothes. They were joined by one of the masters and proceeded to drag me down the old cow path to Mr. Costello's office. He looked scornfully at me and said that he could no longer keep me at the hall. I only wanted him to love me again, but I knew that he, like everyone else, hated me because I had returned.

A few days later I was taken to Lyman School for Boys.

BOOK II

Lyman School for Boys

AUGUST 27, 1959

I ARRIVED AT Lyman School in the early afternoon and was immediately taken to the administration building to see Mr. Wolcott, the superintendent. He was a balding, soft-spoken man of delicate manners. He sat me in a chair across from his desk and told me that he was a good friend of Mr. Costello, who had asked Mr. Wolcott to watch over me. My heart glowed, and my cheeks turned red; Mr. Costello still loved me. But before he ushered me out of his office, he warned me that my shenanigans would not be tolerated at Lyman and that if I kept my nose clean, I might be able to get a Christmas furlough and would probably be paroled home soon after.

A master took me out and put me in a van. He drove along a paved road. As I looked out the window, I saw so many buildings and boys that I felt scared. We arrived at a large two-story brick building. He took me through a door and down a short flight of steps into a locker room. It was larger than any at John Augustus Hall and in the middle of the room was a Ping-Pong table. I was taken past it and was made to stand in front of a small desk. A man with thin, graying hair and a hawklike nose introduced himself as Mr. Kelley and told me that he was my housefather. He logged me in and assigned me to a locker. I looked around and saw about thirty other boys. Unlike my last arrival at John Augustus Hall, when the boys ran up to greet me, no one took any

57

special interest in me. Most merely looked up for a moment and then went back to their funny books, cards, letter writing, or whatever it was they had been doing. This gave me the chance to sneak looks at all of them. Most were much bigger than I was, and I could hear that their voices were as deep as adults'. Some of the boys had tattoos on their hands; I noticed that one boy had *Love* written across one set of his knuckles and *Hate* written across the other. I guessed they were teen-agers, and I felt really scared. Although I had never seen it, I had heard about older boys trying to pressure younger, littler boys into having sex with them. I could defend myself against kids my own size and height, I knew. But I decided that if someone bigger tried to bother me, I would fight him anyway, even if I lost. And if I lose, I would never fink. It was the worst thing an inmate could do; everyone hated a fink.

While I was sitting there, a short, wiry man came over and sat down beside me and said that he was my counselor, Mr. Farber. He explained that all the different buildings on the grounds were cottages in which the boys lived and that the one I was in now was called Lyman Hall. He told me that I wouldn't be in Lyman Hall long and that I would soon be put into a cottage with boys closer to my age. He also told me that I would be attending school on the grounds. I was happy to hear this. I liked to learn, and I remembered Mrs. Shaner. School took my mind off being away from home, too. Mr. Farber told me that he had to leave but that he just wanted to introduce himself and try to put me at ease. I decided that I liked him and hoped we could spend more time together.

Just after he left, I was startled by the sound of a loud whistle. This whistle signaled the end of the day: mail and roll call (also known as count time), supper, and the changing of the guard. After the mail had been distributed and we all had been accounted for, we were assembled outside the building in a row two abreast, smallest first; I stood at the head of the line with another boy. Mr. Kelley stood beside a short, graying lady. She was Mrs. Kelley, and before we could head up the road to the cafeteria, we

had to say in unison, "Good evening, Mr. and Mrs. Kelley." As
I recited the greeting, I decided that Mrs. Kelley looked like one
of the nuns at Sister School; she had their same cheerless, deadpan
expression.

We were marched along a road where I saw other large groups
of boys trooping along in the same fashion. When we arrived at
the cafeteria, I could not believe how big it was. It was a cinder
block and glass structure. One wall was mostly taken up by a
giant picture window, through which I could see a big baseball
field; I thought that maybe I could get to play baseball at Lyman
School. Each dorm had its own long table, where pitchers of milk
were placed several spaces apart. I took my metal tray and went
through the line and then walked to our section and took my
assigned seat. I could not eat and only picked at my food. Mrs.
Kelley poured milk for us under her husband's watchful eye.
When the milk was poured, each of them took a seat at the head
of a different table. Sitting there and looking around me, I decided
that I did not like Lyman School because there were so many
people.

In the evening after supper we spent our time playing in the
locker room. At about 8:00 P.M. we showered. I was given a heavy,
scratchy muslin nightgown and thick-soled leather slippers. We
were lined up and taken up a long staircase to the top-floor dorm.
In it must have been fifty beds.

The next day, after breakfast, Mr. Farber came to see me again.
He took me outside and put me into his car and drove around
the institution. As we drove around, I realized that the place was
even bigger than I had imagined. He explained that the boys at
Lyman School were separated into age-groups and that each of
the cottages where the boys lived had a different name. The
exception to this scheme was Oak, the disciplinary cottage where
the bad boys were put. Mr. Farber made me promise never to go
there. I promised him I never would; I wasn't ever going to be
a bad boy again. He told me that boys sent to Oak lost all their
privileges. That meant TV, movies, visitors, mail, church services,

and conversation, and the boys there were made to work on "the line" all day. Above all, the boys at Oak couldn't accumulate any credits. Mr. Farber explained to me that in order to be paroled, a boy had to earn a certain number of credits. He told me that I would have to earn 700. I gulped. He said that I would accrue 2 credits for every day at Lyman, or 60 a month. If I misbehaved, a master could subtract any amount of credits from my total that he wanted to. At that moment I resolved never to lose a credit. And I believed that I never would.

Mr. Farber continued to drive me around the grounds; he showed me the hospital, the power plant, the clothing room and warehouse, and the houses provided by the state for the superintendent and the assistant superintendent. He showed me where the clergymen's offices, chapel, auditorium, and gymnasium were located. He then drove down to show me the farm. Mr. Farber said there were about fifty or so acres planted with corn, green and yellow string beans, cucumbers, radishes, and other crops. I remembered Mr. Martin and said that I would like to work on the farm. Mr. Farber told me that with the exception of a couple of the older boys who lived at Elm Cottage and who were regular hands, the only boys who worked the farm were those from Oak Cottage.

I stayed at Lyman Hall for two weeks. During that time I became sick with an ear infection; otherwise I had no problem. I was kept in the hospital for a couple of days because I had a fever. The nurse told me that I was getting better and that I would be leaving in the morning. I liked having a woman take care of me so much that the next morning I put my thermometer on the radiator. When Mrs. Malik, the nurse, came back to read my temperature, she told me I had better roll over because I was dead. Then she explained why. We shared a good laugh, and she let me stay an extra day.

Back at Lyman Hall, I found out that a talent show had been planned. I decided to enter. Off our dorm was the locker room. I asked Mr. Kelley if I could make a guitar, and with his consent

I began my project. I shaped it from a piece of plywood, sawed it out, painted it, and then attached thin wires to it along the neck. It was only make-believe and could not make any sounds, but it looked real.

Before the night of the show I asked Mr. Farber to come to the show to see me perform. He agreed. That night, when my turn came, I jumped up on top of the Ping-Pong table and began to sing "Hound Dog," which Elvis Presley had made popular. I strummed my guitar and yelled more than I sang. Some kids laughed, and some kids clapped. After the show Mr. Farber thanked me for inviting him and treated me to an ice cream cone from a store off the grounds. Whenever I saw Mr. Farber after that, I would start singing to him; I liked ice cream.

I was transferred to Overlook Cottage in the beginning of September. I was glad to see that the children there were mostly around my age. I met my houseparents, Mr. and Mrs. Wynn; both were quite old but had full heads of white hair. Mr. and Mrs. Wynn always dressed formally, he in a bow tie and suit, she always in an ankle-length dress.

Now that I was settled in, I was sent to the clothing room to get some standard issue and a Sunday suit. A boy of about thirteen was assigned to take me to see Mr. McKean, the clothing room master. On the way over the boy asked me what crime I was in for. I said I didn't know, but I thought it was because I was a bad boy. He seemed not to believe me and told me he was in for being involved with a stolen car ring. That sounded important, and I thought that he must be really cool. He showed me a pink slip with both our names on it, our destination, the time we had set out, as well as Mr. Wynn's signature. He told me that it was a pass and that if we were caught on the grounds alone without one, we would be sent to Oak for attempted escape. When we arrived at the clothing room, Mr. McKean noted the time and asked the boy what had taken us so long to get there. The boy said he was showing me around a little bit. Satisfied, Mr. McKean gave me some casual wear and a pair of plain black shoes. He also gave me my white Sunday shirt, a suit, and a tie.

I was assigned to the sixth grade. My teacher's name was Mr. Jamison. He was a quiet man who nipped from a bottle in his desk drawer. He was a good teacher, interested in us and in our work. We studied arithmetic, English, history, and science and read stories aloud. We attended school from 9:00 to 11:00 A.M.; then we returned to our cottages to clean up for lunch and resumed classes at 1:00 P.M.. At 4:00 P.M. the whistle blew, marking the end of the afternoon. I hated the whistle because its shrillness always made me jump; besides, I liked school at Lyman. Classes were small since only about a third of the 400 boys attended. My only real problem at school was that I often finished my assignments well before the other students and Mr. Jamison would often give me extra work, which I would still finish up ahead of the others. After a while Mr. Jamison got tired of trying to occupy me and would just let me sit daydreaming.

While I was at Overlook, I saw my mother only once and received very few letters from her. This really saddened me because at John Augustus Hall, which was farther away from Boston than Lyman was, she came to see me every visiting day and wrote often to me. Sometimes she sent me packages of books or toys or plastic model planes or ships and other sorts of things that boys liked. But as these became more infrequent, I became one of only a couple of boys in the cottage who did not regularly receive mail or visits. For this I became known as a State Boy, which was the worse kind of thing to be. A State Boy was looked down upon by everyone; it meant that he was a forgotten kid who was totally dependent on the state. A State Boy never received packages from home, not even at Christmas. Sometimes these packages would consist of everyday items like combs, bars of soap, tubes of toothpaste, hairbrushes, and towels. These things were called outside soap or outside toothpaste. Anything the state provided was called state stuff, like state soap and such. A kid who was a State Boy was easy to spot because he had to use state stuff. Most kids would have first killed themselves rather than have to use state stuff, the humiliation State Boys would be subjected to was that serious. I guess my ostracism by other inmates made me begin to resent and hate my mother. Even though I wrote and told her what I was going through, she never sent me outside soap or outside *anything*. Sometimes the other boys would be cruel and say, "Devlin's a State Boy." That hurt me a lot because I knew it was true. I would want to hide in a corner and never come out. On top of this I was a bed-wetter, and everyone knew it. Except for the hours I spent in the schoolroom, where I excelled, most of the time I felt ugly and inferior.

A few days before Christmas, school was suspended as we prepared for this, the holiest of holy days. There was a lot of activity on the grounds as maintenance men strung up lights on trees and buildings. I loved Christmas because it was such a happy time, and everyone was always so much nicer to each other than usual. I wasn't getting a furlough home, but neither were lots of kids in my cottage. I knew, too, that my mother would be coming to see me. She had indicated as much when she had written to thank me for the little clay Magi I had made for her in school, and I was sure that I would, in turn, receive at least one package from her. I knew as well that the Lions Club and the Rotary Club would give us toys and a party.

As I lay in my bed Christmas night, I stared at the ceiling. My mother had not come, nor had she sent me a package, and there hadn't been any party. During the day I had received a small box along with the other boys. The box was wrapped in red paper and the gold lettering said:

MERRY CHRISTMAS
From the
Archdiocese of
RICHARD CARDINAL CUSHING

Inside the box there was some hard candy and a plastic pen.

I was glad when the holidays were over and school began again. I now hated Christmas, especially when I imagined my mother and my siblings opening presents around their Christmas tree. I thought my family must hate me, and so I started to hate them.

As the second semester of school opened, I was still finishing my assignments ahead of my classmates and left to daydreaming. My teacher took me to see the principal, Mr. Hamlin, and told him that I was capable of eighth-grade work. I was reassigned to the eighth grade in the early part of that second semester—a jump of two levels. My teacher's name was Mr. Renner. He was a chain-smoking Broderick Crawford type, with a rough and gravelly voice to match. I looked forward to the challenge of my new class. Mr. Renner taught the same subjects as Mr. Jamison except that he would not remain in the classroom with us after he had given us an assignment. He would stand out in the corridor and talk to the teacher of the class across the hall. I knew he was doing something wrong because he would say to the other teacher, "Cheese it. There's Hamlin," and return to the classroom and his desk. As soon as the coast was clear, he would go back into the hall. The other boys didn't mind that he did this because they weren't studying anyway. But I missed Mr. Jamison. I did fine in all my subjects, although math was difficult for me and becoming more so as the days wore on. Mr. Renner would teach it so quickly that I couldn't keep up with him. Sometimes I would go out into the hall to ask him for help with a problem, and he would say, "Sure. Sure, kid. I'll be right in." But he never did come in, and by spring I was too far behind to catch up.

One day Mr. Renner told me that I wasn't capable of eighth-grade work. When I challenged him about his standing in the hallway, his face turned beet red and he said, "Why, you insolent little cocksucker!" and kicked me hard in the shin. A sharp, burning pain shot up my leg, and through tears of pain and anger I threw my pencil at him. I knew the minute it left my hand that I was in trouble. Mr. Renner grabbed me by the scruff of the neck so hard that I felt as if I were choking. He dragged me down to Mr. Hamlin's office. I could hear the class cheering as I was taken away. Mr. Renner told the principal that I had thrown my pencil at him. I told Mr. Hamlin that he kicked me hard and showed him my cut shin to prove it. Mr. Renner lied and said I had banged it on a chair when I was fighting with him. I protested, but Mr. Hamlin told me to have a seat, dismissed Mr. Renner, and picked up the phone to call somebody. I sat there wondering what was going to happen to me. Soon a man came and took me out to a pickup truck. I was going to Oak Cottage. At that moment my world crashed in on me. All my perfect behavior was for nothing. Now my mother would really hate me. On the way to the farm where the boys from Oak were at work, all I could think of was how much I hated school and adults.

I was taken into the main farmhouse, where the linemasters were sitting around drinking coffee. It was early afternoon, and I saw the boys standing at attention a few feet from the farmhouse in rows of four abreast. I thought this must be the line. I had seen these boys occasionally around the roads at Lyman and had heard the other inmates laugh at them. But whenever a boy came off the line, he was given a lot of respect.

I was taken before the head lineman, a narrow-eyed, balding man named Mr. Gray. I hated him right away. He told me that he would straighten out my "goddamn ass." He went on to tell me that all boys on the line were fuck-ups, and so was I. I felt tears start to form in my eyes; I didn't want to be a fuck-up. He told me that if I fucked up on his line, he would beat the shit out of me with an ax handle or worse. He then slapped me hard across the face to let me know who he was and then motioned to a deputy to put me on the line. I took my place at the front of the line and stood there at attention and fought back tears. I wondered why everyone, especially my mother, hated me so much. I wondered how she could let people do this to me. Even though I was angry with her, I could not help crying to myself, "Mommy! Mommy! Help me please."

I stood that way for a long time while the other boys on the line tried to ask me through clenched teeth what I had done. I was too afraid I would get beaten with an ax handle to respond.

After a long time the linemasters came out and marched us past the other boys up a road. One master stood in front of us, another to our side, and another in back. We were marched down to the clothing room, and as we were marched, I felt that all those who knew me from Overlook were looking at me and laughing. I kept my head lowered to avoid their eyes. Once at the clothing room I was given army boots and khaki work clothes. After we all had changed, we were marched back to the farm. Each of us was made to get down on our hands and knees and hand-weed rows of vegetables. As I was weeding my row, the boy in the next row was trying to talk to me, but I kept trying to tell him I didn't want to talk. Then I felt a pain more searing than I'd ever felt shoot up from between my legs. I screamed in agony as I lurched forward, and my face came to rest in the dirt. Mr. Gray was standing over me. I would get a worse kick than that if I talked again, he said. He spoke to me as I lay there writhing, begging God and my mother please to help me. He ordered me to stop my whining and get back to my row. The pain subsided, but I was sore all afternoon.

When the day's work was done, we were taken to wash our hands and faces at the cannery. When we finished, we were taken to eat our supper at the cafeteria. We sat alone; we were not permitted to mingle with any of the other population. After supper we were taken to the locker room at Oak, where the night master took charge of us. His name was Mr. Preston. He was short and squat and had a large shovel-shaped nose which, like his chalky face, had red and blue veins running through it. He made a head count and then sat down at his desk. We were made to sit up straight in front of our lockers in silence for the next two hours while he dozed on and off. We dared not move, for he had told us that he had a loaded gun in his desk drawer—and we believed him.

The next morning I met Mr. Reitz, the housefather. He called me to his desk and made me take my pants down. He then whacked me hard across my bottom with a long flat board and told me that it was for nothing, but just to wait until I did do something. Back on the bench again I wept softly to myself. When I had gathered enough courage to look around me, I saw that nobody was laughing. The other boys all had pained expressions on their faces; I could have been any one of them.

Our days began at six in the morning, when we were taken to breakfast. By seven we were assembled to begin our day's work. Sometimes we were simply made to stand in front of the school-hospital while Mr. Gray went inside to have coffee with Mrs. Little, the head nurse, whom he liked. More often than not, though, we were taken directly to the farm and put to weeding. We were also used for odd jobs like unloading the trucks that came to the warehouse. Even though I now hated school, I wished I were there. And even though I liked farming, I didn't like what we were doing.

Above all, I dreaded the nights. Mr. Preston was on duty five nights a week. Whenever he would catch someone whispering, he would make all of us pull our benches away from the lockers and kneel for an hour or more on the hard pockmarked concrete floor. Our backs ached so much from the strain that we would often tremble and the ridges and sharp points in the concrete would dig into our knees until tears sprang to our eyes. One night a boy who we knew was retarded expressed the frustration we all felt: He stood up and put his fist through the window, cutting his arm so deep that we could see the fat hanging out.

If five nights of Preston wasn't enough, I now wet my bed every night, and heavily. I was also beginning to have nightmares; we were told that blood-crazed maniacs from the state hospital nearby lurked alongside a monster who roamed the woods near Oak Cottage, looking for young boys who tried to run away or who were very bad. My nightmares grew so intense—we had been told that when the monster caught a boy, he would cut him up and eat him—that I was taken to see Mrs. Reardon, the institution psychologist. She would talk to me about my dreams and nightmares. It helped but not much. And I remained, all the while, on the line; I was there longer than I had expected; why I did not know. I thought that they were trying to teach me a lesson. I celebrated my twelfth birthday at Oak.

In July I was placed in a cottage for older boys, ages fourteen to sixteen. I think that the masters thought the older boys would keep me on the straight and narrow. The new cottage was called Worcester, and I liked it. For one thing we got to stay up later and to watch TV. Also, we did not have a regular housefather or mother or master, but rather a group of them, who were much younger than most of the masters. I liked them because they were friendlier to us. I think they were studying law at a nearby college.

Worcester was also a smoking cottage. Though I was too young to smoke, I thought it would make me feel big and grown-up. I couldn't wait to be grown-up because the masters always picked on the little kids.

That summer we spent our days playing either on the ballfield or on our own lawn. Most of the guys wouldn't play with me because I was a State Boy and also because I was younger and smaller than they. Still, even though I was considered a State Boy, I was pretty well respected by most of the guys since I had done a long stretch on the line; the longer the stretch, the more they respected you. I really didn't mind that I was not more than casually accepted by the guys; I hated Lyman, and I didn't want to be a part of it. Throughout my incarceration I had felt that I wasn't really guilty of anything, and so if I joined in with the boys or in the program, I would be admitting my guilt. The fact that I had been sent away, and had been away for some time, had to mean in some people's minds that I was guilty of something— but not in my mind.

Langer, a blond, husky kid, came to Worcester soon after I had arrived; he was only a year older than I, and we became friends. A couple of older boys told me that I shouldn't hang around with him because he was queer. This was my first real experience with homosexuality. Even though I knew how queers at Lyman were hated, I decided not to care if Langer was queer because he was my only friend at Worcester. Since he never tried to touch me, no one could connect me with any homosexuality. But when another boy named Trent came to Worcester from Oak, and I learned that he was Langer's special friend, I hung around with Langer less. On one of the few times I did hang around with them, they taught me how to smoke. I didn't like it yet soon found myself lining up after each meal and before bedtime for my daily ration of cigarettes. These were state-supplied cigarettes called Airlines or Wings, and the masters used them to reward or control our behavior. Another time Langer and Trent asked me if I wanted to learn about sex. I was only twelve and didn't know what sex was really about. I became frightened of them after that, and I avoided them.

In the fall of that year, 1960, I was placed back in school, but in the disciplinary class. My teacher was a musclebound man whose name was Mr. Hogan. We called him Superman behind his back. He was feared by both the boys *and* the masters. Beside his desk he kept a wooden paddle which he called his glutus maximus stick. To his credit he was an able teacher, but I hated schoolwork now. The way I got back at school, at all of it, was not to learn. I knew that no matter what the teachers did, they could not make me learn. When I would turn in incomplete assignments or assignments with purposely incorrect answers, Mr. Hogan would threaten me with his stick. I would cry and say that I really was trying to do my best. There was nothing he could do to me, and secretly I gloated.

I devised a whole array of excuses to get excused from school at every opportunity. I would complain of earaches to get to the hospital. I would make up stories of nightmares or other things in order to get appointments to see Mrs. Reardon. I joined the choir so that I could get passes to choir practice. Since I was now considered somewhat of a veteran at Lyman, my passes were not so closely scrutinized; sometimes the issuing master wouldn't even bother to write the time on it, and so I could dillydally on my way to my destination. I discovered that several older boys, teen-agers really, played this pass game, too. A couple of them had stolen pass books from the warehouse, and every once in a while I could barter cigarettes for forged passes. Eventually I got so good at the pass game that I could sometimes get out of class for a day or two at a time.

In October Father D'Angelo was transferred to Lyman and soon started altar boy classes. I was still thinking about the priest-hood, so I joined the altar boy classes. I felt really good about myself for the first time in a long while. Father D'Angelo had changed, though; he wasn't as friendly as he used to be. I liked the altar boy classes and it also gave me another excuse to get out of school. I didn't have a lot going for me, but I was pretty resourceful. It comforted me to think that I was doing my time at Lyman somewhat on my own terms.

During the time I was at Worcester I never saw my mother, and I heard from her only once or twice. But that was okay because I really didn't think about her much anymore since the reality of her seemed so far away and long before. Around Halloween, however, I had to go into Boston to have my ear checked. I wrote and told my mother that I would be in Boston and asked her to come and see me. She wrote back and said she would. I didn't realize how deeply I missed her, and I was so happy that she still wanted to see me. I began preparing for my visit to Boston; it had been a year since I had been away at Lyman. I had no idea how many credits I had earned or when I would ever go home. But I knew I was struggling at Lyman, and I tried not to care about the stupid credits.

The evening before I was due at the hospital I decided to spit-shine my shoes. I was sitting happily by a window in the TV room when I heard a tapping sound on the glass. I looked up to see a hideous bloody face staring back at me. I shrieked, jumped from my seat, and threw my shoebrush and shoes at the monster. The face went away. The master on duty came over to me and tried to calm me, but I stood shaking like a jackhammer; all I could see was the monster looking at me. All of what they had told me at Oak was true, and so were my nightmares: There *were* monsters lurking outside at night, and they were trying to get me because I was such a bad boy. Some of the boys gathered around me and laughed; they all thought it was a big joke. The master left me for a minute and returned with a mask which made me even more frightened. He could not convince me that the lifeless rubber mask and the thing in the window were the same. That evening I could not sleep. And after that I began to have really bad nightmares.

The next morning I was taken to the hospital. Seeing my mother was so wonderful that I almost forgot about the previous night's event. But I told her about it anyway. She tried to make light of it. As she got ready to leave, I clutched her and tried to explain how I didn't want to be a State Boy anymore and how much it hurt being a State Boy, and wouldn't she please come to visit me? She said she was sorry that she hadn't been up but now would try to see me more regularly.

When I returned to Lyman, I became withdrawn and sullen after I found out that the masters had schemed together to scare me. They all knew I was afraid of monsters, yet they still conspired to do this to me. I decided to resume my brand of passive resistance.

Two days after my hospital visit I was caught on the grounds of Lyman without a pass, meaning that I was attempting an escape. I was taken back to Oak Cottage.

The next day, when Mr. Gray saw me, he said, "Welcome back, fuck-up." I wanted to say to him that maybe fuck-ups weren't fuck-ups because they wanted to be or even liked being the way they were. Maybe there was something fucked-up *about* them. It was around this time that I started to think that there must be something retarded about me since I could never seem to do anything right.

After we boys tramped down to the clothing room to receive our boots, work clothes, and bright-colored mackinaw jackets and gloves, we were marched down to the farmhouse, where we were made to stand at attention. During the winter there wasn't much farm work for us to do, so we often just stood in line for the entire day while the linemen sat in the farmhouse office, drinking coffee. By lunchtime we'd be frozen. If the linemen grew bored, they would call some boy into the office and make jokes about his family; masters read and censored incoming mail and therefore knew a lot of personal information about our families.

I was really starting to hate. I hated hating, but I could not help myself. I felt that everyone hated me. Although I tried not to hate, I found myself intently watching everything the masters did or said, and if I saw people—a visitor, a stranger, whoever— talk or act as they did, I would hate them, too. I hated grownups, and I became even determined never to grow up to be a mean adult. Observing and hating were what I always thought about. I would look for anything to hate. But the idea of hating hurt me deeply and sometimes made me cry.

In November I was taken to see a visiting doctor. He tried to get me to talk about myself and Lyman. I made believe I was shy, but I just didn't want to talk to adults anymore. The doctor gave me some pills for my bed-wetting, but they didn't help.

I remained on the line until just before Christmas. I was then placed in Hillside Cottage with boys who were seventeen to eighteen. I thought surely I would be sexually pressured, and I was scared. But the boys there treated me like a kid brother: I had their respect because I had twice been to Oak.

The housefather was named Mr. Carpenter. Even though I wanted to hate him, I couldn't because he was so nice and gentle and grandfatherly. When we met, he told me he was happy to have me in his cottage and to behave myself and I'd be fine. I expected him to call me "fuck-up" or "State Boy" the way most of the masters did. He didn't, and I was grateful.

I was placed back in Mr. Hogan's class, where I continued to refuse to excel; this time it was made easier by the fact that I was really behind in my schoolwork from being on the line. I also went right back to getting passes any way that I could, and sometimes I would sneak a walk around the grounds; I wasn't afraid of Oak anymore. Anyway, it seemed I would never be going home to live again.

With Christmas being near, however, I thought surely I would get a pass home. I knew that I didn't have enough credits to go on parole, but after more than a year I must have earned enough to get a Christmas furlough. I really wanted to go home. I hadn't spent Christmas or Thanksgiving or my birthday there in almost six years. But no pass came. Instead of a pass for home, all I got was a card from my mother. In it was a short message in which she said she was sad that I would not be home for Christmas but that I should cheer up because she was sure I would be paroled soon. As she always did, she went on to tell me how bright and smart I was, and because everyone said so, it must be true. If I was so smart, I thought bitterly, how come I was in jail and why did everyone, my mother included, hate me?

I spent Christmas Eve alone in the dorm. The silence was deafening. I crept from my bed to look out the window. I watched cars moving slowly about the brightly lit grounds. I knew that inside the cars were families coming to pick up their sons to take them home for the holiday. As I watched them go, tears gushed from my eyes and formed small pools on the sills. The reality of my life lay stark against the night, and I wondered what was so awful about me. I hated Christmas and myself. I remembered my rosary beads and someone once telling me that if I said a novena over and over on each little bead each day for nine months, I would get a wish. I lay in my bed and began my novena. My wish: to be a good boy. I began kissing the pictures of Jesus and the Virgin Mary that were on my scapular, which I wore around my neck and which I had received for my confirmation. I fell asleep before finishing. When I awoke, I remembered my novena, kissed my scapular, and began my prayer again.

A couple of days after Christmas the boys who had been furloughed home returned. I saw their happy faces and their new airplane models and games, and I became more determined than ever to complete my novena. After a short time, though, life at the school returned to normal, and I stopped my novena.

Nighttime remained tough for me because I continued to bed-wet and have occasional nightmares. The nightmares started up again in a serious way when at bedtime one night we saw lots of lights on the grounds. When I went to the window to look with the other boys, we saw the red flashing lights of police cars. I became scared because I thought it must mean that the monster was loose again and that the police and masters must be trying to catch him. I didn't say anything because I was with older boys now and I didn't want to act like a little kid or risk their laughing at me. That night, though, I could not sleep. My bed was next to a locked room where linens and cleaning supplies were kept. When Mr. Carpenter, the night master that evening, came around and asked me why I was still awake, I told him I was scared to sleep next to the door. I thought that goblins and ogres and witches were behind it. Mr. Carpenter tried to dispel my fears, but I was still lying there, wondering whether they had caught the monster, when I fell asleep.

I was not asleep long before I woke up screaming. I had felt the monster's cold, strong hand on my neck choking me. The next day I was sent back to see Mrs. Reardon. I didn't mind seeing her again because she wasn't a male and she wasn't a master. I had seen the school shrink, Mr. Swann, a couple of times. I thought his name was nice, but I didn't like him. The only reason I went to see him was that he gave me cigarettes. With my pass in hand I went to see Mrs. Reardon.

She asked me what I was afraid of. I told her I had many fears: dark streets; scary Halloween masks; windows that rattled on windy nights. She smiled and asked me what else. I told her about the monsters. She told me to try to think about something pleasant before I went to sleep, something that I liked to do. I couldn't think of anything, but then I remembered Mr. Milici at John Augustus Hall, and I said, "Fishing!" I promised I would try it

74

that very night and come back to see her the following day.

That night I dreamed I was fishing by a brook on a cloudless and cool summer day. The line tightened, and I smiled as I reeled in a large fish. Then my expression turned to horror as the fish became a monster. I shook and cried and screamed when in my mind I saw its big mouth open up to swallow me.

When I told Mrs. Reardon about it the next day, it sounded almost funny, and we both laughed. She told me to keep trying to think about nice things and to try to calm my fears by saying out loud to the monster, or to the mask, or to the rattling windows, to stop or to go away.

Like "Stop shaking you?" I asked her.

"That's right," she said and smiled again.

I promised I would keep trying.

In addition to my fear of monsters, I had to battle against my fear of Mr. Innis, the evening master who made me his whipping boy. What he liked to do best was to compile a list of our infractions. Then, when it was time for our evening shower, he would call off his list of names. Those of us who were on it—and it seemed I always was—had to stand in front of the line. As we stepped from the shower stall, he would whack us hard on our wet bottoms with a leather slipper. If one of us cried, he would be incited to beat the crying boy even harder. Other times he would order us to sit in front of our lockers for the evening while he played Ping-Pong with his favorites. I would glare at him when he did this because the table was for us boys, and he would hog it for the whole night. More seriously, when he found that I had wet my bed one night and had not reported it, he beat me with his leather belt. I was balled up in the corner of my bed, trying to cover myself against the strapping he was giving me. Suddenly he stopped and said, "Oh, shit." I looked up and saw that his belt had broken in two. If it had not broken, there was no telling when he would have stopped. I thought of all the times I'd asked for God's help and thought perhaps He had finally heard me.

In the spring of 1961 both Langer and Trent were returned to

Hillside. I learned that they had been originally placed in Oak for homosexuality; now at Hillside the guys avoided them or called them names. It was a funny thing about homosexuality: I noticed that the guys who appeared to be the toughest and said most often they hated queers were, in fact, the ones having sex with homosexuals, or were on the receiving end, as they would be sure to qualify, as if this somehow excused them. So, too, many boys fought each other openly for the sexual attentions of particularly attractive, known queers. But it seemed to me that just because these guys were on the receiving end, they were much the same as the queers they said they hated; it confused me. One evening I was sitting on the stairs near the TV room, shining my shoes, when Langer and Trent came out to shine their shoes. They were there for only a couple of minutes when I noticed them touching each other. I asked what they were doing, and they said that they were masturbating and wouldn't I like to know how to do it. After some coaxing and prodding I tried it with them. I felt a warm sensation all over me like when someone hugged me. It was nice, but I did it only a couple of times after that, just when I felt really lonely or unloved.

Every month a couple of boys were assigned to clean the locker room. We called this a GI party. All the boys looked forward to taking their turns because while we were working, we were allowed to listen to the radio and were given extra cigarettes. One evening Langer and Trent and I were assigned together. While I was busy scrubbing the locker room floor, I realized that Langer and Trent were missing. I checked the shower and bath areas: no sign of them. Then I checked a small room off the boiler room. In the room were a couple of clotheslines over which I routinely hanged the sheets that I washed by hand the morning after one of my bed-wetting episodes. When I didn't hear my two coworkers, I stepped inside to have a look. I saw some movement behind my sheet, and coming around it, I found Langer and Trent doing something funny. They told me that they were having intercourse and coaxed me to try it. I did. It was like playing a new game. But before long we were caught by Mr. Napier, the master who was supervising the cleanup. He didn't make a big deal of it, but he nonetheless took away our cigarettes for a week.

Sometimes I would hear the older boys talk about sex with girls. I didn't know anything about girls, although I wanted to; I knew that having sex with a girl someday would mean that I wouldn't be thought of as a little kid anymore. But I had never really been around girls, except for my sisters. And sisters weren't like girls.

When the evenings became warmer and the light stayed longer, Mr. Carpenter would have us take off our shoes and socks and go out onto the big lawn to kick around a ball. What we were doing, he told us, was called soccer; most of us never heard of it before. We felt silly playing it, but Mr. Carpenter was adamant, even as the other boys and masters laughed at us. I heard someone say that Mr. Carpenter was eccentric, and I wondered what it meant. I thought it was a swearword or something.

After soccer Mr. Carpenter would take us on a long walk to a state fish and game reserve. Nearby was a small pond. Mr. Carpenter told us never to go near it. I thought that an odd thing to say because if any one of us were found near it, we would be considered runaways. Someone then said that he'd heard that the masters sometimes killed boys and buried them there. This really upset me, but I put it out of my mind. Then one evening something strange happened.

About a week later, two boys had run away from Hillside when Mr. Innis was on duty. To run away from Lyman was bad enough; to run away during Mr. Innis's shift was inviting even more trouble. The two boys who escaped were duly caught and returned to Hillside, but before being placed in Oak, they were taken to see Mr. Innis; he had let out the word that he wanted them first. When the boys arrived, Mr. Innis said that he was going to show us why we shouldn't try to escape while he was on. He took one of the boys into the boiler room and shut the door. We could hear him beating the boy and the boy begging Innis to stop, promising him that he would never run away again. Suddenly there was silence. Mr. Innis came out of the boiler room, and he was very nervous. He told us to go to our beds even though it was only about seven in the evening. As we changed into our nightclothes, he made a phone call, and we could hear the agitation in his voice. I had never seen him act that way. While lying in bed, I wondered if the boy was dead, and his body dumped in the lake.

In April I celebrated my thirteenth birthday with a visit from my mother and siblings. As a special present I served my first mass. It was my proudest moment. But seeing my brothers and sisters again made me ache to get away from Lyman. I had been locked up for nearly two years. I saw my chance in late May. A boy from our cottage had been sent to the state hospital in Tewksbury. He had gone there to have a circumcision. I asked him how he had done it. He told me to tell the nurse that it burned when I urinated, and they would send me. I did, and I was sent for a circumcision, too.

A couple of days later I was operated on. I liked being at the hospital so much that I never wanted to leave. It felt strange and so good not to have a master telling me what to do. And when I wet the bed, I was immediately given a clean set of sheets. Each day the doctor came to check me, and each day I expected him to send me back to Lyman. But a week passed, and I was still there. The stitches were beginning to hurt. I asked the nurse when the stitches would be removed. She was surprised that no one had told me that they dissolved in water and would disappear after several baths. I had not been taking baths for fear of infection. The doctor had assumed I was. I began taking baths, and in a few days all my stitches had dissolved. But what I saw looked like a butcher job. When I returned to Lyman School, a letter from my mother was waiting for me. She had married Bill, and they had moved to a nice new apartment in Dorchester.

In the latter part of June 1961 I was paroled. To be paroled itself seemed a miracle; to be paroled in the summer was all a kid could ask for.

My mother had moved to a three-decker wooden structure on Nightingale Street, a tree-lined street on which there was a temple. The street was also directly across from Franklin Field. It was a neighborhood much like the one we had lived in before I was taken away. When I arrived at the apartment, I was greeted by my siblings. As before, they regarded me with eager, curious eyes. Cheryl, who was not yet fourteen, was freshly scrubbed and glowing. Kevin was now eleven, Hugh ten, Pat nine, and Donna eight. Right away my brothers wanted to take me to meet their friends, and my mother to meet the neighbors. It all was very exciting and heady.

After I had unpacked my things, my mother introduced me to the landlord, Mr. Steinberg, a friendly middle-aged man who shared his first-floor apartment with his sister. Her name was Sally, and she had a beard of stubble which frightened me at first. My mother next introduced me to her upstairs neighbors, Mr. and Mrs. Wohl. Mrs. Wohl and my mother were good friends. Mrs. Wohl baked Jewish desserts for Chanukah and Rosh Hashanah and shared them with our family. She was very kind, and I liked her right away.

Inside our apartment I was glad to see that my mother had gotten some new parlor furniture. My own room, which was the boys' room, still contained one large bed for the three of us, but it was at least a new one. In the girls' room Cheryl had her own bed, and Donna and Pat shared another.

Tired by all the excitement, I lay down on the firm, soft mattress for a short nap. I cried for happiness that my mother was remarried and living in a nicer home. She seemed calmer, more at peace. Above all, I was home. I never, ever wanted to go away again. Maybe now I would be accepted. Because I had felt responsible for my mother's divorce, maybe now I was in some way responsible for her getting married again. I fell asleep feeling that all was right with the world.

Later that afternoon my two brothers took me across to Franklin Field, where I met some of the neighborhood kids. They greeted me warmly. But I felt shy around them and gave my

79

brothers looks to indicate that I wanted to get going. Hugh and
Kevin were shining shoes every evening in Boston, and that evening I went with them. Once again they showed me off to all their
friends. I felt a little foolish and sad that I did not have outside
friends whom I had grown up with as they did. I felt so different,
so self-conscious and out of place. The boys made a bundle that
night and treated me to whatever I wanted. That evening, at about
ten, I arrived home with them and went through the back door
into the kitchen to find Bill sitting there. Still the besotted bastard,
he spit and made a lunge toward me, but my mother interceded.
He swore at me and cursed me as I ran to the safety of my room.
I lay in bed hating him and feeling very confused. I had thought
he would be nice to me now that I was his adopted son. I fell
asleep listening to Bill rail at my mother about how he hated me
and how someday he'd kill me. I promised myself that when I
got bigger and stronger, I'd beat him up. My brothers, probably
used to Bill's threats and bombast and tired from their work,
snored peacefully through it.

When I awoke, the sun was bright in my face. I roused Kevin
and Hugh. We would go swimming. It felt incredible not to awake
in a big dorm and to know that my day would not be completely
planned for me and that I would not be constantly watched. Hugh
and Kevin always had a few dollars in their pockets from shining
shoes—they gave my mother the bulk of their earnings—and so
we and a couple of their friends took the el to the North End,
which had the biggest and best pool in the city. We stayed until
dusk. It had been nearly two years since I had been outside on
my own after dark. It felt really great but strange.

As soon as we arrived back home, Kevin got ready to go into
town to shine shoes, as he did every night. He was a sensitive,
affectionate boy and was devoted to our mother. Not having lived
at home for so long a time, I did not fully understand their
relationship. But whenever my mother was feeling low or hurt
physically because of Bill's occasional beatings, Kevin took it the
hardest. Hugh, on the other hand, was not as industrious and

went out with Kevin only once or twice a week. He was the brashest of us. He would give my mother only half of what he earned; the rest he would share with me. I suppose I could have worked along with them, but for the moment, at least, I wanted only to have fun, not shine shoes.

I spent most of my time with Hugh. Cheryl was not usually around and had her own circle of older teen-aged friends. Of the children, Hugh seemed most in need of a father, and in a way, I became his father as well as his brother. We went swimming nearly every day, rain or shine. The only things I thought about were having a good time and becoming an altar boy on Sundays. Although I'd only done it in practice at Lyman, I was sure I could do a good job. My mother took me to see the priest, who told me that I was still too young and that he was all filled up anyway.

After I had been home about a month, I began to notice differences in the way I was being treated, not unlike the last time I had been home. While I was away, I was always thinking about parole; now that I was home, I was always fearful of being sent back to Lyman. I had such powerful dreams about being returned that when I awoke, it took me the full day to reorient myself. My mother was of little help. She continually reminded me that should I misbehave, all she needed to do was to pick up the phone. The first time she threatened to call the parole officer was one evening after I had stayed out past my curfew. My mother told me I could not go out the next day. Sometime that afternoon I was sitting alone in the parlor. My siblings and mother had gone out. I noticed framed school pictures of Cheryl, Hugh, Kevin, Donna, and Patrice on a side table. They all were smiling. I didn't understand why I did it, but I took matches, and without actually burning the photos, I used the afterburn of the match to blacken their faces. When my mother returned and discovered the defaced pictures, she called me and extracted a confession. The next day my mother let me out to play but told me to stay near the house. After a while she called me inside. I went into the parlor to find Mr. Wachtel, my parole officer. My heart raced, and I began to perspire; panic and fear enveloped me as images of Lyman and Oak swirled in my mind. I wanted to run and run and run. My mother had betrayed me; I saw no exit.

I stood trembling before him. He questioned me about burning my siblings' pictures. Why, why did I do it? I didn't know, I said over and over, all the while apologizing and pleading with him, crying and begging him and my mother please not to send me back. At last he stood up, marking the end of the conversation. He was letting me off with just a warning. Still, I shook all over the rest of the day. From that day on I began to anticipate my behavior. I lived outside myself. I became quiet and even more withdrawn. How could I be perfect? I thought. But in a few days I relaxed and forgot about it.

My mother had been doing volunteer work for our incumbent ward representative. She told me she was going to introduce me to him and asked me if I would be interested in doing campaign work for him. Always eager to please, I agreed. He lived not far from our home, so I dressed carefully and went with my mother to see him. I immediately liked his easygoing charm. He spoke expansively, and I warmed to him. We talked at length, and I agreed to deliver circulars for his campaign. I forgot about swimming and spent my afternoons distributing flyers and visiting my new friend. He was always jovial, and I enjoyed his company. One day soon after, he told me that if he was reelected, he was going to make me his page. I was ecstatic and now worked even harder for my new friend. To think of it! I, a State Boy, a criminal, was going to be a page! Then he began to ask me questions that I did not understand. How did I like nail polish, girls' clothes? When he asked these questions, his look changed. He told me that after I became his page, we would be much closer and that he would give me a room in his friend's Back Bay home, near the State House. He asked me if I would wear nail polish and girls' clothes from time to time. Frightened and confused, I told my mother. She told me I couldn't go to see him ever again. I pleaded with her to let me; I was going to be his page. I did not understand

82

what was going on. I saw my dream pass before my eyes.

I had been home for a few weeks when I noticed my hair was getting longer. I went nuts. It was wonderful. Its shortness had been an embarrassment to me and a reminder of Lyman. I was beginning to look like my brothers and the other boys in the neighborhood. My hair became an obsession. I, too, could look like outside people. Jesus, I was starting to look like outside people! Jesus fucking Christ!

I scraped together the money to buy a small jar of Vaseline. Vaseline had been contraband at Lyman School, so I felt a special devilish delight in purchasing it. Vaselined hair was considered the emblem of maturity. But my mother scoffed at this practice and would not allow us to use the Vaseline. And so I hid the jar under the first-floor back stairs, where each morning I used it before going out for the day. I'd put gobs of it on my head, and with a small brush I'd sneaked out from our bathroom, I brushed my hair backward and backward until my scalp was raw. And every evening, before my mother came home, I carefully rinsed it out.

The other boys and the neighborhood girls now began to stop ribbing me, and I began to feel as if I belonged. One Saturday morning a few weeks later, just before Labor Day, my mother handed me $2 and told me to get a haircut. I was stunned. I pleaded with her not to make me do it, but she was adamant. Finally she screamed at me to leave for the barbershop right now. Something happened to me; my eyes became wide and wild as she came at me in a threatening way. I put up my fist and said, "Don't, or I'll hit you!" She called to Bill, and I flew down the stairs. I hid in some nearby bushes for the next couple of hours. No! No! I cried to myself. How could I have raised my hand to my mother? The memory of it made me feel sick all over.

I sneaked out of the bushes to find my brothers and to tell them what had happened. They understood and promised to sneak me in later that night. I wandered the streets until it was dark and very late. I did not want to go home ever. But fatigue and remorse drove me to the back door. True to their words Hugh or Kevin had unlocked the back door. I tiptoed through the kitchen, past my mother's room, and crawled in between my brothers. For the moment I found peace in the warmth of their bodies next to mine and in the feeling of their love. I drifted into a disturbed and restless sleep.

My brothers and I woke up to my mother's prodding. She was very sweet to us, and I was happy she'd forgiven me. I thanked my lucky stars and swore to myself I would do whatever she said. She told me she had forgotten about what happened, and my brothers, too, were glad, for they shared my anxiety. She asked me to help around the house that day. I was more than willing; in this way I would atone for my sins and show her that I did love her. In the afternoon Mr. Wachtel drove me back to Lyman School for Boys.

Once back at Lyman I was sent to Hillside. I saw a lot of new faces there and one familiar one, Langer's. During those first weeks I was deeply depressed. One Sunday morning in early October, about a month after I had returned, I was sent downstairs to wash my wet sheets while the others remained in the dorm, making their beds. I threw my sheets into the round washbasin, went to my locker, put on my Sunday clothes, and, in a daze, walked past the many cottages, the farm, and offgrounds—and twenty-eight miles home. I walked around the neighborhood secretly until I saw Hugh playing with friends in Franklin Park. When they saw me approach, the boys all ran to me and cheered, and I cried out of happiness. Hugh and Patrice went home to tell my mother, who in turn told them to have us come home. I would not go for fear that she would turn me in. I was frightened of her and wanted only to see my brothers and sisters again. After a few hours of coaxing, and tired and hungry now, I went home where my mother hugged, kissed, and fed me. Through her smiles and tears she told me it was better that I went back to Lyman. I agreed. We went into her room to watch TV. She lay on her bed, and I sat on the floor with my back against the end of the box spring and mattress. Christmas was still two months away, but Brenda Lee was singing "Rockin' Around the Christmas Tree" as my mother lay there crying. The next day she took me to the Division of Youth Service in Boston, where Mr. Gaspar, whom I remembered from my trips to the parole board, promised me that if I were very good, I could be home again in time for Christmas.

When I arrived back at Lyman, I was put on the line and sent to Oak. For some reason I was taken out again after just two weeks and sent to Hillside. I did not have a history of escapes like other runaways, and the episode was soon forgotten. After a few days at Hillside I was sent to the clothing room to return my Sunday suit, which I had ruined on my first run, and to turn in the outside clothes I had worn back. I was sent unescorted with a pass. The pass did not say how many sets of clothes I was to turn in, when I arrived at the clothing room, I hid my outside clothes in a basement window under the loading dock. The clothing room master took my Sunday suit and issued me a new one. I chuckled on my way back to the dorm and planned my next escape. That evening I schemed with Langer to run away the next night.

After supper the next day, while the other boys were playing on the lawn of the cottage, Langer and I slipped into the locker room and hid in the boiler room. Once it was known we were missing, a general alarm went up, and the boys were called in for count. The housemaster thought we were already offgrounds, so we were safe in our hideaway. When we heard the last footsteps going up the stairs, we slipped out, checked the grounds, and kept close to the shadows until we were past the warehouse and in a dark open field. The only things that now lay between us and Route 9 were the superintendent's house and assistant super's house. We heard the distant barking of a dog. Once on Route 9, we again kept to the shadows, until a long way down the road we came upon a farmer's field in which there sat a big truck. Langer told me to get into the passenger seat while he climbed in on the driver's side. He fumbled at the dashboard, and I heard the engine start. I was frightened when he told me he was going to drive it; I did not think a fourteen-year-old could drive. But drive he did. When we got into Newton, just a few miles west of Boston, he drove up a long, steep hill. Coming down over it toward a red light, he said he was going to run it; he didn't think the truck would make it if he stopped. At the bottom of the hill the old truck sputtered and kicked and bucked. It smashed into the signal pole and stopped. We jumped down and ran through backyards and leaped over fences. Running along Route 9, east toward Boston, we reached the next town, Brookline, where we came to a pond bordered by large private estates and streetlamps. The pond was too open, so we crossed to the darker side of Route 9. We were about to go up a hill into a wooded area when a car drove up. A man stuck his head out to ask for directions. Langer tried to warn me and kept running. They nabbed me and took me back to Lyman.

Two days later, on October 21, I was sent to the granddaddy of them all, the place most feared and respected: the Institute for Juvenile Guidance in Bridgewater.

BOOK III

Institute for Juvenile Guidance

NOVEMBER 20, 1961

1.

I SAT IN THE WINDOW of my cell and leaned against the bars. The grille was rusty and was held together by strong bolts, which creaked and groaned. I sat there as I often did. Though cold, it was the warmest place in my cell; a constant chill emanated through the cinder block walls. Every once in a while I turned my head back inside, my eyes dully wandering past the faded gray bureau, army cot, and faded green walls and then back outside again. Beyond the prison wall I saw empty fields. The November sun bathed the landscape shades of pale gold, beige, and brown. Evergreens and naked trees, on the bony arms of which clung the last shriveled leaves of autumn, formed the horizon.

Sea gulls climbed and soared overhead on air currents that sometimes whipped in fury, creating nonnavigable turbulences from which they quickly recovered. Their mournful screeches echoed the silence; perhaps it was not so much their screams I heard as my own.

I sat and watched more intensely the black tar road that flowed out from between the trees and field past the prison wall, as both time and light dwindled. It was the shining silver beacon of the Greyhound bus from Boston that I sought. It arrived every hour on the hour. Since I could not know the time, I kept a constant vigil; from the fading light I surmised that the next bus would be the last and that she would be on it. In her first and only letter to me during my first month at the IJG my mother promised me she would come. I thought about her letter and her promise to see me. My every waking moment during the two days before revolved around her impending visit. If she came, I would no longer be thought of as a State Boy, with all its mean connotations. To pass the time, I spent hours stuffing my shoes with paper, brushing the stitching with a toothbrush until it was brilliant white, spit-shining my shoes over and over until I could see my happy face in them. I washed and scrubbed my dungarees with a floorbrush in my sink of freezing water, wrung them out by hand, laid them on my bureau, seam to seam, where I flattened out each wrinkle and worked on the creases with the edge of the brush. I laid the pants between sections of newspaper and then under my mattress, where they would dry and look as though they'd been taken to the cleaners and pressed. I combed and brushed my hair and looked constantly in the mirror to see if I still looked the same, hoping my hair and face were perfect so that she would love me.

I pulled myself up onto the sill of my cell and saw for the first time the woods beyond the field. I tried to imagine the many creatures that roamed them. On the trip from Lyman School I had been told stories about boys who had escaped from the IJG to disappear into these woods, never to be seen again, the victims of quicksand or hideous flesh-eating monsters.

I shook the image free and sat and watched the road as a cat watches a mouse. The bus emerged from the shadows. It passed beyond my sight, stopping near the gray cement entrance to this century-old former maximum security prison for women. I lurched from my parapet and walked over to my observation window. Then came the interminable wait and the gripping desperation. I strained my ear for the faint jingling of the guard's keys. I listened and watched and then it came, the faint jingling of keys and footsteps that drew closer and closer. The guard's twisted red face leered inches from mine. Oh, God! Yes! She had come! In a second he turned and walked across to the cell directly facing mine, inserted his key, and took the boy inside it with him.

I slunk to the floor as if my bones had turned to a gel. On my knees I put my head in my hands and stayed there, beyond grief or anguish, hollow and mindless. I must have sat there for at least an hour before I heard the happy, returning voices of celebration and reunion in the corridors. It was then that the reality that my mother had not come, and would not now come, became starkly evident. My body shook, and my jaw quivered as my eyes began to fill with tears. I wanted to cry, to tremble. But for now even this consolation would be denied me as the boy I knew across from me would run to tell me about his visit. I would smile and say, "How wonderful," as my pressed clothes became oppressive, suffocating. And then the master would come to look in my observation window, and I would look at him with a serene face. I would not go to supper and face the smirking, self-satisfied stares of those whom I'd told about my mother's coming. Or own up to the deep shame I could not now bear. I fought back my tears and composed myself. When the master opened my door, I told him I wasn't hungry. He shut my door, and I slunk to the floor out of range of the observation window until I heard the last footsteps and voices of the boys slowly descend into silence.

And then I cried. I cried until I felt my heart squeezing out through my pores. I moved to my bed and lay down in fetal position, caught between the hope and hopelessness I'd felt for so many times over the years. I wondered why she had not come. I thought she was merely being cruel. But then I thought she had stood me up in order to remind me that I was a bad child. I fell asleep with my hands between my pressed pants, everything passing into silence, like the voices in the corridors.

I awoke to find that the boys in D, E, and F Corridors had returned from the dining room, while the boys in A, B, and C Corridors, the first-floor honor corridors below, were in the auditorium, attending the Sunday night movie. The master opened my door and came in to check the heavy grille on my window; it was part of the Sunday evening ritual. After shaking the grille to make sure it was not loose, he ripped off the wall a picture of Boston I had earlier put up with toothpaste and reminded me that we were not allowed to put anything decorative on the walls. When he left, I sat up in the cell window to look out into the black night. The reflected scene changes of the movie in the auditorium across the way made the night seem blacker and stiller. I looked out into the darkness and remembered that only hours before, I had sat there with the hope of seeing and hugging my mother. It seemed so long ago that I had been at home, been a part of a family; I could no longer deny the reality of the walls and bars that were my life.

I longed to read a book. But books were very few and hard to get since there was no library at IJG. Whatever books there were at the institution were the personal property of the boys whose families had either sent or brought them to them. I often wrote home for books; after a time, when I received no packages, I gave up trying.

Perry Mason had become my favorite literary character. That seemed somehow right to me since the IJG was part of the Massachusetts corrections complex containing the state farm for drunks and derelicts and a prison for the criminally insane. Albert De Salvo—the Boston Strangler himself had been here for a time. Before Bridgewater I had not had much exposure to books, but now I would read each one I could get my hands on over and over. The Mason series ignited my interest in words. In one of them Perry had told Della that one of his client's relatives was an "extemporaneous prevaricator." I got out a dictionary and found out that this meant "a quick-thinking liar"—a bullshit artist! I thought it was really cool that you could say that to someone in such a nice way, so I began to call everyone I knew an extemporaneous prevaricator. It gave everyone a good laugh. I also became interested in law and forensic medicine. But my biggest reason for liking Perry Mason was that he always got innocent people off.

In addition to Perry Mason books, there were mostly westerns available to us, and a few hot, contraband sex novels and girlie magazines. These would be confiscated from us in periodic shake-downs, during which our cells would be pulled apart by the masters. In order to get these books we would barter our state-supplied weekly rations of cigarette packs. Some of these guys were known as cigarette merchants; these nonsmokers sold their stashes to boys who had either smoked all theirs before the week was up or gambled their rations away. In my cell that evening I longed for a cigarette, but I would not go to a merchant because the boys who did were sometimes forced to have sex with them to erase the debt. And soon they'd be right back in debt again.

Instead, I fished through the metal trash can in my cell and pulled out all the tobacco butts. I collected whatever tobacco was still left in them and took a small piece of paper from a letter tablet. I made a cigarette with it. It smelled awful, and the puffs burned my throat, but the cigarette helped relieve my loneliness and anxiety. I passed the time pacing back and forth in my cell and daydreaming about nice things like being free and playing. I caught flies off the wall: I had got so good I could catch them in midair. When I tired of doing that, I rolled up a piece of paper and played basketball with my tin can. I played this game until my loneliness and depression drove me under my covers and I drifted to sleep.

I awoke the next morning to the odor of urine and a cold wetness that left me shaking and shivering violently. The sharp sting of ammonia from my repeated bed-wetting had burned deep sores into my hips. I was much too ashamed to tell anyone that I continued to wet the bed, although I was sure that some knew, for the smell coming out of my room surely gave me away. I wished with all my heart that I wouldn't wet the bed. Yet it didn't stop. At least I could look forward to dry sheets when we changed them each week. But even that one night's grace period sometimes eluded me because my mattress would be soaked through. I would take my blanket and fold it over the wet area and place my sheet on top of it; this worked fine, but it also meant that I froze in the night.

On sheet day we were asked to place our dirty sheets in a pile

93

in the middle of the corridor floor. I would put my sheets inside my pillowcase so that the stains could not be seen. Sometimes, though, I wet the bed so thoroughly that the dripping sheets would stain my pillowcase. I would wait until I thought no one was looking, and tensely I would run out to hide my sheets in the pile. I didn't know what I would do if any of the boys found out that I bed-wet; at thirteen and a half I was far too old for this nonsense.

The odor problem caused by my bed-wetting always distressed me. I tried to overcome this by opening my window all the way and placing on the sill a bar of soap, which acted like a deodorizer. This, and the cold air which helped retard the smell, helped somewhat. Whenever I had the chance, I would run down the hall and try to gauge the urine odor coming out from my cell. At best it was a stale one but not as bad as it would have been without the soap. I comforted myself by convincing myself that I was the only one who knew. But all day long I would be preoccupied with how I smelled because we showered in the evening. I could not wait for my birthday because with each new birthday I believed that I would stop for good.

In spite of these efforts, my secret got around when a boy caught me trying to conceal my sheets. He pulled them out, opened them up, and told everyone to come have a look. I tried to deny they were mine and ran to my cell and closed the door. But the boys came up to laugh at me through my observation window. For a time I was teased, but after a couple of weeks, when the novelty wore off, I was left alone. Still, I hid my sheets and put soap in my window.

At this time of my imprisonment I was placed in the ninth grade of a makeshift school consisting of three small rooms off the small lobby separating E and F Corridors from D. Since this wasn't school at Lyman, I became interested in learning again. In the morning I attended Mr. Worth's English and math class, and in the afternoon I had Mr. Colman's geography class. In another classroom Mr. Douglas taught the oldest boys. These boys were generally away for the first time and were well on their way to completing their high school studies. I wanted to be in that class; unlike my teachers, Mr. Douglas never left his classroom to smoke and drink coffee with the other staff. He sat and taught all day. Whatever intellectual potential I had was being undermined with almost perverse calculation. For one thing, the staff had not bothered to test me before assigning me to a classroom, yet I was only at about the sixth-grade level. Nor would Mr. Worth and Mr. Colman take the time to help me with my assignments; no sooner did the day's lesson begin than each would leave the room to join the other and to smoke cigar after cigar. Meanwhile, the seven or eight other boys in my class would pull out funny books and cards. At first I tried to study, but after a time I gave up.

The masters' indifference to our education made school a joke. I lost interest almost immediately. The teachers' attitude reflected the institution's, which was that we all were incorrigible criminals who had to be locked away from society but provided with at least the gesture of an education until we reached the age of sixteen as the law required. That is as far as it went. The masters took it on faith that we were inherently stupid or uninterested in learning and that we'd probably never pursue an education on the outside. And they all assumed we'd be back anyway. Yet when we were paroled, we were expected to return to normal school situations and do well. Our failures there only reinforced the teachers' perceptions that we were unable to learn. Their actions said as much. Mr. Colman, especially, never tired of telling us what punks and shits we were and that we were in Bridgey for one reason only: to pull time. Pretty soon I came to believe him.

Once winter came, we never went out of the building, although many of us would have loved to play in the crisp air and snow. Every evening after dinner we were herded into the rec room. It was a good-size horseshoe-shaped room, but it offered few amenities. Lined along the wall were round tables and chairs which were chained together and bolted to the floor to prevent inmates from smashing them over each other's heads. The inmates liked to play poker or five-card stud for cigarettes. The masters were supposed to break these games up; more often they turned their heads. Certain guards not only allowed our gambling but liked to watch or egg the boys on when their games became heated or violent, as they occasionally did.

It was a pretty violent place. I learned that among these boys were pimps, homosexual prostitutes, car thiefs, and even murderers. On my corridor alone were two boys who had killed their mothers. Understandably, then, my first evening in the rec room was a frightening experience. I fully expected to be sex-pressured, and when I walked into the room that night, I was stared at as though I were an unescorted girl at a local dance. I tried to avoid eye contact, yet I couldn't help searching for a friendly face. There weren't any. What saved me was my young age. Some of the boys were as old as nineteen and twenty; none of them was going to bother with a thirteen-and-a-half-year-old kid who didn't even have one exciting crime to talk about. My corridor, F Corridor, was safer than most because we were relatively newer inmates and we were kept segregated for much of the day from the rest of the population.

But I yearned to have friends. I wanted to be a part of the institution even as I resisted at the same time becoming too involved with the social structure at IJG. As I had at Lyman, it was one way I fought my incarceration; by joining in completely, I would be admitting that I was guilty of something.

And so during that first month I remained on my best behavior. Some boys would be paroled home by the board at the end of every month. This left empty cells in the better corridors for the others to move up into. As an inmate accelerated through the system so did his prestige and privileges. Moving night followed the parole board meeting. As I moved from F to E Corridor, I felt as if I were being paroled, too. My new cell had its own sink with hot and cold running water.

What I liked best of all about my new cell was that I had an older boy on each side of me. On each wall was a narrow hole that allowed us to pass folded funny books from cell to cell or to pass cigarettes on folded pieces of paper. I got to know a boy in the cell below well enough to ask for a cigarette now and then. His name was Bobby Kearny; he was a quiet, sweet-natured guy who was reportedly doing time for hustling queers. I would lie on the floor and pass a string down through the hole where the sink pipes went through the floor, and he would tie a cigarette to the other end, which I would yank back.

When Bobby didn't have a cigarette to share with me, I could always call across the hall to Brian Sayer. He was my favorite of all the guys. I was considered by the others just a little kid to be tolerated at a distance, but Brian let me look up to him as a big brother. He was in on a first offense, and appeared to want a better life for himself than the other inmates I came into contact with. He did this by enrolling in extension courses. Brian would throw the cigarette as close to my door as he could get it. I would try to pull it under with my belt—a long and not always successful process. Sometimes I would have to wait for a master or another boy to come by. And if I ever needed a match, I could easily get one from a boy we called Sparky, because of his freckled complexion and bright orange hair. The name fit his crime: He was a pyromaniac. At least once a week he would set his mattress on fire—until the masters got wise and stopped giving him one.

Another thing that I liked about E Corridor was that it was easy to sneak out of the cell. This was accomplished by closing the cell door, which locked on impact, to just within a hair of being closed so that it looked shut. With a piece of mirror I could see down into the lobby, and if there were no masters in sight, I would sneak out. Once out in the corridor I would go from cell to cell and exchange books with other boys. In this way I got to know what books were around, and I could arrange to wait my turn for them. For this I was risking segregation, but it was worth it to me. I hated being alone in my cell, being poor, and never having anything. I got caught out of my cell once or twice, but since I was just a little kid full of energy, the masters usually tolerated me and just locked me back inside.

On Saturday nights one of the boys in the honor corridor would put his radio in the sill of his window. The empty prison yard and the evening stillness provided natural acoustics. After rec hall and showers we'd return to our cells for the night, and we'd listen to Murray the K in New York "and his swinging soiree." The show consisted of oldies but goodies, and we'd all join in. This was a happy time for us—something we looked forward to all day.

If Saturday night was a high, Sunday morning was a hangover. We never left our cells except for mass, mealtimes, visits, and the weekly adventure movie. I always attended mass and served occasionally on the altar. I still had dreams of one day becoming a priest, yet I could not get close to the IJG priest since he came only for Saturday confession and Sunday mass. And so on Sunday I sat in my window all afternoon watching for the Greyhound bus, knowing I would not be receiving a visitor but hoping that somehow my mother would want to surprise me. It was only when she would write to say she was coming and then not show up that I was thrown into such a terrible depression. I liked being alone in my cell, though. It was my own little world where no one could bother me, where I could laugh or feel sad and remove the mask I had to wear outside in the corridors.

One evening in the rec hall I saw a boy reading a thin glossy page. On the cover was the title of a popular song I liked. I went up to the boy to ask him what he had. I saw a kind of strange hieroglyphics which he said was sheet music. I was very excited. With so little to do in my cell I often sang songs to myself as I paced the floor. There was a part of me that wanted to become a rock 'n' roll singer, and the guys on my hall told me I had a good voice and encouraged me to sing. With these music sheets maybe I could now learn the words to new songs. He told me that he had gotten it from Mr. Dinova, the music teacher. I had never spoken to him but knew who he was; I had often seen him bouncing rhythmically up the stairs from the main lobby heading toward his studio in D Corridor. He always carried a thick, heavy briefcase that looked almost as big as he was, and he left a trail of bittersweet, aromatic cigar smoke swirling behind him.

The very next day I approached his studio door. He sat at a desk in an old swivel chair, his legs dangling a few inches from the floor. He stared at the wall, deeply absorbed in something. I tapped lightly; he did not even blink. He was a Hobbit-like character with a massive head made even more so by his long salt-and-pepper hair. He had thick, bushy eyebrows and large jowls and ears, where tufts of black hair grew from the canals. I stood there silently. He came out of his trancelike concentration and swiveled around. Startled to see me, he cocked his head to the side, raised his eyebrows, and gave me an eager and rich-bodied hello. He stood up and invited me in. He spoke to me in a fine, educated voice as if I were an old friend, with a kindness that reached into a part of me I'd never felt. I liked being near him. When I asked him if I could borrow some sheet music, he directed me to a stack of them. For me, it was like a discovered treasure. He said that they belonged to all the boys and that I was welcome to them. He told me to take as long as I wanted with them, and when I returned them, I could borrow new ones. I took a couple, and he ushered me out and said that he was glad to meet me.

Back in my cell I copied out the lyrics and thought about Mr. Dinova. He was the only adult I had met at IJG who hadn't thrown rough, filthy words at me. I felt as though I'd finally found a friend. For a couple of weeks I went back and forth, exchanging sheets of music, always happy to see him. I'd say hello, and he'd bounce right up to me and inquire about my health and my state of mind. I did not quite know how to take him and his seemingly very genuine concern about me. By the second week of December he asked me if I wanted to learn to play an instrument. I suggested the guitar. No, he said, he didn't teach that. Then he suggested the clarinet and immediately produced a mangled-looking piece of tin. I took one look at it and passed it off as something old fuddy-duddies played. I'd actually seen a wooden clarinet before, and somehow I could not imagine myself accompanied by an accordion player, wearing lederhosen and a Tyrolean hat, and spinning out polkas. I politely declined.

When I returned to my cell, I gave it further thought. It would be something to do, which would be better than doing nothing; and more important, I had really grown to like Mr. Dinova. I was sure I'd hurt his feelings. I confirmed that impression when I went to see him the next day to tell him I would like to study. He could not contain his delight. He sat me down next to him, took out the clarinet, and for the next half hour showed me how to take care of it, put it together, take it apart, where to put my fingers and how to blow through the mouthpiece. Many squeaks, sore fingers, sore jaw, and numb lips later, Mr. Dinova told me to return to my cell and to play around with it for a week to get to know it. The following week, he said, he would give me a lesson. I skipped rec hall that evening and fiddled around with my new toy. After an hour of more painful finger joints, swollen lips, lockjaw, and only a melodious note or two, I was ready to go back to being strictly a crooner. But then I realized that I had been doing something productive and learning from a kind, devoted teacher. In the purposeless day-to-day living of the IJG I had found something, though I wasn't sure just what.

During that month of December a boy showed me a leather purse that he had made in the arts and crafts shop. I thought that it looked nice and that maybe I could make one for my mother. I went to my counselor, Mr. Ellison, and asked him if he could get me excused from school and assigned to the arts and crafts shop. He said that he would try. The truth was that it was really no problem to get out of school; as long as an inmate pulled his time and kept his nose clean, nobody much cared about what he did. Two weeks before Christmas I had my reassignment.

The arts and crafts shop was located in a cage at the back of the dining room. The teacher, Mr. Scott, showed me how to use the different tooling devices for ornamentation and how to sew together the different compartments. Unlike the other masters,

Mr. Scott came around to check our projects, to answer our questions, and to offer his advice and expertise. He taught us so well and was so good-hearted that if a boy needed help with his project, he would practically finish it for him. Mr. Scott made it clear that he did not like the way we were being treated. He cared about our education and his own—every night after work he drove to Rhode Island to continue his studies at the Rhode Island School of Design. I don't think he cared if he was fired; the administration didn't like him, but we boys adored him. He seemed to be one of us; he never degraded us or passed judgments. While we worked on our projects, he would stand at his desk with his foot on the bottom drawer and talk to us about life. "You move with the big hand," he said. "Life goes on." I tried to remember that.

At the end of my two-week term, just barely, I had made a beautiful pocketbook for my mother, which I stained a chestnut brown and into which I tooled her initials. I was proud of my present for her; wouldn't this prove my love and devotion? Wouldn't she now forgive me, take me home, and never send me away again?

I wondered what Christmas would be like. I was certain that the Lions or Rotary Club would come give us a party. Surely in this desolate place the administration would open its hearts to us. During those two weeks before Christmas there was a hint of festivity. Cards and packages of clothing and books and foodstuffs arrived. I received cards from both my grandparents and a jigsaw puzzle from my mother. My father's mother sent me a sweater, and my mother's mother sent instant coffee, Pream, and some cookies. I felt that this time I would not be left out. The fact that I had been remembered was proof that I was still loved. But the week before Christmas my mother sent me a card and a letter describing the things she had gotten for my siblings and closed by saying that she was sorry she hadn't had enough money left to buy me anything else.

I felt sorry for the boys who really were forgotten, who received nothing all year. Not a card, a letter, a visitor, or a package. Most of the time I was just like them. After my initial elation a kind of despair set in. I hated the token cards and my mother's every-thing-was-fine-in-the-world letters, which always reminded me how smart or bright I was and how I should try to be a good boy. I was trying so hard and prayed nightly to God and my mother to help me or at least to explain to me what was so wrong with me and what I had done to be put in this awful place.

On the Friday just before Christmas I was taken to the super-intendent's office in the main lobby. A couple of the counselors and guards and secretaries were there. Another boy named Tommy Bender was in the office. Tommy was in for boosting—stealing clothing from stores to sell on the street. He also was one of four dancers in a well-known Dorchester dance troupe. After the sec-retaries had finished fawning all over me—remarking to each other how young and cute I was—I was asked to sing a song. At the time the Twist was the rage, so I sang Chubby Checker's version of the song while Tommy demonstrated the dance. As I sang, I marveled at how inventive a dancer he was. When it was over, they clapped and cheered, and even the superintendent smiled. Then we were taken back to our cells, our moment of glory behind us.

There was no Lions Club party on Christmas Eve, and we were remanded to our cells for the evening instead. After our showers we received our little boxes, just like at Lyman with the addition of a pack of cigarettes. Christmas Day was a Monday, but the weekday routine was suspended for the holiday. And so I sat in my window, waiting for the bus that never came, staring at the purse I'd made for my mother all the while. I drank a lot of coffee that night so that I awoke with a case of the runs. I called and called from my observation window for a guard to take me to the hopper until I was almost in tears from the stomach pains and pressure. Finally I had to use a paper bag; there were no toilets in our cells.

When Tuesday came, I was glad Christmas was over. Mr. El-

lison came to give me an extra ration of cigarettes and a present
of six funny books from the secretaries. By prison values I was a
rich man. Meanwhile, I began to train for the boxing team. Bridgewater had a team, and when I heard that it went out once a week
to fight around the state, I decided to get on it. I'd do almost
anything to get out of the IJG. The upstairs rec hall was converted
into a makeshift gym on certain weekday afternoons, and on those
days, as soon as school was over, I'd go over to watch. There I
saw boys sparring, hitting punching bags, jumping rope, and
shadowboxing, all to a butta-pa-pataba rhythm. It was exciting
to watch. I was intrigued. Yes. I would definitely join the boxing
team.

I got to work on it right away. It was tough going. I observed
and tried to copy what I could of those in training. I punched the
bag until my knuckles bled, jumped rope until my legs were
rubber, and hit the speed bag until I could do so with my eyes
closed. After my workout I'd sit on a card table and watch the
older boys box. One of those I watched most frequently was not
on the team, but he was a skilled fighter nonetheless. His name
was Darryl Wilson; I hadn't liked him when I had encountered
him before because he was a cigarette merchant who also rented
out pornographic pictures and books. Now, watching him box, I
admired and respected him. But because I was so young, no one
would take the time out to teach or spar with me so that I went
on with my training alone. Then I met Mr. Dalton, a master who
was an ex-boxer and who came to the gym to exercise and to teach
fledgling boxers the techniques of the art. When he saw that I
was serious, he took me under his wing and began teaching me
the rudiments. When the other boys saw how hard I was trying,
they, too, began to help me.

I loved the gym, its sounds and smells, and the camaraderie.
I was getting to know more guys and was beginning to feel a part
of something. When the gym wasn't open, I studied my clarinet.
Although I still wanted to quit, I could now read simple music
and play simple songs. I was also getting to know the other boys

in the music program. Mr. Dinova and I had no more than a superficial relationship until I told him during a lesson that his thick blue office rug was filthy. He gave me his stock cocked-head look, raised his eyebrows, and agreed. He asked me if I would like to help him clean it. I said sure, and the next Saturday morning he took me from my cell. We went to the studio and began moving his furniture out of the office and into the corridor. Once that was completed, I began cleaning the rug. He put cigarettes out for me and bought me sodas from the machine downstairs. This was a real treat. It took me the entire day to finish the work. We joked and laughed and shared stories. Later in my cell I felt very special.

Between my boxing and music I was feeling reasonably happy. These activities kept me busy, made me feel good about myself, and softened the harsh reality of where I was and my feeling of abandonment. But these were diversions, I knew. Parole was always foremost in my mind, and I was always preoccupied with rejoining my family.

In January Max Dinova became less accessible, spending much of the time secreted in his studio, practicing for his Artist's Diploma, the musician's equivalent to a Bachelor's Degree. In the schoolroom I listened to his clarinet, his fluidity, his tone and virtuosity. It was hard to believe I played the same instrument. The corridors proved natural acoustics; his sounds filled them and made the cell bars melt and the hard, dull paint of the walls turn bright and rich in texture. Everyone looked up from his cell or classroom and listened. Of course, Mr. Colman made disparaging remarks. But Mr. Dinova's playing inspired and filled me with a joy and pride I could hardly bear, and I knew that for the first time in years I felt love. He was my hero, my savior.

Now, whenever I was near him, my heart pounded. In preparation for his recital at the New England Conservatory of Music's Jordan Hall, each of us boys was asked if we'd like to do a little work for him. My eyes shining, I nodded yes. He came in the evenings and took us from our cells to the studio, where he sat us at a large rectangular table and closed the door. He brought us two odd-shaped instruments, explaining that one was an alto clarinet, the other a bass clarinet. They looked old. The silver keys were tarnished. Our job was to restore their luster. Assigning each of us a different task, he laid out packs of cigarettes and provided sodas during the time we worked.

It was the first time I'd ever really noticed the studio. Two walls were covered with blue acoustic tile, and the other two walls were painted soft pink. On the two windows were curtains with music notes across the borders, and beside the table where we sat was an upright piano. Along the wall with the windows was a record case and stereo. And tacked on the wall by his desk were glossy pictures of classical music stars Max had played with over the years. He turned on two lamps and the stereo. After working on his horns, we addressed envelopes bearing recital invitations to friends of his all over the world. It felt so cozy sitting there like elves, chatting away and getting to know each other. It was impossible to believe that on just the other side of the door was the gloomy environment of the IJG. Max sat in his swivel chair, and without a word his head moved about like a conductor's baton. I didn't want to go back through that door; I wanted to say with Mr. Dinova. I wanted to be just like him.

Each day I wondered when I would go before the board. My sentence was indeterminate—it could be as short or as long as the administration decided. I was getting older now and not as often feeling that I was being pulled in all different directions the way I had felt at Lyman. My behavior so far had been perfect. Then one evening Darryl Wilson approached me in the rec hall. He brought me over to one of the card tables where a group of other boys were gathered so as not to look too conspicuous. He pulled out a newspaper headline that said the world was going to end. I could hardly believe my eyes. I thought I would never see my mother, brothers, and sisters again. I was terrified. But Darryl said he had devised an escape in which we all could go home. I agreed to the plan without question. It involved overpowering the masters and getting the keys. I wanted to be home with my family when the world ended. The plan was to take place in the dining hall the next night; one of the other conspirators would raise a chair to signal the start of the insurrection.

During lunch on the following day there seemed to be an unusually large number of staff members present, but they appeared unruffled, and so they gave us no real cause for alarm. When we inmates had finished eating, Mr. Fielding, the assistant superintendent, stood up before us. As usual, his hair was unkempt, his drip-dry suit looked rumpled, and his tie was crooked, and he had a cigar sticking out of the corner of his mouth. His single remarkable facial feature was his eyes, which were small, expressionless, yet sadistic. He stood there in his usual posture, rocking back and forth on his heels and rubbing his stomach. His speech was slurred and unclear. What was clear is that he'd somehow uncovered the plot. Someone must have told him.

Our timing could not have been worse since Fielding ran the institution on weekends in Superintendent Richard Johnston's absence. Johnston was a tough man who was feared by the inmates, but he was fair; Fielding was treacherous and serpentlike. We waited. He informed us that he knew our names and that after lunch he wanted each of those involved to come to his office. I returned to my cell and debated what I should do. This was serious business. I decided that I would sit tight. If he knew I was among them, I was in trouble already, and if I didn't step forward, my punishment could hardly be much worse. Then again, if he didn't know, I'd be out of the woods. But he knew. I was called to his office. He told the master who escorted me down to leave. It was the first time I had come face-to-face with him. He acted coy but produced a thick, metal-studded leather belt and assured me that he had ways of making me talk. I promptly confessed, not doubting for a moment that he would whip me. Finally he called the guard, and I was led through B Corridor, down a back flight of stairs, and through two heavy steel doors.

This was segregation, the infamous hole I had heard about again and again since my arrival at Bridgey. All of my clothes except my undershorts were taken. I was led through another steel door into a room containing eight cells. I was taken to the last cell on the left. The guard closed the door and left. The air was so heavy it was hard to breathe, and the acrid odor of disinfectant burned my eyes and nostrils.

The cell was small and dark. I was stunned and stood there not knowing what to do. I felt claustrophobic, but I managed to suppress it. As I began to unwind, I took stock of my cell. On the floor there was a thin, lumpy mattress stained with urine and feces; that was all. I began to pace madly back and forth from wall to wall; it was only four steps. A hundred things ran through my mind. My mother would find out and hate me. Mr. Dinova would hate me. When the world ended, I would die in a dark, musty cell. I was responsible for the troubles in the world, and I felt the weight of the world on my shoulders. I hated myself; I was no good. Hadn't everyone been telling me that for years? I pleaded for my mother to free me. For my God please to help me, please to make me better. For what seemed like hours thoughts and emotions overwhelmed me until I thought I was going insane.

Exhausted now and my back and legs aching, I sat on my mattress in the corner. The only sound I heard was a constant clanking of pipes. I had no idea of the time; there was no sunlight for me to judge, only a square of dull light latticed with the shadows and the small iron grille of my cell. I noticed it was chilly and I was shivering. At the foot of my mattress I found a piece of blanket, which I wrapped about me. It was so scratchy it burned my skin. I tried shifting it into different positions, but still it irritated me. I took the blanket off and got under the mattress; I still felt cold, but that was better than the feel of the blanket. I awoke to the sound of my cell door opening and the scraping of metal. It was suppertime. I heard many voices and a commotion outside my cell. After the master was gone, I heard:

"Hey, Devlin! That you?"

"Yeah!"

"Gilmer ratted," said one voice.

"Yeah, we'll get him," said another voice.

"He sucks Fielding's dick," a third voice added.

"Yeah! Him and Fielding are both faggots," said still another.

And so I was greeted, and throughout supper the chatter continued. I ate half-heartedly. When the guard's key was heard in the latch, we became silent. We were not supposed to talk. Our trays were collected, and each of us was given a turn in the bathroom. Although most of us didn't have to go, it was the only time we'd get out of the cell. I took my turn and made believe I had to defecate. I sat there as the master stood and watched me. I feigned grunting and the like; he kept saying to hurry up all the while. When I was returned to my cell, I listened as the other boys told jokes and sang songs and told stories. The masters could not hear us since they were far away on the next floor and two thick steel doors separated them from us. One of the stories I was told was that a boy had hanged himself in my cell and it was now haunted by his ghost. I fully believed this, and from that moment on I was terrified. As long as we were joking or talking, I didn't worry. During the long night a guard, or screw as he was called, would come down to make a check. When one of the boys told him he had to go to the bathroom, the guard said he would be right back, but he didn't return. After a time the boy gave a cry of agony, "Hopper call!" I could understand why the mattress was stained.

We spoke and joked until from sheer exhaustion, one by one, we turned in. Suddenly it was quiet, and fear gripped me. I expected at any moment to see the apparition of a ghoul approaching me. I wanted to scream but knew that would seem unmanly. That first night I sat on the mattress pulling myself as tightly as I could into the corner. Bleary-eyed, I watched the door of my cell until I fell asleep sitting up. I awoke from a nightmare panting and sweating; the ghost was there, watching me, I knew. I made myself stay awake for what seemed hours until I heard the master's key clank open the door. Breakfast. When he got to my cell, I pleaded with him to put me in another cell. He told me that sorry, no, all the cells were full, and he shoved the tray at me.

I ate my food greedily, licking every corner of the metal plate. Feeling safe, I slept through the morning until lunchtime, whereupon I ate greedily again. Fully rested, I called out to the other guys. No one wanted to talk. I began pacing my cell. It all seemed surreal. The world hadn't ended. But now the ghost took over my thoughts, and I tried to imagine what he looked like. I cowered in horror from what I saw. I had to get out of that cell. I paced and paced for hours until I could not take another step. I lay down on my mattress and realized that so long as it was day, I had nothing to fear.

The need for a cigarette interrupted my thoughts; I dreamed of various brands, Dinova's laid-open packs, butts, snipes, anything. I heard a voice call to me; it was Darryl. We began to talk, and soon we all were at it. I asked if anyone had a cigarette. Nobody did. After supper and well into the night we continued to rap, sing, and play word games. And again, after the others were asleep, I sat in my corner, watching, convinced that as long as I was awake, the ghost would not appear. I was so frightened just by the thought of it that my throat constricted; I felt as if I were choking. Each day I asked to be moved to a different cell, and each day I was told all of them were filled up.

Miraculously one of Darryl's friends assigned to the kitchen managed to smuggle in a pack of cigarettes underneath the mashed potatoes and gravy of our evening meal. Darryl promised to leave me a couple in the bathroom. The first chance I got I went in and took a seat. I saw the cigarettes, a match, and a piece of striker. The trick was to get these items into the elastic band of my underwear without the master seeing. This presented a small problem; he was staring right at me. In the blink of an eye I stood up and had them in my waistband. Back inside my cell I waited for the guard to leave. When he did, I carefully split my match in half and lit my cigarette, the first in a week. I reeled with dizziness. But God, it tasted good, and my troubles dropped from me like dead leaves. I saved the other for later.

I had no idea when I would be released, but one day Fielding came and took out one of the boys, and I was moved to his cell. I was surprised to find that it was better lit. From the back of that cell I could see a window a couple of feet away, out of which I could see a sliver of the prison yard. Glad to be out of the first cell, I relaxed and got into a routine and attempted to mark off the day. As the sun moved across the sky, so the lighted square of my screen moved down and across the wall, and this, after trial and error, gave me a sense of the time of day. Mostly I paced the cell and tried not to think until I managed to tire myself out. Then I'd lie down and take a nap only to awake and pace again. Each day I got stronger until I could actually pace from breakfast until supper without resting. Watching my clock on the wall, pacing, and mealtimes became the focus of my days. After the third week, when only Darryl and I remained, this mindless routine gave the day the quality of not being there; it became only a square of light that moved across my cell and turned to a dull orange. Finally Darryl was released, and I was left alone. By now I had so thoroughly trained myself to mindlessness that I never questioned why I had been singled out for the longest stint. I sang and talked to myself and tried to think about my situation as little as possible. I ate my meals with ritualistic design: two peas, three peas, a dollop of potatoes, an exact tiny spoon-size piece of meat. Each spoonful became a meal within itself. Food was now a concept to imagine rather than to experience, so that when I was finished, I never felt as though I'd eaten.

On my thirtieth day in the hole I was taken out. I was given back my clothes, which had been kept in the bin of a closet; they were cold, wrinkled, and musty-smelling. It was a strange feeling to wear clothes again and even stranger to move around and to smell familiar odors that now smelled new and exotic. I was led through the corridors up the stairs to F block. I would have to start all over again. I was told I could change my clothes and to report to the rec hall. I changed into clean underwear. The ones I had on were disgusting; I threw them away.

Once in the rec hall I was taken aback. All the guys, some of whom had never thought to give me the time of day before, now came up to me and offered me cigarettes or whatever I wanted. I discovered that a stint in the hole was grounds for respect among the inmates; the longer the stint, the more respect it earned you. I had planned an escape and had done a stretch with the in crowd in the institution. I was one of the boys now. Although I was still a State Boy, I now became a sort of honored prisoner.

When I got readjusted to institution routine again, I went back to the music program and to boxing. Max Dinova welcomed me back and passed no judgments. I deeply appreciated this. I was removed from school and assigned to the ironing room as a kind of punishment. Mrs. White, who ran it, gave me a cold stare and led me over to one of the six ironing boards where others were already at work. She showed me how to iron pants, shirts, and sheets. I took up my position and under her watchful eye began to iron. The work was tedious but not difficult. As I finished each piece, I hung it on a hanger and walked over to her and went through the ritual of holding it out, turning it, and asking, "Is this okay, Mrs. White?" She would closely inspect the sleeves, back, front, collar, and yoke and invariably point out to me several areas that I'd missed and reprimand me for my slowness. I got through the first day feeling weary, but I felt I'd done a good job. At least I had made an honest effort. At the day's end Mrs. White complimented my work with a smile. I decided I liked her and was glad she, unlike Mr. Fielding, didn't have the butt of a cigar at the corner of her mouth.

Spring arrived, and with it my fourteenth birthday. I really felt like a teen-ager now. I received the usual cards from home, and unbelievably, I got a small package from my father, a man I almost never thought about. I had last seen him six years ago, in 1956, before I had gone away, and had heard of him only a very few times since then. The package contained some chocolate-covered peanut butter cookies and a card that said "Love, Dad." I was in ecstasy. I had a father! Whom could I tell? For days I looked at the package of cookies. Whenever I was out of my cell, that package was always in my mind, and when I returned, I'd look at it and touch it reverently. Finally I slowly undid the package and one by one devoured each cookie, with each bite trying to experience my father. When they all had been consumed, so were any thoughts of my father.

In May I moved back to E Corridor. This time my cell was on the side of the building that faced the visitors' gate. It was the side we all wanted to move to, and as always I passed the time sitting up in the window, taking in the spring air. Out past the wall I could see the road that led past the IJG and curved around past the set of buildings known as the state farm, the place where the commonwealth sent its drunks for thirty- to ninety-day stretches. I had heard my mother tell of my father's trips there. Just beyond my view was the Institute for the Criminally Insane. This knowledge made me recall the gruesome stories I'd been told about the inmates there and reactivated my nightmares. They were not as bad or as prolonged as the ones I'd had at Lyman perhaps because the prison wall and my cell bars made me feel more secure. I decided it would be best to get off that side of the building, however, reasoning that if I couldn't see the institute, I would not be frightened by the stories.

As summer approached, the routine of institutional life became less regimented, and I was free to divide my time between the prison yard and the music and boxing programs. By August I had made it to the honor corridor. There I would be allowed to have a small transistor radio, curtains on my window, rugs on my floor, foodstuff and coffee, and an extra pack of cigarettes each week. I was sure my mother would be very proud of me. I wrote her and asked her to send me a transistor radio. I didn't need the other things, although I would have liked to have made my empty cell look more homey. My mother wrote and said she could not afford a radio. I was heartbroken. Music was everything to me.

Since I was in a corridor on the honor floor, I now got a chance to look into some of the other boys' rooms. I was amazed at how nicely decorated some of them were; you'd never believe they were prison cells. One boy I knew gave me his old radio because he had gotten a new one. I was finally happy. In my cell I felt fulfilled. Every Saturday afternoon I'd listen to the top forty songs, and with paper and pencil I'd copy down the words of the songs I heard. I also went before the board that month, and on August 31, 1962, just ten months after being brought to the IJG, I was paroled.

When my mother came to take me home, I was surprised to find that she had not moved; it had seemed that her moves and my releases were always related. My sister Cheryl once again had cleaned the apartment for my return. I hoped to feel as though I had never left, but instead, I felt as though I had never really been there; I supposed I really hadn't. When I'd been home about a week, my mother took me to see our parish priest. She explained my desire to become an altar boy, and the priest promised he'd try me soon. I was elated. Certainly this be proof to God and my mother of my good intentions! I resolved to be a perfect Catholic and a perfect boy.

I was not, however, a perfect student. My mother had enrolled me in the eighth grade, and I failed miserably. I had missed too many months of classes during the past year or two, and I could not understand the work. To hide my shame, I would often be tardy, and a couple of times a week I was sent home with a note. I didn't know which was worse: the humiliation of my ignorance being revealed before the other kids or my mother's warnings to shape up or be sent back to the IJG.

After my second week at school I was called by the priest to serve the 7:00 A.M. mass. Now nothing else mattered. I was going to be a real altar boy. I reviewed my Latin day and night and mentally rehearsed the procedure. My mother was proud of me;

I was proud of myself. Soon, very soon I would be Father Devlin, a priest. I skipped up to the church, donned my garments, and with the priest beside me walked from the vestry into the inner sanctum of the altar. I was sure my face was filled with serenity. The feeling of holiness pervaded my every sense. All went well, and early each morning I could be found back at the vestry, eager to serve. On the fifth morning, during the canon, I had to bring the altar book from the left to the right side, and as I went to genuflect before crossing, I dropped the book. The priest turned, and my guilt-stricken eyes shot up to him. Furious, he glared at me. I picked up the book and brought it to him on the altar. He thumbed through the text with a look of exasperation. After mass I said nothing, and neither did he. The other altar boy snickered at me as I left. Later that day, when I returned from school, my mother berated me: The priest would no longer need me to serve mass.

It was at this time in my life that I started to notice girls. I fell in love with Nancy Karper. Each day after school I would walk her to her religious school classes—Nancy was Jewish—and wait for her and then walk her home, all the while talking about the normal sorts of things that teen-agers talk about. Nancy made me forget the pain of all the years. Because of her, I settled down in school and felt the world was new and beautiful again. I knew now that I would never go back to the IJG and that God had finally forgiven and freed me. My mother was remarried and living in a respectable neighborhood; I was home, and the most beautiful girl in school liked me. What better proof had I that I had at last atoned for my sins, for wrecking my mother's marriage?

I decided to ask Nancy to be my steady girl friend. I walked to her house, and on the way I picked a rose. She was waiting for me on her front porch. I gave her the rose, and we looked lovingly into each other's eyes. Then her expression changed to a pained one, and she told me she could no longer see me. She gave no reason, and she went inside. I whirled around so as not to betray the tears that formed in my eyes. On the way home I

cried openly. I would never carry Nancy's books again. I wondered
if she had found out about my past. I had felt no need to tell her
that I had been to jail, to reform school—I didn't feel as though
I had committed any crime. Besides, everybody in our lower-class
neighborhood knew I had done time; it seemed to be no big deal.
It was only much later that I found out that Nancy's parents
wouldn't let her go out with me simply because I was not of their
faith.

Still, it was a devastating blow. Thereafter I took very little
interest in my schoolwork and in the things around me. My grades
slipped. And since I still had no friends of my own in the neighborhood, my social life ground to an abrupt halt. A short time
later my adolescent wounds began to heal, and I was digging in
my heels again at school.

One morning in November I noticed that my hair was once
more at the point where I could start training it. I wanted to get
some Vaseline, so Hughey and I decided to play hooky. We spent
the day downtown having such fun that I forgot all about the
Vaseline. Later, when we got back to Dorchester, we swiped a
jar at a local store, returned home, and hid it under the back
stairs on the first floor. My mother knew we had skipped school.
She told us to go into our rooms, to take off all our clothes, and
to go to bed. Then she came in and began to yell at us. Her words
stung and finally made me scream out with all the resentment
that had built up for years. I called her many swearwords. My
outburst made her stop. Her jaw dropped, and she informed me
she was calling my parole officer. I felt so shaken that a wisp of
wind could have blown me up and away. Exhausted, I lay beside
Hugh. He cried for me, and I for myself. He pleaded for me not
to go away again. We held each other and drifted to sleep.

That night I had many dreams of being away. They were so
real that when I awoke the next morning, I was amazed to find
that I was still at home and not in a cell. During the evening my
mother had had a change of heart. She was not sending me back.
In gratitude I decided I would be perfect. I watched my every

movement and thought every minute of every day until I thought I was perfect.

Across the street from us lived Jane. It was said that she was the neighborhood whore. Certainly there were always boys outside her house calling to her to come out. I had seen her leaning out her window, talking down to them in a teasing way, her breasts partly exposed underneath her full sweater. This made me feel good, but funny all over. I had never felt that way with Nancy. Jane looked like the girls I'd seen in the dirty picture books in Bridgewater. I watched her from my second-story window and wondered if she'd let me do things to her. I asked some of the older boys in the neighborhood. They told me if I wrote her a note saying, "Jane, can I fuck you?" she would. It was that simple. Oh, that's how it worked. Just by repeating those magic words was how you did it. Yeah, I thought, that's what really makes you a big teen-ager.

Jane was in my homeroom. The very next day of school I wrote the note and handed it to her confidently. I waited all day with excited anticipation, although for just what I didn't know. After school I entered the apartment through the back door. My mother was standing there with a strap and the piece of paper with my note in her hand. I was punished and sent to bed without supper. I lay there until the anxiety of what would happen to me had worn my body to a frazzle, and I slept fitfully, again dreaming of being back at Bridgewater. In time the incident was forgotten by everybody except Jane, who gave me stern looks from her window, where the boys forever called up to her to come out.

Sometime shortly after, my brother Kevin became sick and was quarantined to his room. I was to sleep with my younger sister Patrice. One night, as I climbed in beside her, curiosity overwhelmed me. I had to see what a girl looked like. She was asleep and lying on her back. I lifted her nightgown and looked. My eyes opened wide as I stared with a sense of wonder and puzzlement. I mustered up my courage and touched her vagina. My hand flew away since I sensed it was somehow wrong to violate her that way. I went to sleep and awoke the next morning, having completely forgotten about it. But later in the day I became more curious than ever and suggested to my sister, who was ten, that we play around. She seemed scared, but I said I had a safe, just what I had heard the teen-age boys at Bridgewater say when they sat around telling each other stories of their sexual exploits. I told Patrice that I had Vaseline, too, since the big boys at Bridgewater often said they had to use that. Anyway, nothing happened. Then, a few days later, Pat and her girl friends found Hughey's and my jar of Vaseline under the stairs. My sister told my mother she thought I was going to use it on her. My mother went into hysterics. My parole officer was called in, and I was questioned about sexual things I didn't even know about. The questions came so fast that I became confused. Hugh was called into the parlor, too, and corroborated that all we intended to do was to use the Vaseline in our hair. He asked my parole officer not to take me away.

I was taken from my home to the courthouse in Dorchester. I was asked many questions by the judge. I tried to defend myself. I was accused of many things that were not true. The fact that I had been in Bridgewater—long associated as a place for the sexually deviant and criminally insane—was a strike against me. Then, too, because my records made reference to my having participated in homosexual acts, the court assumed the worst. It was as if the judge, court officers, and spectators all were voyeurs looking for sordid stories to believe for their own excitement. I had merely touched my sister and asked her if she wanted to have sex. I did not myself fully know what sex was; I had done all this innocently, not malevolently. But the court decided I was a perverted sex maniac.

On the way back to Bridgewater I was in a confused daze. As always, I did not really know why I was being sent away. I had been home less than two months.

2.

October 23, 1962

Back again at the IJG I went through less of the soul-searching that usually had accompanied my returns; it didn't last nearly as long as, and was far less intense than, previously. I looked forward to the boxing program and to seeing Mr. Dinova again, although I was ashamed to face him and anticipated the disappointment in his eyes. I wondered why no one understood me; I wondered what was going on. I wanted so much for someone to understand me, to love me, and, most of all, to believe in me. I believed that Max Dinova did. I knew that he would welcome me and shelter me from a world I found increasingly bewildering and that he would smile at me through understanding and comforting eyes. Bridgewater, for all its walls and cells and cold impersonality, did not bother me. My desire for love and understanding transcended everything.

For a few days I remained in my cell, hoping to see him. Inside, I knew he would never come to me. Deeply ashamed, I fought the urge to go to him until my loneliness and hunger for love drove me to his door. When he saw me, he gave me a cold stare and told me to sit down in the chair next to him. I sat with my head bowed, feeling naked and uncertain. He remained silent. Secretly I felt excited to be near him. We sat in silence for a time; my love and respect for him were so great that I would have sat there day and night just to be near him. When he told me he was angry and disappointed in me, my head sank lower. Eventually he softened, and my head became lighter, and I raised it slowly to look at him. I wanted to reach out and squeeze him and never let him go. I asked him if I could study clarinet again. He said that he didn't have any instruments available, but when one became free, yes, I could, certainly. He stood up, indicating that he had work to do. He put his arm around me and with a smile welcomed me back. As I walked back to my cell, I felt happy again; over and over again I told myself that he was the only one who really loved me and I was the most special boy in his life. The world seemed a wonderful place. I promised myself that this time I would be on my best behavior. I wouldn't hurt or disappoint him ever again. And so I began my new sentence with revived hope and vigor.

Although it was fall and school was in session, I was not required to attend and was instead assigned to different shops. I especially liked arts and crafts, and luckily I was assigned there as often as I wanted to be. Mr. Scott taught me how to make plaster-cast molds and how to draw; they kept me busy all day. Mr. Scott did not seem to mind having me assigned to him; we had a fine relationship. I was eager to learn, and he to teach. But the nine-to-five crafts schedule often interfered with my getting to the gym or to music practice so that after a few weeks I chose to work in the dish room and the dining room, where I could be free after an hour or two of work.

It wasn't very long before I had a clarinet again, and each day I divided my time between practicing my music and boxing. In the gym I worked out with a devotion unmatched by the other boys. The assistant coach, a huge man with a baby face, sat and surveyed the young new contenders. Generally he did nothing but sit there and watch us. Because he was one of Richard Johnston's cronies, his job was secure. But while I trained, I'd steal glances at Coach Bailey, who was in charge of the boxing team, to see if he was considering me; this time I was determined to make the team.

Mr. Dinova, too, stressed to us boys in the music program the need to practice every day. Yet here practice for me was difficult. I wanted to play only the songs I already knew from the sheet music or to pick out tunes by ear. During the week I'd try to practice in my cell after lunch or supper. I was usually discouraged by the shouts of offended sensibilities from the boys on my corridor. At times, though, I really loved to practice and took pleasure in hearing my embouchure become clearer and seeing and feeling my fingers glide more smoothly over the keys, and developing the skills to play more complex studies. A more important incentive for practicing was that if my lesson were not down perfect, or near perfect, I would be made to repeat it for the following week. This, and my desire to please Max, made me resolve to work harder.

Thanksgiving, Christmas, and winter passed. I was now in E Corridor and preoccupied by my boxing and music interests. I heard very little from home and didn't think about my family as often as I used to, except on Sunday visiting day or at the end of every month, when the parole board met and my friends went home. I went through an agonizing metamorphosis each time. All that I had worked so hard to repress would be ripped away from my subconscious, and for the few days after, I wandered around, neither boxing nor playing music. When I did play, I sat in my window and blew in the lower register so as to hear with my ears the painful sounds I heard in my mind. When moving night came, I again metamorphosed. The thought of moving closer to the honor corridors brought me back into the institution.

From my windowed room in E Corridor I could see the entrance gate, and on visiting days I would watch the visitors come and go, knowing that no one was coming to see me but vicariously sharing the experience through the others coming in. I always secretly hoped that I would see my mother enter and would sit for hours watching, wondering, and waiting; I hated the intensity of it all. When the last visitor passed through the gate, I'd cry until I had no more tears. Each visiting day became a little easier when I no longer watched, or wondered, or cared.

Spring came, and on April 16, 1963, I celebrated my fifteenth birthday. I received a card from my mother and a note explaining that she wouldn't be up to see me because the children's chronic knee problems had her constantly taking them to the hospital. My siblings had nail patella syndrome, which meant that they had been born without fingernails and that their kneecaps occasionally fell out of place, inevitably requiring surgical correction. Each of them had already undergone at least one operation. The syndrome also caused the children's hands to gnarl and their arms and legs to grow crooked. Of all of us only I had escaped the syndrome. Still, I really did not understand how my mother could neglect me. Didn't she know how mangled inside I was?

I kept myself busy with music and the gym. All my exercising was now turning my baby fat into hardened muscle. Although I wasn't tall, I was one of the best-built boys at Bridgewater, and I thought that surely I would be invited to play baseball with the institute's team, which played regular round robin matches with outside teams. Sometimes, before or after a game, we would be allowed to meet the other players, and they were always friendly. I was surprised because I thought that outside people were supposed to hate criminals.

The first spring day we were let out into the prison yard we all ran around and around and played or wrestled until we were pooped and our muscles hurt. After being cooped up in one building all winter long, we needed several days to wind down and to get rid of all our stored-up tensions.

The masters took up their positions at each corner of the wall. There was Mr. Billings, who was English. Tall and very quiet, he was fairly young and had a nervous facial tic, the result of being hit with a wrench by an inmate trying to escape. There was also Mr. Newley. He was tall, stocky and always had a leering look on his face. It was generally conceded that he was queer and that he would watch us boys through our observation windows and masturbate. And finally there was Mr. Manning, who had a deep, robust voice. He was a former military man and used to tell us that anyone who wasn't American was either Communist or queer.

When sides were chosen for baseball, I was not picked. I was still too little. I ran to a corner of the yard where I knew I could always get into a football game. That failing, the only other activity available to us was horseshoes, which I never liked. During the summer, as the heat became oppressive and our desire for running and sports was sated, we would sit around the prison yard, listen to the radio, and talk about home and all the things we would be doing there. Some of the older boys, those very few who were away for the first time, would talk about seeing the Boston Red Sox and would wish that they were allowed to see the games on television. They talked about concerts and going to the circus, too; I wished along with them. In all the time I spent in prison, we were taken to see the circus only once, and people there looked at us so strangely that I couldn't enjoy it.

The guys also liked to talk about the crimes that had brought them to Bridgey in the first place and to share their tricks of the trade. One boy, for example, told us how he used Band-Aids to tape up windows before breaking and entering them so that there wouldn't be any noise. At other times the guys would talk about the plans they had for after their paroles. "Man, when I get outta here," one of them said, "I'm gonna buy me a bad pair of alligator shoes and a sharkskin suit and have all kinds of bitches working the block for me."

"Shit!" he was told. "To hell with bitches, man; they ain't nothin' but trouble. I've learned a lotta slick shit in here, and I already got some scores lined up with this dude on my corridor when we get out."

Whenever the guys got to talking like this, I would just sit there and listen quietly; their stories impressed and thrilled me. But I had no crimes, or plans for crimes, of my own to contribute. I hated jail, and I didn't want to go away anymore. I knew in my heart I could never do such things. I wanted to go to the Boston Conservatory of Music and study to be a virtuoso clarinetist and play in the Boston Symphony; more than anything, I wanted to be just like Max Dinova.

Some afternoons a few of the boys would gather under a large spreading elm and sing songs like "In the Still of the Night," as well as popular songs of the times. We would take turns singing lead and harmony. We weren't bad. Masters, staff, and other boys would come by and listen. My voice had matured from the yelling days of "Hound Dog," and many people said that I should be a singer. That always made me feel happy and good about myself.

Although I loved going out into the prison yard, whenever Max was at the institution, I would sit in his office and do work for him instead or would practice my clarinet in the practice room directly opposite his studio. Sometimes I would practice so earnestly that Max would tell me that I sounded like a conservatory student. Max's praise filled me with joy. My playing had in fact become more proficient, and I had progressed from being a beginning to an intermediate player. This, in turn, made Max more serious about my lessons. He taught me the advanced chromatic scales and alternate fingering. One day he even sat me down, and we played a series of short duets together. I felt so warm and so loved, sitting there with him. Music enriched my life, and through my newly-trained ears I now heard the sounds and rhythms of life.

That summer Max began to teach us how to listen to and appreciate more diverse and sophisticated kinds of music than the simple classical melodies we were accustomed to playing. One day he presented us with Richard Strauss's intricate *Till Eulenspiegel* and proceeded to explain to us how certain orchestral instruments stood for the voices of the main characters and how other instruments stood for the supporting ones. He put on the record and passed out copies of the score and then showed us how to read it and how to listen simultaneously along with the record.

As the work opened, he told us that the E flat clarinet, high-pitched and squeaky, was Till and that the violin strings carrying the melody represented Till devising some merry prank to play. Then the strings would hush, and Till would be off. The townspeople, musically the trumpets, French horns, and flutes, would become angered with him. Then Till—to the sounds of oboes and cellos—would become sad and contrite. But very soon he would again be devising another of his merry pranks and be brightly off once more. Max explained that sometimes Till's pranks unintentionally hurt people; that was why he was finally taken before the judges—all bass clarinets, tubas, and trombones. Here the narrow minds and condescending attitudes of the city fathers and their representatives became apparent: Till must hang for his deeds. After his death the townspeople immediately realized how much they loved Till and his merry pranks, even though it was now too late. I listened in rapture. I loved the music, and I loved learning how to read the score. But more important, I saw myself in Till: All my life I had been trying to tell my mother and the authorities that I was only a merry prankster who did not fully comprehend the gravity of what I did. The authorities—the Youth Service Board—had hanged me, like Till.

In the middle of the summer a new boy joined the music program, and he was already proficient on piano; this was good, because we needed a piano player. His name was Williams. He was tall, with even features, and had a superior air about him. It was rumored that he had axed his mother to death and that he came from a rich family who owned a corporation in Rhode Island. I did not doubt this because his father could visit him at any time, and I could tell his clothes were expensive. Except for the fact that he was very stingy, he wasn't a bad kid, I thought. What was curious to us, however, was that even though he had been at IJG for only a couple of months, thick, plush rugs were installed in his room along with fine curtains, nice bedwear, and a big expensive shortwave radio. When I saw these things, my barren little room seemed even emptier than before. Williams also always had plenty of cigarettes and so much food that he rarely came down to the dining hall. Sometimes he would even be permitted to go home for the weekend, a privilege extended to the rest of us only if there was an emergency or tragedy at home.

Now that we had a piano player—making a full complement of musicians—Max decided we were going to have an ensemble. He arranged our chairs and music stands in a semicircle, where we found the parts we would play. Our hearts pounded with joy; this is what we'd studied for so long; it marked us as legitimate musicians.

There was Blake, whose crime I never knew, and I, Stubborn Child, on clarinet; McQueen, who'd organized a car theft ring, and Pat on alto sax; Kurtz, in for homosexual prostitution, and Molina, in for car theft, and Kessler, in for raping a girl and biting off her nipple, on tenor saxes. Peters, who had killed his mother with a shotgun, played trumpet, and Williams played piano.

The first tune we performed was Fats Domino's "Blue Heaven," with the clarinets taking the lead. I was nervous and made mistakes, while McQueen and Molina rushed the beat, so that it took awhile until we played it through. Done, we congratulated ourselves. It was a simple melody with simple harmonies but for us, it was a Brandenburg Concerto, a Mozart symphony. Next we played Sarah Vaughan's "Broken-Hearted Melody," with Max playing the melody. He sat on a high-legged stool and played a raunchy, wailing lead to our amateur embouchures. The melody and the sound of the alto sax moved me so that I knew I would have to learn how to play it. Soon we heard noises from the prison yard below. When we finished the tune, we jumped up to look out the window. A flock of prisoners looked up from below with pleading eyes as others danced around them. It was sad that they were so starved for music. I guess Max agreed, too, because on a Friday afternoon a short time later all classes, shops, and activities were suspended, and we were herded into the auditorium. The boys in the music program were seated in the row directly in front of the stage where a big band was setting up. Max introduced the ensemble members as his students at the Berklee College of Music. They began to play, and we went wild, all of us. I watched my hero, Max, up there conducting, his roly-poly body bouncing rhythmically, his arms waving spasmodically, and his salt-and-pepper tousled mane flying out in all directions. The final tune was called "Harlem Nocturne." Before he played, Max asked us to picture New York City during the early-morning hours and to listen for the special eerie, haunting, and melodic sound of the alto sax, the sound of New York, seeping through its glass and steel canyons. Max was not only a fine musician but also a wonderful storyteller. When the band began to play and one musician began an alto sax solo, I almost cried from happiness. I resolved that one day I, too, would go to Berklee and study the alto sax.

We were not allowed to lend our instruments to any of the other boys or even to share them among ourselves. Max was very strict about this. But I was going crazy with lust for the alto. I was too ashamed to tell Max; I didn't want to hurt him. And I was afraid he'd tell me that I couldn't switch instruments. I begged the guys who played alto to let me borrow theirs until they finally relented. Each occasion cost me a pack of cigarettes, but it was well worth it. To prevent Max from discovering our indiscretion, I would borrow the sax at night while the others went to the rec hall and would play my heart out. The fingering was similar to that of the clarinet so that playing it really wasn't all that difficult. Occasionally I sneaked a go on the sax on random Saturday afternoons when Max usually was not at the institution. But on one such afternoon he caught me in my room, blowing away. He took me to his studio, extracted the name of my accomplice, and, when the other boy arrived, gave us both a tongue-lashing about honesty and trust; this seemed to me rather out of place considering where we were, yet I felt bad. He dismissed us with a warning. As I was leaving the studio, he called to me. I turned. With a smile he said, "You sounded pretty good." If he only knew how much I wanted to be like him. I smiled and thanked him and still sneaked a sax whenever I could.

In late fall of 1963 I made it to D Corridor. There were many new faces there, and one surprising old one—my corridor friend of my last stint, Brian Sayer, who had been paroled and returned. He, in turn, introduced me to Eric Reilly. He seemed to be a nice, quiet kid, but Brian warned me he could become dangerous if he was bothered; prior to Bridgey, he had been beaten up by a boy in a street fight and had retaliated by placing a big stone in a sock and beating the boy over the head with it. Brian was sweet on Eric's sister, Angela, whom he had met one Sunday when he was a runner. A runner was someone who stood downstairs in the lobby when visiting hours began. As each boy received a visitor, the runner came upstairs and informed the master. Each floor had two runners. Being selected to be a runner was a consolation prize to those boys who never received visitors of their own. Angela and her mother came to see Eric every Sunday, and since Brian was almost always the runner, he got to meet Angela. They started to write to each other, and Angela sent him a picture of herself. When he showed it to me, I told him I thought she was pretty. I was happy for Brian because like me, he didn't have anyone.

In one of the cells next to me was a boy named Gilmer. He was Fielding's infamous confidant as well as a well-known homosexual. He was so ugly that the boys would tease him and say that his face would make a train take a dirt road. I felt sorry for him—his head was kind of lopsided, and his ears were cauliflowered and not centered on his head—and I would talk to him since many of the guys wouldn't. I would even pass him a cigarette through the hole between our wall. One evening he passed a note through it asking me if he could give me a blow job. Disgusted, I told him no. Even if I were gay, I wouldn't have fooled around with him. But the next morning I was called into Fielding's office; Gilmer had told him that I had. Despite my protestations, Fielding put me in the hole.

This time I was all alone, and I felt claustrophobic. I picked up my mattress and had a fit as I threw it around and screamed that I hated God and my mother. I remained for a week in the hole, where I paced back and forth all day and put myself into a trancelike state. When I was released, I was surprised to find myself back in D Corridor, not F, which was where boys returning from the hole were usually sent. Maybe Gilmer had confessed. As soon as I was out, I went to see Max and cried on his shoulder, insisting on my innocence. I feared that if Max thought I was queer, he would hate me. I thought, too, that when I saw Gilmer again, I would beat his head in, yet when I did see him, all I could feel was compassion for him. Compassion was something else Max taught me.

It was now the middle of December, and I was in a new cell now. One of the boys next to me was named Howie. One day he began to act strangely. He became uncharacteristically quiet, walked around making jerky motions, and his eyes took on a glazed look. All the kids in D were worried about him; he was one of us, and when the chips fell, we were all for one. We knew he was acting funny, and when we told the masters they merely laughed and said he'd be okay. Finally, after a day or two, he went to see the nurse. She gave him a couple of aspirin and assigned him to sick bay, which merely meant he was told to stay in his bed, was given a pitcher of juice, and had his meals brought up to him. I looked in on him that evening as I returned to my room after rec hall and thought he looked really sick. And he was. That night, as I slept, Howie died of spinal meningitis.

Howie's death was only a more dramatic reminder to me that I was locked up in prison, and the realization triggered another depression. During these times I would go see Max and he would help me to sort out my feelings about the Youth Service Board. He explained that I was an individualist, like him, and that I should always try to be my own person, but he cautioned that the more of an individual you were, the more people would dislike you.

The idea that I was like him fed my secret fantasy that he wanted to adopt me. I knew he had two daughters but no son. I became convinced that he wanted me as his son. I mused that he had never missed not having a son before, but when he met me and saw all the love, affection, and spirit I had to offer, he had recognized the gap in his life. This idea grew stronger in my mind when, one Saturday near Christmas, he took McQueen and me to his house, where we spent the day clearing his barn of wood and other junk. It was a wonderful day and made me forget that I lived just down the road in a cell behind gray walls. We met his horse, Fleet, his two daughters, and his wife, Annie. I immediately liked her. She was a strong, intense-looking woman with bright blue eyes. I was glad she was going to be my mother. Ellen, the older daughter, was tomboyish, very outgoing and friendly. Julie gave me cause for concern. She was felinelike—sleek and graceful—but wary and said little. When we finished our work that evening, we were treated to a delicious homemade meal. Seated at the table, I felt shy and self-conscious. I had not eaten in a family setting for many, many years. Finally, with Max's coaxing, I dug in.

Back in my cell that evening I was convinced Max was setting things up to work me slowly into his family and that he'd brought McQueen along only to throw me off his true intentions. Confident that he was going to become my father, I took more and more liberties with his time. I knew he didn't like anyone getting too familiar with him; he had told me so. But that was okay; I was his son. I wanted him to spend every available moment with me, loving me, teaching me, guiding me out of this nightmare. It was only a few days later that I received a shock. I was sitting in my cell window, looking out toward the gate, when I saw Max and Williams leaving together, Max's arm around Williams's shoulder. I couldn't believe it. Max loved *me*, not Williams.

The first chance I had the following day I ran to see Max. I stopped outside his door to compose myself. When I entered, I asked him if I could help him in the studio. He said no because Williams had just been assigned to him as a full-time secretary. I tried to shake the news off. I persisted until finally Max became exasperated with me and said bluntly, "I'm not your father, Mark."

It jolted me to think that all the time he had known what I was thinking. I wheeled around and ran to my cell.

I lay on my bed and cried for a long time. I knew now that I would never become Max's son. I wanted him to love me and to teach me the clarinet so that I could become a virtuoso musician with the Boston Symphony—a son a father would be proud of. But I knew I was just a State Boy who wasn't worthy of anything. I had no musical talent, and that is why he wouldn't adopt me. Max was all the world to me, and losing him made a large part of me dry up and blow away. For a while I avoided him, and when I saw him again, he said he had missed me and gave me a cheerful smile. I still loved him, but the magic was gone.

I never wondered about my own father. I had heard nothing from him directly since he'd sent me the cookies on my fourteenth birthday. Once or twice in the intervening years a master would tell me that my father had said hello; he was then at the state farm for alcoholics across the road. I had found that hard to believe until one day in the late fall of 1963 I saw him seated beside another man on the horse-drawn wagon that was used to pick up garbage from the various Bridgewater detention centers. I wanted to call out to him, but my voice locked in my throat. I felt I would have been calling to a stranger. By the time I was finally able to get the sound past my throat, the swill wagon had already passed up the road to the state farm, and all I could see of him was the slow, rhythmic bobbing of his head and body.

I had always dreaded the holidays, and now they were again upon us. This year they were more agonizing for me than usual. My year-long study of music, which had given me a sense of worth and identity, now meant nothing. Whom had I been fooling? I was a State Boy; that's all I'd ever be. All around me I was reminded of the fact as the other boys received their cards and letters and gift packages from home. Once again all I got was a perfunctory card bearing an insipid psalm. It almost seemed cruel. I'd have been better off without it. I waited for the holidays to be over and prayed that the desolation that tore through me would subside. When the new year did arrive, I was told I was going before the board. I was to be paroled on January 31, 1964. Max congratulated me and hugged me the day I left.

3.

I found that my mother had moved again, this time to a new two-decker on a tree-shaded street. It was one of the nicest streets and neighborhoods I had known. I felt as if I'd stepped into another world through a time zone and as though I'd tussled from within a cocoon to emerge as a newly transformed being. I really did feel there was something different going on inside me. I felt a sense of newness I'd not known during previous paroles. It seemed as if I had never been away. On the next street was my grandmother's house, where I'd often gone before I was ever incarcerated. The first time I saw it all the memories of my happy early-childhood days were freed up, and with those memories came a rush of joy. I was older now, too, and felt that I had achieved some things while I was away. I almost felt whole again, not the collection of spinning parts I'd felt like for so long.

My mother bought me some clothing and enrolled me in the ninth grade at the local junior high. At first I was very shy and kept my head lowered. I applied myself diligently to catching up with my studies as best I could since I'd not really been in school for two years. My reading ability saved me from complete failure since I could not even calculate simple fractions. After a few days in school I was surprised to see Brian Sayer's girl friend, Angela. I was beginning to notice girls now and I wanted to introduce myself to her, but she was in another homeroom. Even from a distance I liked her because she seemed to be shy like myself.

One of the girls in my classroom was named Terry. She was well built but not too pretty; like other girls at that time, she had a wild-looking hairdo brought about by teasing her hair and dusting it with hair spray until her hair looked as stiff as molded plastic. I felt bad about the names boys sometimes called Terry; she had a reputation. I wanted to ask her out and to protect her from what I thought were vicious lies. When I worked up the nerve to ask her out on a date, she surprised me by saying yes.

On the night of our date, which was around St. Valentine's Day, I showered, dressed, and left my house. We were to go to a movie, and then I would take her home. I knew almost nothing about girls—what they talked about, what they liked—only what I'd seen in the movies. I stopped to buy Terry flowers and a huge valentine card. I arrived at the address she had given me to find a dilapidated gray Victorian house surrounded by a low wrought-iron fence and a weed-infested yard. I made my way up the short walk to the stairs and rang the bell. Terry admitted me to her third-floor apartment, where I met her mother and older sister. They were pleasant and offered me a seat. Terry went off, she said, to get ready. I looked around me. The apartment was strewn with many kinds of women's clothing, from feathery boas to leopard-skin capes. A thick and ghastly perfume hung in the air. Neither Terry's mother nor her sister spoke to me, but both went about the business of covering their faces with makeup and trying on odd assortments of clothing. I felt as if I were in a witches' den. When Terry at last emerged from her room a half hour later, she informed me that she didn't want to go out and complained of a cold. Stunned, I left the apartment, leaving the card and flowers behind. It was a bitter disappointment. I soon got over it, however, when Ronni DiPietro entered my life.

Once a week during the school season I was required to attend catechism classes at the local parish. It was there that I saw her. There were thirty or so neighborhood girls and boys in the classroom, girls on one side, boys on the other. I caught her looking at me, and when I looked back, I felt my whole body tingle. Throughout the lesson I wondered who she was. But when the class broke up, I simply left. I could never have considered talking to her, let alone asking her out. Over the next few weeks I was content just to see her at church class, where we stole glances at each other. I thought her very beautiful. One day in school I was surprised to see her in the corridor holding books. She must have known I was there because she walked by my homeroom and gave me a wink and teasing smile. I could not understand why she was doing these things, and since I had had so pathetically little experience with girls, she frightened me. I asked some of the kids in my class about her. I found out that she was in the precollege class and was one of the most popular girls in the school. Not very long after, Ronni sent me a note that said she liked me and wanted to meet me. Well, fireworks rocked my head. After school I met her and walked her home. We talked about many things, but all the while I couldn't keep my eyes from her face, with its blue eyes and creamy skin. She spoke with a hint of a lisp, which for some reason excited me. When we arrived at the door of her home, I was surprised to discover that she lived in a house, not an apartment. I was sure that once she knew I lived in an apartment, she would not want to see me.

Love transcended my preconceptions. Over the next few weeks I saw much of her, at church and after school, from which I would walk her home. Her father was very strict, and on school nights she had to stay home. After about a month I invited her to come over to my house. I brought her up to the apartment and introduced her to my mother. She and my mother talked for a while and seemed to forget about me. I tried to keep her attention, but she was more interested in my mother, who had started a casual conversation and was now telling her about my past. A few hours later I walked her home. The next day I sent her a note to meet me after school. I waited for an hour for her in the rain, but she didn't come. The next day I received a note from her that said she didn't want to go out with me anymore. I tried to tell myself the apartment had something to do with it. But it hurt. I moped around for a few days until my mother told me that my homeroom teacher had told her that I would not graduate from junior high school unless I could perform a small miracle. I immediately buckled down. I was motivated by the fact that I knew Ronni was going to graduate, and I didn't want her to laugh at me. I'd show her that I was as smart as she was. And I did graduate, even though I failed in math. I still couldn't do fractions.

My best grade came in drawing class. Somewhere along the line I had become interested in pursuing a career in architecture; perhaps it sprang out of a desire for a permanent home. My junior high counselor told me that although there weren't any public trade schools that taught architectural drawing, I might be able to enroll at Boston Trade High, which taught mechanical drawing. I said I'd like to try that. On the day before my graduation the guidance counselor told me I had been accepted for the following academic year.

In the first days of late spring, when I was sixteen, I began meeting kids in the neighborhood. I began to hang out with a small group of seven boys and three girls. Our hangout was, of all places, on the low stone wall of the Dorchester Courthouse. They said that they knew I'd been away and that they didn't care—I think my brother Hughey had told them. It was difficult for me to comprehend that I was with outside kids and that they easily accepted me as one of them. I felt stupid and childish among them; I didn't know a thing about cars or girls or major-league sports or beaches or outside stuff in general. And I did not know how to conduct myself in social situations—meeting their parents, for instance. But they were always warm and kind to me; it was as though my having been locked up were past history.

Although I often felt awkward around my new friends, I was happy to be with them. These were simple, decent, good kids who didn't drink or smoke or swear, who respected their elders, and who were comfortable with themselves. I had dreamed about being with kids like these. It was a summer unlike any I had ever known.

134

That summer we often went to Nantasket Beach, returning late at night, singing songs along with the radio, crowded together in the front and back seats of a borrowed family car, telling jokes and laughing all the way home. On one of those outings I was seated next to the window on the trip home. In their merriment they did not notice that tears of gratitude were running down my cheeks as I watched the silent forest go by. I remembered that Max Dinova had once told me what he most admired about me was my enthusiasm. And it was true, or at least in prison I was always bouncy and eager to take on new challenges. But on the street I was shy and introverted. These kids had helped me break through it. In rare moments I could be funny and clever and hold the group spellbound. Afterward they'd say how surprised they were, that they hadn't known I was like that. I hadn't known it either. Everything was fine at home, too. My mother was nice to me, and Bill, whom I almost never saw, did not attack me anymore. Everyone said that I was doing so well.

My favorite new friend in the group was Mike McKenna. He and I got jobs together working in the cafeteria of the First National Bank of Boston/Data Processing Center in Dorchester. It was only part-time work, but it was also the first time I had ever earned my own money, and it felt really good. After each shift Mike and I were allowed a meal and a piece of dessert. But Mike, who was athletic and very playful, had this thing about custard pie. He would often filch a whole pie when no one was looking and down the whole thing in the locker room. Bonnie, one of the serving women, would tell the manager, Mr. Howell, whenever she caught Mike in the act. And Mike would retaliate by teasing her about being overweight. I did not join in because she was an adult, and I feared that she could send me back to jail. She didn't know anything about my past, but I always just assumed that the adults could tell. But although I didn't tease her, I did not like her. Having been in prison, I had a contempt for finks. And she also reminded me of a housemother at Lyman School.

One day, after a barrage of Mike's wisecracks, Bonnie apparently had had enough. She went crying to her son. When we left work the next evening, two good-size boys approached us. "Are you Devlin and McKenna?"

"Yeah, that's us."

They came at each of us, swinging. After the bad, really bad guys I'd mixed it up with in IJG, I was able to dispatch my attacker with relative ease; I knocked him cold. Mike, on the other hand, was no fighter. He was on the ground, getting the shit kicked out of him. I grabbed the other boy by the shirt and used his head like a speed bag, unleashing as I hit him all those years of pent-up rage. I was close to putting the lights out on Mike's attacker when a bank guard emerged and broke it up. We brushed ourselves off, shook hands, and, funny as it sounds, asked our attackers for a ride home. On the way we explained about how Bonnie was always trying to boss us around. She had told them the story about our teasing her, but she had exaggerated it. By now the guys were in awe of my boxing abilities and asked me how I had learned to fight like that. My anger having subsided, I slipped back into my shyness and said, "It's over, forget it." I didn't want to talk about Bridgey. They, especially Mike, wouldn't let up, though. He had never known that I could kick ass like that. I became a hero to him. He spread the word, and for a day or two I was a kind of conversation piece. I loved it. And at work Bonnie never bothered us again.

One of the boys we knew was an older guy named Pitt who thought he was "bad," a real tough. He'd heard of my big day and was told that I could whip his ass. Pitt began to speak to me with a bit more respect. I was actually scared of him, but *he* seemed to be more afraid of me. I was thankful for that. Pitt had a girl friend, Roberta Chiger, who was a beautiful green-eyed blonde. In the vernacular of the time, she was "stacked." To the rest of us she seemed untouchable. Roberta liked tough guys; the tougher they were, the more she liked them. Well, she had heard about my big fight and saw the way the guys looked up to me and the way Pitt lowered his tail a bit when I was around. She started to give me those knowing looks, and I started to gulp.

Everyone knew that Roberta "did it"; the very idea of sex with girls was our main preoccupation at that time. "Hey, Mark," a friend would ask, "see those two girls walking down the street? Do you think they do it?"

"I don't know. Maybe."

"See those two sitting on the bench. Do you think that they do it?"

And so we speculated, on and on.

Pitt had told us that Roberta had done it with him. Often. Like all the guys, I would have given my right arm to go with Roberta. And here she was spreading the word she dug me. I shied away. I wasn't into taking another guy's girl friend, and I certainly wanted no part of Pitt. Roberta somehow got word of that, and she broke off with him. That signaled me she wanted me to be her man. And so Roberta became my girl friend. The word went around that summer that Mark Devlin was king of the hill. But I was still scared of Pitt. I knew he could beat me. Miraculously, though, he never bothered me.

On our first date Roberta and I went down to Malibu Beach in Dorchester. We lay beside each other, talking and listening to the radio. Lying beside her, I was ready to take on Pitt and half of Dorchester. When it grew dark, we began to "make out." I closed my eyes and kissed her. It was the first time for me. The kissing and squeezing got heavier; Roberta began to moan in my ear. At this my body shook like a pneumatic drill. I wanted to touch her, but I didn't know how to. I thought that since she had "done it," she'd show me. I finally remembered that I should try to give her a hickey; that was the magic trick, I'd heard. Still, nothing more came of our groping, and we packed up to go home.

On the way back I felt such a pain in my groin that I thought I'd injured myself; I had to walk home bowlegged. When I got home, I felt as if I had to go to the bathroom. I grunted and groaned, but nothing happened, and the pain worsened. Frightened, I told my mother. With a knowing look she asked me if I'd been out with a girl. I said yes, and she told me to go to bed and promised that I would feel fine in the morning. Once in bed I thought that girls can do some powerful things to a guy. I fantasied about Roberta until I fell asleep. When I saw her the next day, she invited me into her house. Her parents weren't at home, and it wasn't long before we were going at it hot and heavy again. Still, I had no idea about what to do or even if she wanted me to do anything. And so after a time she said she had something she had to do, and I left. The next day she was back with Pitt. He gave me a smirking look. He'd known she'd be back. Frankly I was glad. She was too much woman for me, and I did not like being the star of the team. I didn't like heroes, good or bad. I decided to forget about girls; they were too much trouble.

With much relief I went back to hanging around with Mike. One August afternoon we went to see the Red Sox—my first major-league baseball game. I'd often dreamed of being like outside kids or being like the older boys at Bridgey who talked about the baseball games they had been to. Inside the ball park I looked around me in wonder. I, a State Boy, was at Fenway Park! I couldn't believe it. In front of us were sitting two girls who looked about our age. Mike struck up a conversation with one of them and tried to get me involved. The other girl appeared to be interested in talking with me. I was polite but more interested in my first baseball game. Besides, girls only made a guy's balls hurt and demanded a lot of attention. Soon Mike and this girl got into an argument about sports; I was surprised to find she really seemed to know what she was talking about. The argument ended with Mike hitting her on the head with his popcorn box; they were in love.

Mike now began to go to Brighton to see her, and I hardly saw him for the next week or more. Then one day he told me that Kit, his girl, had broken off with him and had told him that he had better not come around anymore because she had a new boyfriend who knew karate. But Mike was hopelessly in love and had to see her. He asked me to come along with him in case Kit's friend got violent. I didn't know what karate was, but it sounded pretty lethal to me. I said sure. I would go as a dispassionate observer. We borrowed bikes and rode over. When we arrived at Kit's building, I remained on the curb with my bike while Mike rang the bell. A short, skinny kid came to the door. It was Mr. Karate, and he looked as if he wouldn't even be afraid of Pitt. He told Mike to leave, that Kit didn't want to see him. Mike returned to his bike and began throwing insults at him. As he started toward Mike, we both got on our bikes and quickly pedaled home.

My sister Cheryl was then working at a Dunkin Donuts. She had a boyfriend named Gary, who was a few years older than she and quite friendly toward me. The new school term was almost upon us, and Cheryl, whom I rarely saw, invited me one Sunday morning to go horseback riding with them as a present for my outstanding behavior.

We went to the Blue Hills stables in Milton. I had never been around horses and was scared of them but willing nonetheless to sit on the huge, powerful monster they gave me. When the stable hand left us, Cheryl and Gary rode off in a blaze of dust, hoofs flying everywhere. My horse and I were content just to clop lazily along the trail. Then suddenly the horse stopped. My eyes bugged out. What do I do now? I thought. The horse just turned and moseyed back to the stable. With a look of exasperation the stableboy galloped over and said he'd try it one more time. Back on the trail and alone again I was sure that horse would stop at the very same spot and go back. When it didn't, I relaxed and began to sing loudly—"I'm an old cowhand from the Rio Grande." I was really getting into it. No sooner had I finished singing than that damn nag stopped, turned around, and headed back to the stables. My singing, no doubt. I was just thankful it hadn't reared up, toppled me, and stomped on me with its hoofs the way I'd seen in the movies.

When we arrived back at the stables, the stableboy came galloping up to me again and took the reins. Laughing, he led us into a corral. I was excited because I knew the horse would start galloping around. I wanted to feel its thundering hoofs and the odor of sweat and leather fill my nostrils. It lowered its head and didn't budge. I sat there dumfounded and afraid to move for a good half hour. Cheryl and Gary came cantering up from the trail; when they saw me, they broke out into laughter. Although it humiliated me to have to ask, I beseeched them to help get me off; I didn't know how.

I approached technical school in the fall with a fervent desire to be a good student. I took my seat in a classroom of ten or fifteen boys. My desk was a drafting table. There were no girls in my class or in the school, and I liked that; there would be no distractions from my studies. Almost immediately I had trouble. I had a good hand, a very good hand for drawing. But the math was extremely difficult for me, and I didn't know how to do it. At first I was able to fake my way through.

In drafting class I met a boy named Daniel. We tried out for the school football team together. It meant a lot to me to be a part of the team. I always loved being involved in programs. Daniel, who was bigger than I and a gymnast, was picked; I was not. But we had, respectively, the two best hands in the class. We often walked home from school together and talked about drafting. Daniel told me that he was planning to go to the Wentworth Institute of Technology directly across the street to study mechanical engineering. I had not thought about what I would do with my mechanical drawing until Daniel mentioned Wentworth, and then I knew. I told Daniel I had been planning the same thing. We smiled at each other; we had a mutual respect for each other's drawing and technical abilities and became good friends. But by my third week in school the math was becoming too difficult for me. I was rapidly falling behind and tried to make excuses. I didn't want to admit that I couldn't do the math. I didn't want ever to stop drawing, and I thought if Daniel, who was really good at math, knew I was not equal to the work, he would not want me for his friend. I was too ashamed to tell anyone.

I was saved by a series of events. I woke up one morning at

about three, sweating profusely and burning up; I was delirious, and when my mother came in to check on me, I thought she was going to send me back to IJG. She calmed me down and took my temperature; it read 104 degrees. I was rushed to the hospital, but in my delirium I first ran down the street, believing that the hospital was the police station and that she was taking me back. She convinced me I was at the children's medical center, where I'd been seen over the past few years for a chronic ear infection. The doctor suspected spinal meningitis, which frightened me, remembering what happened to Howie at the IJG. The doctor gave me a lumbar puncture which felt as if someone had dug a hand into my back and was ripping my spine out. I passed out and awoke the next day in a hospital bed. I sat up and asked for food. The nurses explained that I had had a serious infection of the middle ear, and that the doctors had had to remove my eardrum. I felt woozy but much better and was released the next week with a gargantuan bandage around my head. I was excused from school for a couple of weeks while I got my strength back and before long was back at the courthouse wall, spending the afternoons and evenings with my friends.

One evening a kid I'd not seen before but who was known to the others came by in a car. He looked like Michael J. Pollard, with small eyes and a pug nose. His name was Jesse, and he got out of the car and sat down with us. He had a six-pack of beer with him and offered me one. I'd never drunk beer before. For some reason I wanted to try it that night. As we sat around and talked, the beer made me feel tipsy but less shy. Jesse asked me if I wanted to go for a ride. I said sure. Mike and the other kids warned me not to go with him, but I didn't see any harm in it, so I went. He handed me another beer and began cruising around the streets. He asked me if I wanted to help him steal a pocketbook. I said no, but he convinced me it would be okay, and I finally gave in. I don't know why except to say that somewhere in my mind I knew that home wasn't real and that I'd be going back to prison. I honestly did not understand right from wrong.

In my other world crime was what was right. Now Jesse told me I would do it, and I did: I snatched an old woman's purse and knocked her down as I took it. I jumped back into his car, and he sped off; he circled around, parked his car, and we got out. Walking up the street, Jesse noticed someone he knew. We walked up to him, and Jesse told the boy to give him his watch. I protested. But he hit the boy in the face with his fist and took his watch anyway. Frightened, I ran back to the car. Jesse returned and drove around for a short time. Then he drove to the police station and told them what we'd done. I was taken to the Youth Service Board and charged with robbery and assault. I was taken to court, where I saw the woman I had knocked down. She looked like my grandmother. She gave me a sad look as though she felt bad for me. Seeing her was punishment enough.

I resolved that if I got off on probation—a possibility since this was my first offense—I would go to her house and help her in every way I could. But on October 2, 1964, just two days after the trial, I was back in F Corridor again, staring out my window. I could not get that poor woman off my mind. It took me a long time to get over it. I remained in a sort of limbo.

Before long I was Mark Devlin, State Boy, again, back in the music program and back in the gym. Although I knew Max did not want me to be his son, I still loved him and thought he still cared for me.

I had now reached my full height of five feet eight inches and I had a sturdy, muscular frame. I had had a taste of earning my own money, so that when I heard that IJG boxers were paid $13 a fight, I wanted more than ever to join the team. Coach Bailey still would not consent until one day the team had an away match scheduled and a boy on the team, in my weight class, got into trouble and was put in the hole. The coach told me to get ready. I was going out that night! I believed it only when my hands were taped and I was given a team jacket.

That evening we drove over to Fall River for the match. I was scared, very scared. When it came time for me to fight, I almost ran out the door. I stepped into the ring and looked at my opponent. He looked pretty rough. The bell rang. I came to my senses, danced in, and started throwing leather. I forgot all my boxing skills as I threw wild, swinging overhead punches called haymakers. I threw haymaker after haymaker, managing to connect with quite a few of them. It wasn't classic boxing, but the crowd loved it. They loved a fighter who'd get in there and start brawling. When it was over, I had won. Inside the dressing room I was so drained and weak I passed out. On the way back to prison I sat in the back of the bus with my plastic trophy. I had been the only winner that night; I was very proud. Over the next couple of months I won four more fights and qualified for the semifinals of the Golden Gloves. I won my first Golden Glove fight handily. But my next fight at the Lowell Arena proved to be my last.

I stood in my corner and looked at my opponent to see that he was about six feet three inches, skinny but wiry. During the first round we felt each other out. I wasn't rushing in to mix it up with this guy. In the second round I tried to get in under his long reach, to beat on his body, and, I hoped, to wear him down so that he'd drop his arms and I could get to his head. That strategy worked fine, and I almost knocked him out, but I didn't follow up, and he came back to stagger me. The referee called a TKO. I threw my rubber mouthpiece on the canvas and protested. But a decision was a decision. I had lost my first fight and my last: I had to go to the hospital in Boston to have a tube put in my ear because fluid was building up in it, and when I returned I was taken off the boxing team. On May 28, 1965, just eight months later, I was paroled again.

In the interim my mother and Bill had moved again, this time to a treeless working-class neighborhood in the Codman Square section of Dorchester. Where there had seemed to be a cohesiveness at the last house, there was only confusion now. Just across the street from our new apartment was an empty lot where broken beer bottles and used condoms were strewn about. It was the kind of neighborhood where welfare mothers lived with their too many kids and where their husbands or boyfriends drank heavily and beat the kids. These kids were, in turn, afraid to go back to homes where they weren't really missed anyway. They stayed out late, hung out in packs, drank liquor, popped pills, vandalized property, and pulled minor scores.

Patrice and Hugh, who were now thirteen and fourteen, fell in with this crowd. Kevin, who was fifteen, was still shining shoes in town. I got the impression that the other kids made fun of Kevin because he had a funny sort of bowlegged walk and a weak left eye that made him look a little cross-eyed. They nicknamed him Goober after the character on "The Andy Griffith Show." Hugh was now heavy into drinking and thinking of himself as a kind of tough guy. His toughness was mostly bravado, but he tried to use Kevin as his patsy. It was sad to see them. Kevin had a good mind and would have done better in a nicer environment. And even though Hugh was acting the tough guy, I watched him go to sleep every night wearing his baseball cap and glove. Hugh had dreams of becoming a baseball player. Yet his chronic nail patella problem crippled his legs, and he could not straighten out his arms all the way. Consequently, I think, his drinking sometimes made him vicious, but for the most part he was a sweet, funny kid and now very definitely my mother's favorite. Although I longed to get close to my brothers, their relationships with their friends and to each other had evolved to such a point that I really did not know or understand them. And they began to call me jailbird when they wanted to hurt me.

My mother was now working as a telephone operator, and she had really lost control of the kids. She tried to keep Patrice out of trouble by giving her lots of housework. I guess she didn't want her to become pregnant out of wedlock like some of the other girls in the neighborhood had done. Donna was still the "baby" and rather spoiled; she did not have to help out with the housework.

My estrangement from my family felt complete. I had grown in such different ways from them that they thought I was a weirdo because I played clarinet, listened to jazz and classical music, and could read and was even beginning to write a little music. I was starting to dream about becoming a composer, and it irritated them that I talked about it all the time. In my enthusiasm I wanted to try to teach my brothers and sisters about music, but they only laughed at me until I felt that maybe I *was* a weirdo and a square.

I applied for my Social Security card and took my first full-time summer job, working in the bakery of a supermarket chain. I worked hard, pulling in as much overtime pay as I could. With my money I rented a saxophone and a clarinet. In preparation for school I bought some clothes and drafting tools; I was pretty proud of myself.

After my first few days back in technical school my composer daydreams increased as each day passed and the math became harder. Somehow I found out that the Berklee College of Music, which I'd heard about from Max, was not a long walk from Boston Trade, where I was a student. And so, one afternoon, after school was over for the day, I found myself on the steps of Berklee. I went inside and heard the rich sounds of musical ensembles and lone musicians practicing. It filled me with joy; I felt warm and safe and secure because here were people who were just like me. People who played music were my peers; people who didn't, I distrusted. Everyone was or wasn't Max Dinova. It was that simple.

I went to Berklee after school as often as I could, just to hang around and make believe I was a student there, pretending that I was part of a positive, growth-oriented group. I'd spend the day reading the want ads on the bulletin board and, when I had money, I'd buy books that related to the theory and practice of composing. I did not always understand what I read; nonetheless, I kept them close to me since they made me feel close to Berklee. Whenever I was home, I'd line the books up on a table, look at them, thumb through first this one, then that one. And my subsequent purchase

145

of my very own copy of the album *Jazz in the Classroom*—a collection of tunes played by a Berklee band—brought me one step closer to my dream. With the purchase came a full score. Rather than go to Berklee after school, I would now go home, put on the album, and read the score along with each composition over and over again until I knew the score so well I could picture it in my head. I passed hours doing this while in the living room sat my two brothers and Pat and their friends, drinking alcohol, listening to the Four Tops, and calling me weirdo. I countered that at least I didn't pop pills like uppers and downers, as I suspected they were doing. I was going to be a fine composer. In the meantime, my schoolwork became so difficult that I was forced to quit. I had been in trade school less than a month.

Shortly after I withdrew from Boston Trade, I met my friend Brian Sayer's girl friend and my former schoolmate Angela Reilly again. She had spotted me on the rapid transit and had come over to say hello. Back at public school I had always thought her too pretty to be interested in me, and that she was also painfully shy, so I was very surprised that she sought me out. She had curly blond hair, wide green eyes, creamy skin, and nicely shaped lips. She told me that she had written some lyrics and had sent them with a dollar to a record company in Tennessee, which had set a tune to it. She wanted to hear how it sounded. I agreed to go to her house and play it for her on my clarinet.

When I arrived at her apartment building, I knew that in comparison to the little my own family had, Angela's had even less. When I went inside, I saw that the apartment's floor was sagging, that the windows and doors were crooked, and that the wallpaper looked old and stained. I was taken to the kitchen, which consisted of some old appliances and a broken table and chairs. It was now mid-fall, and turning cold, and the only heat coming into the apartment was from the oven of a stove. I met Angela's mother, whom I had seen before when she had come to see her son, Eric, at Bridgewater. I played the tune composed for Angela's lyrics; it was an extremely simple melody with a country-

and-western flavor. When I finished, Angela and her mother thanked me and gave me some tea. On my way home I thought about Angela and her mother, and I became disturbed. Her mother had next to nothing; the meager wages from her factory job with its long, tiring hours went toward providing her daughter, who was still in school, with decent clothes, food, and a roof over her head. Yet she had found the time every week to see her son in Bridgewater. At that moment I hated my mother.

A week later, without an invitation, I went back to Angela's, loaded down with a rented sax and clarinet. She laughed when she saw me. I asked her to go to the movies. She said yes. In the movie we kissed and held hands. Back at her apartment Angela brought out a record player, put on a Beatles album, and with the cold wind whistling and rattling outside, we danced. I had never danced with a girl before. Now I was sure I was in love. We danced slowly, drawing away from our lonely worlds through each other's synchronized steps. Then I heard a loud, screaming voice. It came from the kitchen. Angela's mother was swearing at her, calling her a whore. Angela hid her face in shame. I did not understand what was going on; I thought her mother must be insane. Angela asked me to leave. Her eyes pleaded with me not to think too badly of her. I left. It was past midnight. As I walked home past the deserted factory-lined streets, the railroad tracks, and the empty weed-covered lots—my footsteps in a kind of metallic echo—I decided I wouldn't go back. A week later I did. I worshiped Angela. She was the only woman I knew who seemed to be really in pain like me, who needed someone to protect her, to make her feel loved, needed, just as I did.

Now that I had left technical school for good, I went to Berklee for an application and a brochure. I turned to the section for composition majors. I read about all the things I'd be studying. I filled out the application then and there, even though I did it for make-believe. In preparation for earning my tuition, I took a job as a supermarket stock boy. I called Mr. Dinova in Bridge-water, as I did from time to time, to tell him my good news. He said he thought that my idea was a good one but said that I needed a high school diploma. I was stunned. My dream of going to Berklee and of becoming a composer vanished. I knew I would never get a high school diploma. I knew from my previous attempts that I wasn't smart enough. Disillusioned, I gave up the idea of going to Berklee, but not of composing. It crept slowly back into my subconscious until one time I even saw myself being hailed at an imaginary ceremony as a bright new composer. I presented a speech, and at the end of it the people cheered and clapped for me as tears of gratitude filled my eyes.

Why did I have to have a high school diploma? I didn't need one. What did the three Rs have to do with music? I didn't care what anyone said. I resolved to be a composer anyway. I decided to study on my own. Yet secretly I knew I never would be a composer, just as I would never be a priest. This, too, was just another diversion to keep the tormented child in me shackled to memory. OK. If I couldn't become a composer, I would become a virtuoso clarinetist. I decided to enlist in the navy and apply to the naval music school. I was sure I'd be accepted. My dream, though temporarily sidelined, was still possible. I felt at peace.

I told Angela of my intentions. She cried and pleaded for me not to go. At first I took almost a perverse pleasure in the unaccustomed awareness of my power to hurt another person. Then I snapped back, and my sense of compassion took over. I convinced Angela that we would still be together and that I'd never leave her. She acquiesced. I went to the Charlestown Navy Yard and took a daylong battery of tests. I called Max, who was proud to hear of my decision. He, too, had gone to the naval music academy. I told all those whom I knew of my plan; my mother and sisters and brothers and acquaintances.

Two weeks after taking my tests I received a letter from the navy. Excitedly I tore open the envelope and read that I had not passed the tests. I was not accepted. Angrily I threw it away. I walked down to the marine recruiting center and said I wanted to enlist for the marines' music academy. I filled out an application and went back two days later to get a testing date. I was informed that my jail record made me unacceptable. Confused and disillusioned, I walked the streets in a daze. After a time I decided the hell with the military anyway; from what I had heard about the army, it sounded just like the Youth Service Board. Besides, I decided to make new plans for my life. I would get a good job, marry Angela, and build a home.

I pored over the Sunday help wanted section until I found the perfect job: Pratt & Whitney Aircraft in Connecticut was hiring trainees for its jet engine-building program. I was sure I would be hired. After all, hadn't I studied mechanical drawing? Except for math, wasn't I a solid B student? Early Monday morning I hitchhiked from Boston to Hartford, Connecticut. I arrived near the Pratt & Whitney office at dusk. All around the area were small houses. The warm glow of their lamp-lights stirred up fantasies of Angela and me living cozily in one of them. When I got to the office, I was handed a two-page application. I meticulously began to complete it. When I was nearly finished, I came to a question that dashed my dream as driftwood against jagged rocks. The question: "Do you have a criminal record?"

I could not control the stream of tears that stung my cheeks as I ran out the door to the highway. I arrived back in Boston around eleven o'clock that night, barely escaping a man who picked me up, brandished a large knife, and talked of murdering young boys.

It was during this time that I would bolt up out of a deep sleep to the sound of my heart pounding so fiercely that I could hear it with my ears. I'd run out to the porch in terror until the night air calmed me down. But even when I went back to bed, I was still shaking. After a time it stopped. Another thing that frightened me and that I could not explain was that whenever I would watch TV and saw shows about happy people, I would get a feeling that some great weight was traveling up through me, first lodging itself in my chest and then as if it were trying to push its way out of me. A chill would come over my body, and my scalp would tingle. Relief came when the tears did. It frightened me but continued for so long that watching TV finally ceased to upset me.

I was beginning to feel better, and free at last of the nightmare, of the years of persecution, depravity, and punishment. I was ready to conquer the world. I wanted to practice my clarinet and sax. But I had no practice room. My mother had a large closet in the hallway. I decided to practice there, reasoning that the clothing would absorb the sound. One Saturday afternoon, when nobody was home, I began to clean up the messy, cluttered interior. About halfway through the task I noticed one of the Magi I had painstakingly made for my mother at Lyman, six years before, lying decapitated among the rubble of bags and baggage. Frantically I pushed the rubble aside to find some of the other figures I had made. Some of them were gone. Some of the ones I did find were broken. I looked for the manger; surely that was intact. But it was gone. I took the fact that my mother kept my Magi out of sight in a closet as further proof that she felt I still had not atoned for my sins. And I knew now I never would. Nevertheless, I still believed in God, and I kept asking Him to help me.

When I finished cleaning the closet, I moved in a chair and the music stand I'd purchased. I began my études and dreamed of Max Dinova, but my reverie soon faded into despair. The sound was indeed absorbed by the clothing, but so much so that I could not hear it with my ears but could only hear it compressed in my head. And Max was not there. I went to lie on my bed, as I had done in Bridgewater when I felt depressed and when there was no one else to talk to. I lay there, tacking back and forth between hope and hopelessness, and dreamed through moist eyes of the things I would do someday.

My desire to become a great composer again consumed me. On the Saturdays when I didn't work, I'd spend my day at the Boston Music Company, buying sheet music and score pads. A score pad is a sheet of lined music paper that composers and arrangers use to write in the various parts for the band. I knew little about composing or arranging instrumentation and nothing at all about writing counterpoint and harmonies. I had only an

150

idea about scoring. But I'd sit there anyway, writing out whole arrangements for melodies I made up on my clarinet. I knew how to write in the clarinet notes but not how to add in the note values. Still, it was enough for me.

I continued to practice in my makeshift closet-studio on days when nobody was home. It was hard and lonely work without Max beside me. When my mother came home early from work one afternoon, she told me I couldn't practice there anymore. The only place remaining to me was our back porch. That ended during one afternoon practice when my mother came out and told me to "shut that goddamn thing off." I knew then that I had no talent. I had played my full repertoire that day, as brightly and sweetly as my skills allowed, knowing full well that she was in the house, secretly listening to me. I had wanted to make her proud of me, her son, the soon-to-be virtuoso principal clarinetist with the Boston Symphony. I was devastated for a time, but I still was determined to play. I called a friend I'd made at the market, Debbie Lombardi, and asked her if I could rent a space in her father's garage for an hour every day. But she said no. I decided to run away, to be rid of the pressures and paranoia I'd felt at home. Sometime during December of 1965 I boarded the bus with no plan or timetable except to become a great musician and to play torch songs on a wailing alto. On the bus to New York that ever-with-me sense of hope and hopelessness shifted back and forth inside me until I slept. I arrived at the New York bus station with my instruments, music sheets, and score pad in hand. I had only a few dollars on me and no idea of where I was or where I was going.

I began walking the streets close to the bus station. I walked past the theaters on Forty-second Street and Broadway. A man approached me and asked me for directions. I said that I had just arrived in New York and that I didn't know my way. He talked for a while and confessed that he, too, was new to the city and suggested we have a drink together in a nearby restaurant. Happy for his company, I went with him. He ordered two beers. As we sat, he confessed to me that he actually lived in Brooklyn and asked me if I had a place to stay. I said I did not. He began making suggestive remarks to me. He told me that he would let me stay the night with him if I would let him see my body naked. I was frightened, but I didn't say a thing for fear he would kill me. Finally he said that he was going to the men's room and that if I were still there when he returned, we'd have a deal. If he had offered me a place to stay without getting funny, I probably would have gone with him. But as soon as he was safely in the bathroom, I left and ran down the street. That night I roamed Times Square, crying and wondering why I was so fucked up. Tired and cold, I sat in a restaurant and, with my last $2, had breakfast. It was around 6:00 A.M. and getting light. I was thankful that a night I thought wouldn't end was over.

I roamed the streets for a while longer. With my last spare change I called Max. He was startled when I told him I was in New York. I thought he'd be proud of me. Instead, he told me to get right back home. Without questioning him further, I set out to return. I needed that shot of reality. When I got home late that evening, I telephoned Max to let him know I was okay. He lectured me about the dangers of New York and told me not to do it again. I hung up feeling hollow and in need of something from him that he never was able to satisfy.

Within days I was feeling positive again. I would take any kind of work, marry Angela, and settle down. That was all I wanted, really. To be like normal outside people, without all the pulling and tugging and loneliness and longing. I would forget the past and begin a new life. I took a job as a stock boy at a store that sold lamps and chandeliers. I soon established myself as a hard worker with good organizational skills and a facility for remembering all the stock numbers and inventory levels, better even than Robert, the store's manager. But then again Robert was a bright guy with ambitions for an electronics degree, who was in the process of getting together the tuition.

For a time I was quite happy with my job. I got on well with the owners, who respected my earnestness and ability. Needing constant approval, I did whatever they asked and stayed as long as they needed me. When I was finished for the day, I would go over to see Angela. I'd spend the entire evening with her sitting on my lap, a blanket spread around us to keep us from freezing. The only heat came from the kitchen stove, and from that room we could hear Angela's mother ranting and raving to herself or hurling insults at Angela; it seemed clear to me that Angela's mother must be insane: why else would she be so hurtful? We'd try to ignore her and watch TV and talk until just after midnight, when I'd leave and trudge through the biting cold and snow.

Christmas came, and we spoke of exchanging gifts. Over and over I said to her, "No gifts." The thought of receiving a Christmas present frightened me; I don't know why. But I took a week's pay and bought Angela a new dress and matching accessories. She, too, had gotten me a present. As I held it in my hands, a panic coursed through me. I began to sweat profusely; it felt as if it took me years to open the box. I tried to want the sweater Angela gave me and to share in the Christmas spirit; I tried so hard, but I couldn't. I'd forgotten how to experience Christmas.

In early January Robert left to return to school, and I was promoted with a raise to the position of head shipper-receiver. I had been there for just a short time, but I knew the system inside out. Then my personality began to change, little by little each day. One afternoon, following a small dispute about stock, I told Mary Ann, the owner's daughter, to whom I had always been polite, to go fuck herself. I knew immediately I had made a mistake. I had tried to be perfect, but I had failed. I could not control the anger that welled up in me, and hated myself for it. I was let off with a warning. I again applied myself to the job, settling down for a month or more until I began to lose interest in my work. Just before the spring of 1966 I found I could no longer handle concentrating on both my job and fighting my feelings of anxiety and depression. I left my job.

Within a week I took a new job, this time as an encyclopedia salesman. I reported for work at 9:00 A.M., spent the morning learning the pitch, and after lunch, with three or four other future hotshot salesmen in tow, the crew manager took us out to canvass some of the outlying towns in the Boston area. Arriving back downtown at around five o'clock, we were given the next week's assignments. I was accompanied by a veteran salesman, Matt Curtis. We'd work until eleven o'clock at night, going door to door. This job appealed to that part of me which was the child in need of attention: It allowed me to play to a whole audience of people. And at first I did fairly well as a salesman, but I grew more interested in winning looks of assurance and approval from my customers than in obtaining orders.

In April I celebrated my eighteenth birthday and in May I was officially discharged from the Youth Service Board.

My mother now knew she could never send me back, and so did I. I did not seek revenge but gloated to myself or to her whenever we had a confrontation that in the past would surely have earned me a ride to the YSB. The realization that I could never be sent back to the IJG or any part of the YSB at first confused me because I was so used to it. This wore off as I began to focus on my career of supersalesman and to anticipate its financial rewards. But although I was convinced that I was a good salesman, I'd often leave a person's home after a couple of hours of conversation without a contract. I tried hard but never understood the basic principles of salesmanship.

By October of that year my feet were cold and my arms hurt from lugging a forty-pound briefcase for miles. I had also grown tired of being chased away by dogs and people and of feeling scared being by myself on long, dark roads with houses set a half mile apart. I abandoned my career of supersalesman.

About that time I developed an abscessed tooth. I went to a neighborhood dentist. The tooth was extracted under sodium pentothal. When I awoke, I was crying hysterically. The detention center, John Augustus Hall, Lyman School, and the IJG—images and memories from all of them had swooped around my brain without chronology, like some montage. I felt as if I had gone mad. I reached out and grabbed at the dentist, the nurse, someone to anchor me. The doctor calmed me down with a tranquilizer. I left the doctor's office feeling alternately light and disoriented. When I got home, I collapsed onto the bed closest to the front door, my mother's, and fell asleep. I awoke to a gruff voice and saw Bill at the door, home unusually early, drunk and looking at me menacingly from his cold blue eyes. In an instant he was upon me. He had his hand around my neck and was pulling me up. I was still groggy, but something in me snapped as I felt his hands rip into me. I took his powerful hand in mine and tore it from me. I began hitting his face until I had him on the floor semi-comatose. Realizing what I'd done, I ran from the house and went to Angela's. All the way over my heart beat proudly. I didn't care if I got sent away for assault and battery; I had finally given him back a taste of his own medicine. The elation wore off when I returned the next day and my mother told me I had to move out.

I was overcome with the same feelings I'd had when I was first taken from her in 1956, ten years before. I could not understand how she could protect this man who had once driven my sister Cheryl from home, whom my other brothers and sisters were frightened of and hated, and who had beaten her so many times. How could she prefer him to me, her own son? For a week she allowed me to sneak into my room at one or two o'clock in the morning when he'd be asleep, but I had to be out again by six o'clock, before he was up. She herself would awaken me to get out. I went into a manic swing, determined to make it on my own. I took a job at a factory, where I hauled steel boxes of parts around the floor with a hook. I saved my first week's pay and answered an ad for a roommate.

The ad had been placed by Wayne Nelson, a freshman composition major at Berklee. I could not believe my good fortune. I told him of my composing aspirations and explained I was working to save up the tuition. Berklee and score pads filled my head again, and my strange wanderings through the corridors of Berklee filled up my free time. No matter how I tried to deny it, I felt inspired only when I was dreaming of being a composer. I imagined this composer's world so fully that it seemed to me that it was actually happening. I decided the only way to make it happen would be to enroll in a course in music composition. Yet I could not get past reading the course descriptions in the catalogue. I read and read and tried to make it real until I felt every muscle in my body straining against my skin, ready to burst out. I went through this action/inaction cycle almost every day until finally I was able to register for a night course in theory and scoring. I paid the tuition, bought a score pad, and went to my first private lesson. I was now a composition major. Meanwhile, Wayne and I got along well. He introduced me to two senior composition majors. I told them I was studying theory and scoring; surely I would be accepted as one of them. They appeared uninterested. I thought that in time they would come to accept me as Wayne had.

The Back Bay apartment Wayne rented was small but comfortably furnished. He and I shared a large bedroom. Most weekends Wayne went home to Connecticut. But on the weekends when he stayed in town, he'd invite his friends over to party, and there'd be a lot of drinking, a lot of noise, and a lot of fun. I'd never been to a party. I didn't drink, but I had as much fun as anyone. Once in a while Angela would come to them. But she would cling to me like a spider monkey and hardly say a word all night. I didn't like it, but I worshiped Angela. I thought in time she would relax enough to join in the fun, but she never did. She was always timid. On weekends when Wayne was away, Angela and I would be free to enjoy each other alone and especially be free from the clutches of her crazy mother. Alone with Angela, I actually liked her timidity, her thoughtfulness. I felt protected against being betrayed.

For a time everything was fine; then I lost my job. I got another one right away, but I loathed it. To make things worse, I was not doing well in my theory and scoring classes. No matter how hard I tried to study or to understand the theory of chord construction

I just couldn't grasp it. It seemed too difficult to be surmounted. By my third lesson I could see that my teacher, Mr. Sirota, a respected bass player and arranger, was losing patience with me. I was not able to master the elementary concepts of chords and chord building. He went over and over them with me. What little I was able to retain I forgot as soon as we went to the next step. I dropped out after my fourth lesson. In February 1967 I lost my job, and I couldn't pay the rent. I knew Wayne would take the keys. Knowing I had no place to go, I had a duplicate set made. At the end of the month Wayne kicked me out.

It was cold, and for a week or more I was able to sneak back to the apartment to filch food and get a nap. Then, one afternoon, while I was making a sandwich, I heard a key in the door. I ran under Wayne's bed, trying to breathe as softly as I could. Wayne found me, took the keys, and I left. I called my mother, who agreed to let me sneak in and out until I found another job. I felt my head and the world whirling around in a state of confusion when Angela told me she was pregnant. What would I do? What would I do? I thought for days until I came out of my depression. I would leave Massachusetts, get away from my family, away from a city and state where I had nothing but horrible memories. I would build a life for Angela and the baby and me. I knew I could never do it in my present environment. I elected to run away to Florida, where I would try to get a good job and bring Angela there with me once I got established. I returned to my old neighborhood and started asking around if anyone wanted to run away with me. In that kind of neighborhood finding traveling companions was no problem. Although Joe was sixteen, and Dennis was fifteen, both were experienced car thieves, and they quickly provided us with transportation. We each scraped together as much money as we could. I sold my instruments and music books, the only real possessions I had. It broke my heart to do so because they were my only link to becoming a composer. I felt a part of me was now gone. But with a few dollars to tide me over, we headed south.

Three days later we were arrested in South Carolina. I was in serious trouble. We were charged with transporting a stolen vehicle across state lines. I celebrated my nineteenth birthday in a Sumter County jail. During the next two months I was shuttled from jail to jail, finally ending up in the Aiken, South Carolina, jail near the Georgia border. There we ate corn bread and black-eyed peas, and in the evening hordes of cockroaches crawled all over us as we lay in bed, leaving painful bites. After five days I was taken before a federal judge. A presentencing report sent by the Dorchester police was read. I was sentenced to a zip-six— sixty days to six years. A week later I was brought to Petersburg Federal Reformatory in Virginia to begin my sentence.

BOOK IV

United States Federal Reformatory

MAY 24, 1967

"FUCK, FIGHT, OR HIT the fence," said a stocky red-headed redneck inmate to me as he stood with another inmate, who, in turn, stared coldly at me. At first I could not decipher his message, but I knew from their demeanors that they were not from the local Welcome Wagon. It was about four-thirty: count time. Never had I been happier to hear the whistle that had always "made misery mark time." Before they left to return to their dorms, they told me they would return after supper for my answer.

I went to sit on my bunk, and I wondered what I would do. It hadn't taken me long to figure out that I was being sex-pressured. Going to a guard was out of the question; to fink on another inmate was an automatic death sentence; inmates had unwritten rules that one never went to a hack to work out one's problems. My choices were either to fight or, better still, to try to escape because they would kill me. I had no doubts about that. In the bed next to me was a tall black kid in for dealing junk. One evening, a southern white had sliced his throat with a razor. I knew then that I was in with some pretty hardened criminals.

As usual, I seemed to be the youngest. Most of the guys had anywhere from five to ten years on me, at nineteen. In my eleven years of on and off incarceration, I had never faced this kind of problem. Now I did, and when the whistle blew again, signifying that the count had checked, I knew what I had to do. I wondered if the rednecks would be armed with knives or razors, as most inmates were. All I could hope for was that the fight would be fair. They returned as they had promised. And when I told them of my decision, I was led to a place behind one of the dorms where we would not be seen by any of the guards in the four gun towers. The redhead put up his fists while his buddy looked on. I put up mine and threw the first blow; it was all I needed. It crunched into his face, and he dropped like a sack of flour. A surge of strength and anger welled up in me as I fell on top of him and began to hit his face with bone-jarring rights until his face turned crimson and he went limp. I turned to his friend, but he took off in a flash. When I calmed down, I returned to my dorm to read. I felt damn good but frightened about a reprisal.

The next morning I went to the chow hall for breakfast and took my place in one of the two lines. I kept my eyes aloof but noticed that some of the inmates were looking at someone close to the head of the line I was standing in. There was a general hubbub of discussion, and I noticed that I was getting some unfriendly stares. As the line moved around, I saw the guy I had beaten. In my rage I had not known how badly I had hurt him, but his face was purple and blue and swollen, and he wore a bandage near his mouth. He looked as if he'd been hit by a baseball bat. I imagined that everyone at Petersburg was his friend and that now all of them were going to kill me. I thought about asking to go into lockup at the cell house, fabricating some phony excuse. But I knew if I did a wimpy thing like that, I would have even more trouble when I came back out onto the compound. I determined I would have to stand my ground.

I ate my food quickly and went down to the basketball court to throw a few hoops and steady my nerves. Beside the two basketball courts there were two tennis courts and a dilapidated miniature golf course. Tired of basketball, I wanted to do something else, but I didn't know how to golf or play tennis. I was back to throwing hoops when a tall black approached me. I was already tense and scared into thinking it was only a question of time before I was stabbed to death. He told me that his name was Pratt and that he was from Harlem. He told me that a bunch of dudes were at my dorm, waiting to kill me. He told me that I had better go with him. I refused because I thought he was just using a ruse to set me up for the kill. I went back to playing basketball. As I played, I imagined myself flipping and flopping on the ground with blood spurting out of me from all directions. I ran after Pratt, hoping he was sincere.

When we arrived at the dorm, I saw the guys had divided into two separate groups. One group was all white; these were the friends of the boy I had beaten. Actually they weren't all his friends, but they all were southerners who weren't going to let a Yankee beat one of theirs. I thought, this is crazy, in a place like this they're still fighting the Civil War. The other group was made up of northern whites, blacks, and Hispanics. Pratt explained they were there to make sure nobody bothered me. A smile so wide that it nearly ripped at the corners crossed my mouth. The guys from the Northeast all were smiling at me and patting my back because they were glad to have another good fighter from their section of the country.

The deal that had been struck between the two factions was that the southern kid had to fight me again. We moved off to an area in the compound where the gun tower guards couldn't see us. The redneck looked so pathetic that I simply told him I didn't want to fight him anymore. He was so glad that he almost kissed me. His friend, who I suppose might have challenged me, wouldn't come within twenty feet of me. After that incident I had many new friends, and I never had a problem.

I had arrived at the Petersburg Federal Reformatory only two weeks before. I was placed in the arrival and orientation dorm, where we were held until we could be classified by the classification committee. During the day we watched TV or played cards or chess, which was a new game to me but one that I liked right away. Most of the time we had to listen to lectures given to us by various department heads at the reformatory, which basically were designed to give us a picture of life at the prison.

We learned that there were different types of custody: close, medium, and minimum. "Close custody" meant an inmate must never be found outside the gate; "medium" meant that it was okay to go outside it if you were accompanied by a guard escort; and "minimum" meant that an inmate could go outside the gate without supervision. Minimum custody was necessary to have because the reformatory had its own farm with cattle and crops and a dairy. Outside the compound as well was a motor pool where inmates served as mechanics. This constituted one of the reformatory's vocational training programs, which also included cooking, baking, masonry, and construction work. If an inmate was not enrolled in a vocational training unit, he was expected to work on one of the details inside the grounds, such as maintenance, laundry, or clerical detail. And those inmates who qualified were allowed to work in either the tire-recapping or furniture-refinishing factories located on the grounds; there an inmate could work a full day or evening shift and earn a few cents an hour. We also learned there was a school program in which inmates could earn high school equivalency certificates.

The day after my arrival at Petersburg I was taken along with other new inmates on a tour of the compound. The main building housed the offices of the warden and assistant warden, as well as the visiting room, library, and classrooms. The building next to it was called the cell house. It contained a small but adequate hospital, the offices of the caseworkers, and, in the basement, holding cells for new arrivals and the clothing room, where our outside clothes had been taken and we had been issued army surplus clothing and boots. We had also been fingerprinted and photographed with our inmate numbers. I was 32543. Our tour concluded at the segregation cells, where those who committed major offenses, such as fighting or attempted escape, were disciplined.

As opposed to the IJG, at least the reformatory allowed an

inmate the opportunity to defend himself. The system was thus: If a guy was charged with a major offense, or even a minor offense, such as insubordination or insolence, it was written up on a piece of paper called a shot. The inmate would then be required to pack his gear into his pillowcase and report to the guard. He would be stripped to his undershorts and placed overnight in a holding cell. The next morning he would be given back his clothes and taken before a trial board, which usually consisted of a captain or lieutenant, a caseworker, and a "dispassionate observer." The arresting officer would be on hand along with the inmate, both of whom would speak before a punishment would be meted out. Generally a major shot meant segregation for one to two weeks. But segregation at Petersburg meant only that the inmate was confined to a special cell in his undershorts; he could still write and receive letters. A minor shot meant the loss of privileges, like the Saturday movie, or extra duty—weekend work detail.

The classification process I was undergoing involved taking tests to determine my education level as well as my interests and abilities. After all the information had been gathered, I was assigned a caseworker, who went over the results with me. I told my caseworker that I had a pregnant girl friend and that I was interested in going to work in one of the reformatory's industries to earn money to send to her and to have a little left over for myself. I had already been a State Boy; I didn't want to be a Fed Boy. He said that because I had tested only at the mid-ninth-grade educational level and showed a strong weakness in math, I would probably have to attend school but that maybe I could learn a trade as well. I put down "baking" as my interest.

I had not heard from Angela or my mother in the first month, although I had written several letters to tell them where I was. I knew that this time I was really on my own; there would be no Thomas Costello or Max Dinova. I would have to learn to fend for myself, and I would have to get work in the factory. I knew I'd never receive a dime from anybody at home, nor would I ask. When the weekly assignment, or popsheet came out, I found I had been assigned to close custody and to the bakery as well as to general education development classes. I was upset and angry about my custody assignment, but I had been told that if I didn't "go along with the program" that had been set up for me, I wouldn't make parole.

I was sure that I would be paroled after sixty days. When I had been in Sumter County Jail awaiting trial, I had been put into a cell with two ex-cons who were well into their forties. I was damn scared. Fortunately they had other things on their minds—like escape. They had been working on the old bars for some time, sawing them with strips of a sheet and Ajax cleanser. I was amazed to see that they'd sawed off one bar and through half of another. I helped them partly out of a sense of camaraderie but mostly out of cowardice; I wanted them to be out of the cell even more than they wanted to be. On the night of their escape they asked me if I wanted to go with them, and I said that I didn't. They tousled my hair and gave me a sawbuck. As I lay in bed, I was sure that the fact I hadn't tried to escape would get me a suspended sentence. When it didn't, I knew that at least I would be paroled after my required sixty days.

I was moved to a regular dorm in mid-June 1967 after being assigned a program. My behavior was excellent, for I was anticipating an early release. About this time I finally heard from my mother, who basically wrote that she had given up on me. It was the only letter I received from her. Angela wrote also and continued to write at least every day. Her first letter was confused. She said she didn't know whether to keep the baby, which was due in December, nor was she sure that she wanted to continue a relationship with me. I should have told her to forget about me, but I loved her and begged her not to give up the baby. I wrote her that I was sure that I would be released soon; this seemed to brighten her spirits, and her letters became more positive. In each letter I tried to keep her spirits high as we exchanged ideas about names for our baby. Eventually we settled on Joseph since we were sure it would be a boy.

I applied myself to "the program," and in August I was told that I would be going before the parole examiner in September. This was mandatory procedure following an inmate's first sixty days, but it only convinced me that I was going to be paroled; after all, I was not a dangerous criminal. In preparation for my hearing I had to fill out a paper with a parole plan. This would be attached to the progress report made out by my caseworker. In my plan I had to list where I would live and work and who would be able to help me financially until I got on my feet or if I got into financial trouble. I also had to have a parole adviser who was not part of my family. All this planning convinced me I was going home, even though my caseworker cautioned that I would probably receive a year's "setoff," which meant that I wouldn't be paroled but would be given a new date to see the board again. I honestly didn't believe him. I went before the parole examiner and waited a month to receive a decision. And it floored me: fourteen months. In angry reaction I decided that I wouldn't go along with the stupid program and that I would do the whole six years. I refused to get involved in any part of prison life.

I immediately started getting in trouble. I was insolent and insubordinate with all of the kitchen and bakery personnel. I received plenty of minor shots and lost many movie privileges and pulled plenty of extra duty. I thought about refusing to work and checking into the cell house to stay until my sentence was complete. Yet I could not help thinking about Angela and the unborn baby. The news of my setoff had shattered her, and she began to write again about giving up our baby. I pleaded with her not to. I really, sincerely wanted to come home and be a good father. What bothered me most about Angela's giving up the baby was that the child would probably grow up thinking that I had abandoned it. The thought devastated me. But I was in deep conflict about fighting the feds and going along with the program. Although I tried to be good, at times I just could not get my childlike emotions under control. I was such a fucking mess. I sent in a cop-out to my caseworker—con talk for a formal request—to ask him if I could please go on work release, but it was denied. I wrote to the warden and pleaded with him to let me go home on a special furlough to marry Angela and to see the birth of the baby: denied. This all seemed terribly cruel to me. I was a mixed-up young man, to be sure; still, I only wanted to do what was right and proper. But the feds were totally inflexible and uncaring. I hated them.

In the late part of November I received a letter from Angela telling me that she was going to give up the baby and that she would be saying good-bye to me. Nothing hurts like a "Dear John" letter.

In early December I earned a major shot for giving a hamburger to an inmate while he repaired the big rotary oven in the bakery. As a result, I ended up in segregation. I didn't care about segregation, but not hearing from Angela was killing me. In my cell I mostly paced. I felt that at nineteen I had nothing to live for. There were a couple of guys also locked up in cells on my tier, but none of us had much to say. Each day was quiet and un-eventful, and I got through the afternoons hoping I would get a letter that evening from Angela. When I didn't, I would write her long, passionate letters of love in an attempt to win her back.

Sometimes I thought that I should let her go. I was no fucking good. In the evenings I would look out through the bars on my window and see cornfields and the small landing strip for the light aircraft used by pilots of the Fort Lee army camp just down the road. The strip had strings of red and blue lights that made me long for the neon of the city. Sometimes I would imagine myself taking off in one of the planes down the runway, bound for home. I imagined a lot about escaping and made elaborate plans about tunneling out or trying to stow away in a garbage truck. These thoughts kept me entertained and also gave me a feeling of control, a feeling that I was doing something about my situation. I believed that escaping was the one right I had. I had considered trying to make it over the fence; it wasn't impossible. During the summer two guys had made it over at dusk while we were on the ball field.

I don't know how the guard who shot at them had missed, but I decided not to take my chances that way. And when the returned escapees received an additional two years on their sentences, I forgot about it altogether.

I was returned to my cell a couple of days before Christmas. The compound was decorated with lights, and each dorm had its own tree. Christmas didn't mean much to me; in fact, I hated it now more than ever. On Christmas Day we all received a little box of candy and a pack of cigarettes. When the guard came by my cell to give my present to me, I, like most of the other inmates, told him to shove it.

In early January I learned through a letter from Angela that our six-pound son had been born on December 11, 1967. He was named Joseph, and he had been given up for adoption. Tears flooded my eyes as I gripped the post of my bunk bed.

At this time I had been taken out of the bakery and placed on inside maintenance. It was a dirty job, which involved sweeping the walks and policing the grounds. Inside maintenance was where the fuck-ups were assigned. I hated being assigned to this detail, and I did not like Mr. Horton, the detail officer. He was everything I now associated with the feds: He was totally straight, heartless, and conformist. I once told him that if he'd had another brain, he would have a rock collection; it earned me an extra shot of duty. Undeterred, I kept going out of my way to bother him until he was ready to pull his hair out. At that point he had me thrown in segregation for leaving my work area without permission.

When I came out, I was put to work in the laundry. Mr. Bassett was its detail officer. He was an older man, peaceful and polite. I liked him so much that I found myself performing my work diligently. But I was there for only about a month before he retired. The man who took his place was Mr. Purcell, a hard-looking, tobacco-chewing man. He gave those of us assigned to him a short lecture in a thick Texas drawl, warning us that we had better toe the line with him. My first impression was that he thought he was a real hard ass. Well, I thought, he hadn't met

Mark Devlin yet. If he gave me any shit, I swore to myself I'd cut him right down to the height of his cowboy boots.

It wasn't long before we had an altercation. He began to write out a shot on me, and before I left, I told him to his face that all guards sucked because if an inmate said boo to them, they'd lock him up since that was the only way they knew how to deal with things. I left in a huff and went to the cell house without packing my shit. If they were going to lock me up, they could pack it themselves.

When I arrived at the cell house, the guard there told me to go back to the laundry room because Mr. Purcell wanted to see me. This threw me. When I got back there, Mr. Purcell sat me down and asked me to tell him what was going on with me, and I told him about my situation. He looked on with understanding eyes and then told me that I had taught him a lesson that day. He told me how much he hated being a guard but that he was only a year away from retirement. After our talk I had so much respect for him that I immediately went on my best behavior. Mr. Purcell's whole demeanor changed, too, and he became a great guy to work for. As a result of his talking with me, I became the hardest worker in the laundry. Mr. Purcell knew that I did not have any money to buy things from the PX, which sold cigarettes, candy, and magazines, so even though he knew it was premature, he put me in for a meritorious service award, which provided stipends to inmates for exemplary work over a period of time. The award could be as much as $20 a month; my award was approved for $10 a month. Mr. Purcell and I became good friends after that, and we called each other Hoss, like the character in "Bonanza." But after working at the laundry for a couple of months, I realized I didn't want to be a laundry worker all my life, so I decided to ask to take the masonry vocational training course.

In June 1968 I was placed in the masonry shop. My teacher, Mr. Adler, was a nice man and a good teacher. In the evenings I went to school, where I continued to study for my high school equivalency certificate. Angela was writing to me again, and my life was going along pretty smoothly.

The Vietnam War was in full flower at this time, and many of the inmates at the reformatory were either conscientious objectors or Jehovah's Witnesses. The inmate population also included "flower children" in on drug charges, Black Muslims, and southern rednecks in for making illegal moonshine, or white lightning. Among the prisoners was also the expected assortment of smugglers, bank robbers, and stock manipulators. There was even one guy incarcerated for posing as a doctor and as an airline pilot. I didn't feel I had much in common with anyone, and I kept to myself.

On the weekends I attended all the religious services, including the Jewish and Quaker services. I was beginning to question religion now. There had been a whole influx of exotic religions in the country, everything from the religion of yoga to the religion of drugs. These were strange times, and with so many new religions and philosophies abroad, one could hardly keep up with them. It seemed to me that each religion tried to make the universal values—love, compassion, kindness—exclusively its. I began to think that organized religion was a bunch of crap. I walked the compound and thought a great deal about it. I came to the conclusion that man could not accept his own mortality. The saying "And in the beginning man created God" began to make sense to me. If God were compassionate and loving, then how could He let me suffer as I did? My Catholicism and blind faith had stood me well over the years, but now I no longer believed.

Obviously I had little faith in the political system either, and I read widely, as often as I could, trying to divine some meaning from the books I encountered. I read works by Ayn Rand, Hermann Hesse, and Kahlil Gibran; I was very into Ayn Rand's ideas about individuality. I also liked Hesse's stories; *Beneath the Wheel* and *Demian* were my favorites. I no longer consoled myself with the parables of Jesus but found comfort in the words of Gibran:

"The deeper that sorrow carves into a being the more joy that being can contain."

In November I went before the parole examiner. This time I didn't need a parole plan because I wasn't going to be paroled but released through a community treatment center known as a halfway house. I would stay at the house along with other federal and state prisoners for three months, and depending on my adjustment to the community, I would be paroled or sent back to the reformatory or have my time extended at the halfway house.

On January 6, 1969, after a year and a half of incarceration, I was put on a bus bound for the Brooke House in Boston, where I was to stay. I was met there by the house director, Arthur Harris, a big, intense-looking man with a gift of affability and familiarity. I liked him right away. He took me to his office and ran down the rules of the program. I was expected to get a job and to be back at six in the evening for mandatory house meetings and rap sessions. I was expected to participate in the upkeep of the house as well as to contribute a small sum of money toward my room and to put some of my money into a savings account. I would also have a ten o'clock curfew; if I violated it, I would be restricted to the house after supper. No weapons, drugs, or alcohol were ever allowed, and women were not allowed in the rooms.

I was also introduced to my counselor, Eli Bergen. He was a graduate student studying psychology at Boston University and I immediately had a good feeling about him. He had soft, gentle eyes; he certainly looked like an intellectual. He was slight of build, bearded, and his hair was already thinning. I found him easy to talk with. We talked about me mostly, my interests and plans and such. By coincidence he was a piano player, so I told him of my dream to attend the Berklee College of Music. Eli told me that this might be possible through the Massachusetts Rehabilitation Commission, which helped handicapped people; President Johnson had just expanded its jurisdiction by signing legislation making behavorial disorders a handicap, too. I perked up at this suggestion and began to plan my years at Berklee, but first I had to marry Angela.

That evening I called her, and she came over right away. We went to a park bench in the Boston Common and kissed and hugged madly until it was time for me to go in. The next day I made an appointment at the commission for an interview and then went to Berklee and picked up a brochure describing all the courses I would be taking as a composition major. I was excited and happy. I was sure that I would be sent to Berklee and that all the awful years were now over.

In preparation for my entrance to Berklee I rented a clarinet and study books and practiced as often as I could. One evening Eli and I even played the first movement of the Mozart clarinet concert for the house residents. I had fallen in love with this concerto after I had first heard Max Dinova play it, more than seven years before. Hearing it again made me get in touch with Max and tell him about my plans. He encouraged me and offered to write a reference for me should I need it. I went to my appointment at the commission and met my counselor, a nondescript paper pusher type. He told me that the commission would pay only for courses in liberal arts education. I tried to argue my case, telling him that besides music, I had never really had any interests and that sending me to music school was the least the state could do for me after not educating me for so many years. The counselor was uninterested and said that the commmission would instead offer to pay for psychiatric help. I refused.

I was disheartened, and Eli hurt for me. He tried to tell me that perhaps I could save up the money and go to Berklee by myself; this seemed beyond my ability even to imagine. After a time I decided to pursue a career as a mason. I applied to the bricklayers' union for an apprentice's card. I was informed that I would have to be tested first and that the next available test date was six months away. Instead, I found a job selling women's shoes in a discount store. I settled into my job and forgot about going to school, but not about marrying Angela.

I felt I owed it to her; she had stuck by me, and I really did love her. We made arrangements with a justice of the peace, got our license and blood tests, and set our wedding date for the following week. I didn't say anything to anyone at the house because I wanted to keep it a secret. The night before Angela and I were to get married I was put on restriction for staying out with her past my curfew. This shook me up because I had rented a tuxedo, bought rings, and made arrangements with my mother and sister Donna for a simple postwedding celebration. I finally went to the housemaster and begged him for a pass home for a couple of days, telling him I had to attend the wedding of a friend, a very good friend. I was issued a pass, and the next night, March 15, 1969, we were married. We went to a hotel for our honeymoon night, but our reservations had gotten lost so that we had to go sleep at Angela's house; her mother was quite surprised to see us and somewhat nasty about it, too.

When I returned to the halfway house and told everyone my good news, I was put on restriction. It was against policy for an inmate to marry without permission. It meant that I could even be sent back to Petersburg. Fortunately the feds were lenient with me: On April 18, 1969, just after my twenty-first birthday, I was paroled.

Angela and I took a one-room efficiency to save money. We both were working, she as a bank teller and I at an exclusive women's shoe store. Angela became pregnant almost immediately. I was happy and grateful to be getting a second chance at fatherhood. We spent our evenings going to the movies, dinner, jazz concerts, and, occasionally, the theater. Angela took driving lessons, and I went up to Max Dinova's home in Bridgewater for clarinet lessons. He wouldn't charge me, although I wanted to pay him; I was making good money now from my commissions. We moved to a one-bedroom apartment, and soon after, on December 6, 1969, Angela had a beautiful seven-pound girl. She had a full head of hair, big button eyes, and a rosy complexion. We named her Marie. Angela stayed at home, and I became the breadwinner. We were proud parents and still loving with each other.

Our troubles began when one of my customers got my address through the telephone book and sent me a card with all sorts of love notes. Angela opened the letter and called me at work and cried to me. I assured her that the girl was only a customer and that she knew I was married; I had no idea she had had designs on me. I liked to look at pretty girls, but I was devoted to Angela. I even got the girl to tell Angela that I never went out with her or did anything with her beyond selling her shoes. Angela refused to believe me and became suspicious, jealous, and possessive. If I even looked at another girl, she became angry, and so to please her, I kept my head and eyes straight ahead whenever we went out. Soon she never wanted to go out at all, and we began to fight. I was really weary of trying to reassure her of my devotion to her and Marie. Most of the time I think I was a decent father and husband.

One day at work I was broke and needed some cash. I decided that I would try a little trick to get it. Because I always wanted to seem perfect, I felt too ashamed to ask the manager, Mr. Romano, for an advance on my pay. I sold a lady three or four pairs of shoes and neglected to write one pair of them down. When she handed me cash, I pocketed the amount of the pair I didn't write down, about $60. I began to do this regularly. I never really felt that I was doing anything wrong or that I was betraying the store's trust or putting my family in jeopardy. One evening, while I was home, the store called to say that a woman had returned a pair of shoes, one of a multiple order, and that the shoe number had not been recorded on the slip. Shocked back into reality now, I told Angela what I had been doing. She took out money to reimburse the store for the shoes and went down to the store and told Mr. Romano the truth. Mr. Romano told Angela how sad and disappointed he was in me; he thought I was bright and had hoped to give me a promotion one day. Because he liked me, he wasn't going to prosecute, but he was firing me.

I felt bad for a while, but I was under pressure to get another job. I foolishly took one that required my living for three months in Virginia, of all places. The job was as a manager trainee for a fast-food restaurant chain called Gino's that was expanding to the Northeast. I was glad to have a job and also excited about learning something new. I gave up the apartment and sold the furniture.

It was now late April 1970, and I was twenty-two. Angela and Marie and I flew to Washington, where we were met by Gino's personnel. They informed me that Angela and Marie could not stay. I wondered why the hell they hadn't told me that when I'd been notified I'd been accepted for the job. I was ready to turn back. We spent the night in a motel, and in the morning Angela left with Marie and returned to Boston. I was put up in an apartment in Alexandria with three other men, and each day we went to train in Fairfax. At first I liked the work, and every weekend I flew up to Boston to be with Angela and the baby, who were now living with my mother. But after working only one month, I decided I didn't like the job and being separated from my family. The biggest problem with the job was its structure: I felt as though the older managers were guards, and the young trainees inmates, so I began to have severe anxiety attacks. My confidence shaky, I ran away from Virginia and home to Boston.

Angela and I did not have enough money to rent an apartment, although she had saved some of what I had been sending her. We went to live with my older sister, Cheryl, in Jamaica Plain. I had a hard time finding work, and we went on welfare. Soon, though, we were able to get an apartment around the corner from Cheryl's, and I got a job as assistant night manager of a fast-food deli.

Back on track again, I decided I really did have more on the ball and decided to pursue a liberal arts degree. I applied to the Massachusetts Rehabilitation Commission, which told me it would send me back to school if I first, as a show of good faith, enrolled in a course on my own, paid for it, and completed it. I took a course in accounting at a local college. Just before finals I told my teacher I needed a letter for the commission. He wrote one saying that I was the best accounting student he had in his three years at the college and that he had no doubt I would surely receive an A at the end of the course. But as finals approached, I panicked and began to drink to calm my nerves. All that I had studied was lost to me. I failed my final, and I failed the course.

Nonetheless, the commission sent me to a special day school it had just founded for underachievers who weren't doing well in other school settings. It was called the Thirteenth Year. The school's philosophy was that certain individuals spent so much time avoiding failure they never got anything done, and the school tried to teach its students to accept responsibility for their lives. As part of the program we students were required to keep journals with entry headings like "What's Good for Me" as well as to attend group therapy sessions. We were taught math through playing games such as chess, which allowed us to see how the pieces moved in mathematical ways and how strategies were formulated.

I liked the school, but I had a conflict right away. Most of the students were teen-agers who were into James Taylor, Janis Joplin, drugs, and other things associated with the counterculture. I was into my young married father identity. My hair was short and parted down the side, and I wore double-knit clothing. Obviously with my past history and with my responsibilities to my wife and child and job, I didn't fit in at all with these kids. Each night after school, while they were free to party, I went to my job. But one evening, before closing, two girls who were classmates of mine happened into the deli. We talked a bit, and they asked me if I wanted to go back to their dorm room to smoke some marijuana with them. I had never smoked grass before; I felt disoriented enough, but I figured that it was harmless and that they would tell the other students the next day that I wasn't the square they thought I was.

At first the dope had no effect on me as we sat around toking and talking genially about school and other things. Suddenly the girls' voices seemed to be far away yet loud, and the walls began to close in on me until I felt as if I were sitting in the room of a dollhouse while I was still human size. I ran out into the street; my legs felt as if they were sinking deep into the concrete, and my heart pounded as if it would explode. When I got home, after what seemed years of traveling, I began to come out of it. But at school the next day the same feelings returned. This time it seemed as though my skin were burning up. I ran from the school and never went back. I had been attending for just two months.

I didn't know what was the matter with me, but I was sure that the Thirteenth Year was starting to reach the emotionally mangled child inside me. I had spent years successfully erecting barriers to protect myself from others and to repress the long years of pain and hurt, but one of the school's avowed aims was to help students break down false confidences. This was extremely threatening. My confidence was the falsest of all, but it was all I had.

I was incredibly uptight all the time. It became so bad that I could not even sleep next to Angela. I would lie on the couch and roll myself into a little ball, put the TV on, and just stare at it. I even experienced stomach cramps and chest pains and became convinced I was going to die of a heart attack, even though there was no history of heart disease in my family. I would try to soothe myself and avert the attack by telling myself that I was too young to be sick in this way, but the symptoms persisted. I reasoned that only by leaving the state of Massachusetts could I prevent something horrible from befalling me. I began to make plans for getting the fuck out of Dodge.

I convinced myself that I should go to Hollywood to get into acting. It was foolhardy, I know, but I convinced Angela that everything would be fine once we got there. We sold our furniture and possessions against my mother's and Cheryl's advice. The fact that I was still on parole and would be jumping it bothered me, certainly, and added to my anxious state. But I was tired of always being on parole or in jail, and I figured that the feds

178

wouldn't bother to look for me in California. So with the $1,200 we had scraped together, I rented a car and outfitted it with all the things we would need on the trip; we even bought a car seat for Marie. On June 11, 1971, we headed west. When we reached Las Vegas, I decided to stay there and become a singer like Jerry Vale. We put up in a Holiday Inn and stayed for about a week. I soon forgot about my reason for wanting to stay there. We moved on to Los Angeles; we stayed for three days, and again I forgot why I was there. We arrived back in Boston a little more than a month after starting out, broke and homeless. Again my sister took us in. I returned the car to the rental shop early the next morning before it opened; whatever I owed, I could not pay.

However distressed I was about our situation, Angela was worse. I could not find a job, and by August we were back on welfare, and Angela and I were at each other's throats. One afternoon, while I was out looking for a job, Angela attempted suicide. I called home to find out she was in intensive care. I ran through a whole gamut of emotions until I was exhausted. Everyone— my mother, my family, Angela's mother—were against me; I was nothing but a no-good bastard. I was not allowed to see Angela, but I called every day to check on her condition. After three days she was taken out of intensive care and placed in the psychiatric ward. Marie went to stay with Angela's mother, and I just sort of wandered around.

Meanwhile, I was wanted by the feds; my mother had told the authorities I had left the state without permission. I owed a huge bill on the rental car; Angela was in a psychiatric ward; and I was broke and homeless. I wished at that point that *I* could have committed suicide. I managed to scrape up a few bucks, and I rented a car to live in until I could get on my feet. I had no intention of returning it or paying for it, and when I did not return it on the day it was due back, a warrant was issued for my arrest. I was caught and arraigned at Brookline district court. Fortunately my case was continued, and I was freed on personal recognizance. I knew the feds were looking for me because of my parole violation, and I thought they might be waiting for me at court, but they weren't.

In September Angela was released from the hospital, and she and I went to live with her mother. I got a job selling cars. It seemed as though things might start to get better for us, and for a while they did. But I managed to get fired from my job after a week, and when the company refused to pay me the commissions it owed me, I decided not to return the car that went along with the job. The company, in turn, had a warrant issued for my arrest. Later that month I was again arrested, and again I managed to get off on personal recognizance. I knew that the feds would catch up with me now, so I decided to run away. I went to the Greyhound bus station and bought a ticket for Montreal. I had just missed the last bus of the night, so I slept on a park bench. I awoke early and had some time to kill before the first bus left for Canada. I decided to steal a suit since I had only a few changes of clothing with me. I was caught and arrested.

It did not take the feds long to find me this time, and I was charged with auto theft and six counts of parole violation. With all these charges, I still tried to fight being sent back to Petersburg. I tried to deny that I had gone to California, but my mother testified to the contrary and sealed my fate. On December 20, 1971, I was back in Petersburg. In the two years I had been out on parole, I had managed to fail at just about everything I had attempted as well as to send Angela off on a nightmarish voyage. At least she was writing to me and trying to lift my spirits. I felt totally responsible for her situation, and I vowed in my mind that if I didn't beat the parole revocation hearing scheduled three months hence, I would somehow get out on work release.

On March 8, 1972, my parole was revoked but with the proviso that a special progress report be submitted for review in September of that same year. I was jubilant; it meant that if I did well for the next few months, chances were good that I would be paroled soon after. I wrote Angela to tell her the news. I also told her to hang in there because I was sure that I could get on work release and send her money. I buckled down and worked hard.

In June I managed to get my custody changed from close to minimum and went to work at the piggery. I really enjoyed feeding the pigs and watching them have babies and driving a tractor along the dirt roads. I didn't like getting up at 4:30 A.M., and I hated working in the slaughterhouse, where each week we killed enough pigs and steers for the week's meat supply. It made me feel sick, but I had to do it if I was to make work release and parole.

One morning, as another inmate and I were leaving the dorm, we noticed something small on the ground. We stooped down and saw that it was a tiny bird. It appeared to be either dead or unconscious. We figured that it must have flown into the glass door of our dorm. I took the bird inside and guessed it was a hummingbird because it was so tiny and because it also had a long tongue, which was now hanging out of its little mouth. I knew hummingbirds liked nectar, so I mixed some honey I had in my locker with some water in a flat plastic cap. I gently placed the bird's tongue into the solution and waited. Soon it began to stir, and its tongue moved in and out, lapping up all the liquid. When it was sufficiently revived, I found an empty plastic bucket and filled it with dirt and a broken branch to make a little treehouse. I then placed the hummingbird in it along with the honey mixture and left. Later that day, when I finished my work at the farm, I went to the library to look up hummingbirds. I found that my little bird was a ruby-throated hummingbird, the only kind of hummingbird found on the East Coast.

I was very proud. I had never seen a hummingbird before, much less had one. My plan was to get it well enough to go free. I called it Ruby, and each day I fed and bathed it in a little flat container. It was necessary to use a soft toothbrush to wash the bird because the sticky honey somehow got all over its feathers. After the bath the throat feathers would dry and fluff up and shine bright red and jade green. The hummingbird seemed to be getting stronger and stronger each day. Sometimes I would put it on my shoulder and walk around with it. But one afternoon, when I came back from work, Ruby was gone. I searched around frantically and found it on the ground just outside my window. I was glad that it was getting stronger. Soon it was beginning to use its wings again and flying short distances; I figured it would soon be flying away for good. I debated about leaving it in a small tree near one of the halls, thinking it would be better off there. But I remembered the tiny foxes and skunks that slipped through the spaces in the gate and roamed the compound at night. I decided to keep it in my room one more night. That night I slept with dreams of walking with Ruby through flowered meadows, its plumage as bright as the wild flowers. The next morning, when I awoke, the bird was dead. I was shattered; I took it outside and buried it, and I wondered for days whether I had killed it or whether I had given it a few more days of life.

In the middle of June, just as I was put on work release, Angela stopped writing to me. My mother wrote and said that Angela had been going to nightclubs every night and hanging out with a fast crowd. This did not sound at all like Angela. But there was nothing I could do except to hope that as soon as I could start sending her some money, she would be okay again.

I went to work as a bricklayer's apprentice for $2.25 an hour. After the feds had subtracted my room and board, which came to $25 a week, I was able to send her the balance, about $50 a week. But I was still not hearing from her. Then one day Angela called the reformatory and demanded to speak with me. When I came to the phone, she spoke so strangely that I wasn't sure it was she. She was rambling and incoherent; she said that Marie— who was two—was a teen-ager now but that I should not worry because Marie was on birth control pills. I tried unsuccessfully to reason with her, and I asked her to write as she hung up.

What I didn't know until later, when my mother wrote, was that Angela had attempted suicide that day. She had been found wandering the streets, naked and talking to herself; someone had brought her to the hospital, where she had been diagnosed as an "acute schizophrenic" and placed in the psychiatric ward. When

I heard this, I knew that I had to get home to her somehow. I went to my caseworker and showed him the letter from my mother and pleaded with him to let me go home. He said that nothing could be done until September, when my progress report would be processed. I felt very confused and decided to escape. I told my boss that I had to go back to the reformatory for a dental appointment. It was payday, so he gave me my check. I walked off the work site and headed into downtown Petersburg and to the Trailways bus station. But I just could not seem to buy a ticket. I wanted to be with Angela, but I didn't want to risk another two-year sentence. Depressed and dizzy, I just sat down. A short time later a guard and my caseworker found me. They said I was acting like a child; it was exactly how I felt. I was taken back to the reformatory and to an almost certain stint in segregation. Through my tears I asked them if they couldn't see that I was suffering enough. Miraculously they did not put me in the cell house, but my custody was changed from minimum to close, and I was put back on inside maintenance. In a matter of weeks I'd gone from model prisoner to model failure. It was also now the middle of July, and I had but six weeks to shape up before my special progress report was to be sent in. To help Angela as much as to keep my mind off her, I worked hard and diligently.

On September 18, 1972, I reported once again to the Brooke Halfway House. When I stepped off the bus, Angela was waiting. Her appearance had changed drastically. She was bloated from tranquilizers, she was garishly dressed, and her lipstick was smeared and her hair unkempt. She looked like a broken doll. I cried inside for her and swore to myself I'd make it all right for her.

My old friend from IJG Brian Sayer, who had pulled himself together sometime before, gave me a job as a restaurant manager. Angela flipped out again within a week of my return and was put in the psychiatric ward of the New England Medical Center of Tufts University. My job required long hours, from 7:00 A.M. to 7:30 P.M., but it was well paying, and I managed to save $600 in two months. I was under incredible strain, trying to readjust to life outside and to hold down the job. And as always, I was concerned and guilty about Angela. There was no time to see her since I had to be back at the house right after work for meetings, which I was required to attend. But I often slept through them; that would, in turn, earn me a reprimand. The strain was getting to me. To relieve it, I got drunk a few times and stayed away all night. Between my job, my past, and Angela, I was a mess. The house director left a note for me to see him at ten one morning. I couldn't. I had to open and set up the restaurant. He called me at work and told me that if I didn't leave work that instant, he'd send me back to Petersburg. Brian and I went over to Brooke, where the director explained to Brian that I could not work as many hours as I did. Brian agreed. Once we were outside, he told me that he would have to look for someone else. Angry and frustrated, I told Brian I would not hold him up any longer and quit. A few days later the director called me to his office, where two U.S. marshals handcuffed me and took me to Walpole State Prison. On November 11, 1972, two weeks later, I was taken back to the reformatory to serve out the remaining six months of my sentence.

Back at Petersburg once again, I kept to myself, refusing to become involved in any of the prison's rehabilitative programs or recreational activities. I would have to be let out in six months, good or bad, unless I committed another crime during this incarceration. I made sure that this wouldn't happen by asking the prison officials if I could be placed in segregation for the rest of my time. When they wouldn't let me, I refused my quarters and prison job so that they would have to lock me up. I stayed in segregation for the next two months; when I finally came out, I was rid of my anger. I spent the remaining three months of my sentence working on the prison's farm, and on May 11, 1973, I "maxed out." I was given $20 and a one-way bus ticket home. I finally felt freer than I had since the age of seven. I was twenty-five years old, a young adult. It had been seventeen years since

I had first been declared a Stubborn Child. Now, I would no longer have to answer to my mother or family, and I was at long last free from any probation or parole.

B O O K V

Stubborn Child

M A Y 1 2, 1 9 7 3

WHEN I ARRIVED IN BOSTON, I went directly to the Boston Garden to sit for a while and to savor my freedom. In the back of my mind I wanted to get away from Angela and all the bad associations I had with her. I wanted to run and run and never stop running. After a period of enjoying the weeping willows and the ducks on the pond I went to her mother's house.

Angela had recently been released from the hospital. I could not believe my eyes when I saw her. She was once again bloated from the many drugs she had been given; her eyes were glazed, and her look was faraway. Too much Thorazine had reduced her to a zombielike state. Marie was with her and seemed to be well. I got a job selling cars. Things went smoothly for a while, and Angela seemed to be getting better. Then one night her mother began again. She attacked me, but I sidestepped her. In rage and frustration I hit the wall and dislocated my hand. I jumped into the car I had been provided with at work, went to the hospital, and had my hand set. I slept in my car that night and every night after.

Soon after, a young woman walked into the car showroom and turned everyone's head; tall with gold-flecked auburn hair and hazel eyes, she was stunning. It was my turn to take the next customer, so I was able to wait on her. Her name was Rosalind and although I was unable to sell her a car, I had her telephone

number and called and asked her for a date; I had already decided
that I wasn't going back to Angela and all her madness. Rosalind
said that she had a five-year-old daughter and asked if I would
mind going over to her house. I brought a bottle of cheap champagne and two plastic champagne glasses. We sat at her kitchen
table as she told me about herself. She had developed an ulcer at
the age of sixteen because of her parents' constant pressure for
her to succeed. The following year her best girl friend had died
in her arms, and when she turned eighteen, Rosalind had run
away to New York to attend the Art Students League. Not long
after that she married a stand-up comedian, who had abandoned
her and their daughter, Carrie, for a chance at the brass ring, the
Sunset Strip. She had returned to Boston only eighteen months
before. I listened enraptured. She, too, had had a hard time, but
she had endured. Yet I told her nothing about myself. As we sat
and drank and laughed, a storm that had been brewing all night
at last erupted and knocked out the lights. I felt Rosalind's leg
under the table. She looked over toward me and said, "Do you
want to fuck?" I was taken by surprise. I'd never met a woman
like Rosalind. I whispered yes, and when we finished, she said
that I had potential.

About a month later I moved into her Brookline apartment.
The apartment was on the second floor of a duplex that had an
attic which Rosalind used as her studio. The flat was sparsely but
neatly furnished and contained so many plants that I dubbed
Rosalind the Plant Lady. When I was settled in, I bought a flute,
which I had recently learned to play, and record albums like *Jazz
in the Classroom* and *A Tribute to Benny Golson* and played along
with them while Rosalind drew or painted. I felt really wonderful,
very masculine. It was a feeling I had never experienced. Rosalind
and I got on beautifully, and I became attached to her daughter,
Carrie. I began to think of them as my family. Rosalind had a
suspicion that I was married, but I lied and told her I wasn't. I
knew that I was truly in love and that I had never really been in
love with Angela. I knew that I had married her out of guilt and

obligation and because I would take any woman who would take me.

And now I had Rosalind. During that summer of 1973 she was trying to get the money together to attend art school in the fall. One of the more resourceful ways in which she did this would be to drive out to the rich suburbs surrounding Boston and pick through the trash, which surprisingly yielded up many small treasures. In just that summer she had managed to find thirteen Oriental rugs, twelve of which she had cleaned and sold for upwards of $800. She kept the other one; it was a museum piece. She netted a couple of hundred more when she found some old stained glass pieces. But her outings weren't always so lucrative. One evening we came upon a load of boxes filled with gloves of every kind. There was everything from woolen mittens to silver and gold lamé gloves. At home we sorted them; they all were for left hands. In bed we laughed and joked about it, and when we heard a tapping sound from somewhere Rosalind said that it must be the right hands looking for the left hands. We laughed until our ribs hurt. We made love to the strains of Nina Simone singing "Brown-Eyed Handsome Man," which Rosalind dedicated to me.

In the fall Rosalind celebrated her twenty-fifth birthday, and I confessed to her that I was married. She said that she hated men who ran out on their obligations, who chased other women and hurt the ones who loved them. I wanted to tell her the circumstances of my marriage, of my life going all the way back to 1956. I wanted to tell Rosalind everything. But I couldn't; the words stuck in my throat. The next day I got a notebook and began to write my story down. I believed Rosalind loved me so much that it didn't matter that I was married, that I was just a car salesman, that I had spent half of my life in jail. When I had assembled a fair-size notebook, I told Rosalind about it and said that I wanted to read it to her; she told me that she had been reading it all along and as far as she was concerned, my past was the past and it didn't matter to her. Nothing she could have said could have made me feel better.

One evening a few days later I stuffed and roasted a duckling. It was delicious, but two hours later we were literally fighting each other for the toilet. I didn't know that first I had to cook off the fat of the duck at a higher temperature before I turned the oven down to the roasting temperature, so all the fat had soaked into the stuffing. Between turns on the commode we laughed and joked about it. I loved Rosalind's easygoing, wonderful sense of humor and the way it challenged my ability to be comically creative.

Rosalind used to sniff me all over and tell me she was crazy about me. This would make me so happy because it reinforced my certainty that she deeply loved me. That is, until shortly before we went out on our first real date. Miles Davis was playing at the Jazz Workshop in Boston, and we decided to go and make a special night of it. I had never seen Rosalind dress up or wear makeup before, and I was astounded. She looked as though she had just stepped off a magazine cover. Once inside the club Rosalind's mood turned from festive to pensive and melancholic. I asked her what was wrong, but she said that it was nothing. I knew she was thinking of her ex-husband, whom I suspected she had not stopped loving. He was still living in California and was working out a new comedy routine with his partner. After eighteen months he had begun calling her. She would gather Carrie at the phone, their faces smiling and glowing into the receiver, while I stood there watching them, my heart breaking. I loved her so much, but I knew Rosalind had changed; she was moving out of my life. I understood or thought I did. I was sure that my past ultimately had triggered the breakup, even though Rosalind had said it hadn't mattered. I was sure it did. In October I moved out. Out of anger I decided never to tell another woman I had been locked up.

I found a studio apartment on Beacon Street and soon after lost my job selling cars. My rent was a reasonable $45 a week, and I had enough to last me for about a month or two. After licking my wounds and pining for Rosalind, I realized that I still had a wife and daughter to take care of. During my relationship with Rosalind I had tried not to think of Angela and Marie, although I knew I had substituted Rosalind and Carrie for the love and peace I wanted with my own family but never had. Now I decided I would forget Rosalind and assume again my responsibilities to them.

I brought Angela and Marie to my studio in November. Within a week Angela cracked again. She grabbed a roll of toilet paper and began hitting the air around her, crying out for something or someone to leave her alone, and talking incoherently about somebody's trying to get her. I could only watch in stunned disbelief, feeling terrible and wondering how I could help her. Suddenly she ran out the door and into the night. I tried to follow her, but I could not leave Marie alone. When I was finally able to get in touch with my mother, I found out that Angela had been taken back to the state hospital. My mother knew that I had Marie and that I was without a job. Still believing that I was some kind of sex pervert, she made up a story that I was touching my own daughter. For this I hated her even more than ever; I'd have killed myself first before even contemplating such a thing. But it was true that I was out of work, and without a steady income I could not support Marie. Rather than go on welfare or risk an episode with the child welfare authorities, I brought Marie to Angela's mother. I promised I would come take Marie back as soon as I found work. I was so depressed by then about everything that I was lucky if I could just get up in the morning. I wanted to visit Angela in the hospital, but her doctors advised me not to.

I needed someone to talk to, someone who knew me, knew Angela. I got in touch with Brian Sayer again. It was good to talk and be comforted by an old friend, and he, in turn, introduced me to a girl named Catharine. We didn't become anything more than good friends—she was still a teen-ager—but we were drawn together by the feeling that each of us felt as if we were losers. She was so young and lovely, yet she was also a manic-depressive. I couldn't quite understand why she was so troubled—problems at home, she said. I could identify with that and tried, without much success, to help her unravel things.

In January 1974 I hit rock bottom. I lost my studio and ended up in a rooming house where drunks and derelicts slept on the stairs. For the first time I feared that I would become like my father. I made believe this wasn't happening by applying for $30,000- and $40,000-a-year salesman positions. I would answer want ads in my finest hand and receive invitations for interviews, which I never answered. Two weeks after moving to my room, I was kicked out of there as well; I stood in the street on a cold and rainy day with all my possessions in a green plastic bag. I called my mother to see if she would let me stay awhile with her; she wouldn't. A guy I knew who worked in a doughnut shop agreed to hold my bag at the store until I could find a place to put it.

Lost and confused, I began to walk down Cambridge Street near Massachusetts General Hospital. I had been out of prison less than a year, and I now found myself broke and homeless. I began to experience terrible pains in my stomach, and my chest felt so compressed that I thought it would explode. I ran into the emergency room of Massachusetts General Hospital and said I didn't feel good. One of the orderlies showed me to a room with an examining table and told me to wait for the doctor. When he came in, I lay down on the table and began to cry convulsively. He asked me what was wrong. Through my sobs I told him that I didn't have any friends or family, or home, or nothing, and that I never had. He sedated me. When I awoke, he took me to the psychiatric clinic. The prospect of ending up in the state hospital like Angela made me even more paranoid than going back out on the street. I screwed up my courage and walked out. I thought, I'm not crazy, just emotionally a mess, but I didn't know how to change it. Back on the streets I wondered what the hell was wrong with me. What had happened to the Stubborn Child who was going to be a priest or a great composer? I decided that I was lazy, simply lazy, and that I didn't want to work or own up to my responsibilities, that no matter how I tried to think or act like an adult, I couldn't, or at least not for very long.

To show myself otherwise, I got a job in a deli and slept in doorways until I had enough money to get a room. And, as the worst of that winter weather passed, I began to feel that I was getting well. I had my job and a few bucks in my pocket. Across the street from my rooming house was a bar popular with the night crowd, called Daisy Buchanan's. My loneliness drew me there most evenings. I would sit and drink and observe the well-groomed men. I wished I could be like them: suave and sophisticated and always in control of themselves. I got the idea in my head that if I dressed in fashionable clothes as they did, I would be magically transformed and be just like them. Yes. I would be an outside person. So I set about my plan to assume my rightful identity. I invested a portion of my weekly salary in expensive clothing until I had three nice suits and shirts and shoes. At first I felt good, but my confidence broke down quickly when I realized that the young professionals whom I was trying to emulate had spent lifetimes building their friendships, business associations, and a comfortableness in themselves that I couldn't begin to internalize. I even tried lying about myself, telling people that my mother was a stockbroker and that my father was a trial attorney. None of it worked, and soon I was left without an identity.

Before long I was also without a job. I had begun to fall victim to a persecution complex; as soon as my boss or a co-worker would correct me about something, even something minor, such as slicing or wrapping meat, I would fly into a defensive posture, which served only to antagonize them. I didn't want to alienate other people, but I felt fragile, as if I could break up into little pieces at any time.

Jobless now, I started to go up to Berklee again to look around and to make believe once more that I was going to become a composer. Alternatively, I'd sometimes sit in a nearby Greek pizza shop and listen to the jukebox and daydream about becoming a rock 'n' roll singer. Evenings, dressed in my still-new suits, I'd visit a local nightclub featuring a live band and singer. The music mesmerized me. Now I decided I would become a nightclub singer in Las Vegas! That became my dream.

195

While sitting at the bar one Friday night, I met a man who'd lost in love. I told him that not long before I, too, had lost in love, and we shared our stories over a bottle of bourbon. It turned out that he was opening a hairdressing school and was looking for a director. I started work that Monday. I had found my niche. I was an executive. But I lasted only two weeks, and with it I lost my room.

I celebrated my twenty-sixth birthday back on the streets. Again I wondered what was so wrong with me. Why couldn't I sustain a job, a relationship? What secret for living were outside people holding back from me? I ran the gamut of emotions each day, thinking and thinking until my head hurt badly and my body felt as if it had been beaten like a punching bag. I searched for answers: Yes, it was this, or no, it was that. Once I'd discovered what was wrong with me, I was certain I'd be clear and confident again. My daily investigations even took me into bookstores, where I'd stand in front of the psychology section, leafing through whatever looked promising, hoping I'd find the key and, like magic, be cured. But all I came up with were dead ends.

I never thought about Angela and Marie. Survival and self-absorption consumed me. There was no time to think of anyone but myself. I still had no job, but I managed to find a cheap room. I lived for a while by my wits. I ate by dressing up, going to a fine restaurant, and making sure I had two means of egress. I would order the most expensive entrée on the menu and a good bottle of wine. I was always very nervous, and the wine calmed me down. By the end of the meal I'd be drunk enough to escape or not to care if I was caught: my stomach was full. I'd order dessert and coffee, ask for the men's room, and then dash through the nearest exit. I did this for weeks; it was almost a good life.

For pocket money I'd steal copies of best sellers and then sell them at half price in Harvard Square. More often I'd walk into a department store, ask for a shopping bag, and walk through the store until I found a register slip on the floor. After checking the date, I'd find the same priced items and put them in my bag. Then I would go to the returns section and explain to the clerk how I had told my wife not to spend any more money. The clerk would eye me suspiciously but always gave me the refund.

I became almost like an animal trying to survive. I lost all moral restraint when I stole. I didn't want to steal, but I was in a manic cycle. When I woke, my only thoughts were of surviving that day while continuing my efforts to figure out what was wrong with me. I was still spending my mornings at the bookstores reading Karen Horney and Sigmund Freud and others. Afterward I usually proceeded to the Greek pizza shop near Berklee, understanding nothing about myself except that for some reason I could not take care of myself as I should. At the pizza shop I listened to Greek music over the speaker system. It made me feel happy and light. It brought peace to my deeply troubled, chaotic mind. And then one day I heard a Greek song I just had to learn. One of the men behind the counter wrote out the lyrics for me. I memorized them and sang along to the tape when the pizza shop was empty, and the Greek employees would call and say, "Bravo, Marco! Bravo! *Aftós íne polí oréos tragoudhistís*"—I was a good singer. In my painful world these smiling, uncomplicated people made me happy.

When I fell behind in my rent, I lost my room. That night I thumbed through the telephone directory and picked out the name of a doctor living in a wealthy suburb. Then I called a Boston hotel and made a late-arrival reservation in his name. I arrived and, feigning tiredness, quickly filled out the registration card and went to my room. The next morning I phoned the desk and explained that because of a pressing business engagement, I would have to stay in my room for a couple of extra days. For the next few days I slept and ate well on room service, and then I sneaked out. I went from hotel to hotel, doing this for a couple of weeks.

Finally I ran out of living options. In May I went to see Theo, a friend I had made at the Greek pizza shop, and he agreed to let me sleep on the floor of his room in a brownstone on Marlborough

Street. During the day he attended Boston University, and each night he worked as a dishwasher at a downtown Greek supper club. I would sometimes go to the back door, where he would slip me something to eat. He and his Greek friends could not understand how an American could not have even the basics of life.

I hadn't been living with him long when four student nurses moved into an apartment downstairs. They, and the influx of other returning students, brought ideas of getting an education back into my head. I decided that this time I would study law. I was once again thinking about Angela and Marie and building a home for them. I dressed up and went to a bookstore, where I looked through an LSAT study guide. Thumbing through it, I first came to the invented language section and was sure I could pass the exam. I knew I had good analytical skills; I had scored very high on a Watson-Glaser Critical Thinking Appraisal test. And hadn't I read all the Perry Mason books ever written? Wasn't I a self-taught, perceptive observer of human behavior? Hadn't I walked the streets studying everybody to learn how to become an outside person, buying the same button-down collar shirts and cuffed pants, scrutinizing and copying every detail? And certainly I was argumentative; after all, when I was little, I had challenged the masters at Bridgewater and had sometimes won. Best of all, I had kept up my end of conversations with Max Dinova, an educated man with an extensive vocabulary. It was decided then. Mark Devlin was now whole again. I got a job at a deli and set about the business of becoming a fine lawyer. I walked over to a local department store, imagining myself in the courtroom dispatching DAs with a flick of my double-edged tongue. Yes. Everyone would want me to be his attorney. I would be another Clarence Darrow or Louis Nizer or, better yet, Perry Mason. I would be brilliant but highly ethical and moral. Once inside the department store I stole a new suit and briefcase.

I dressed and filled my briefcase with pencils and legal pads. I went to the Suffolk University School of Law and got myself a catalogue to read about the courses I would be taking. Throughout the rest of that day I walked the streets making believe I was like outside people. I was certain that the real outside people could not tell that I had been imprisoned most of my life, that I had slept in wet beds, or that I had been a State Boy.

I made an appointment with an admissions counselor at Suffolk and told him that I wanted to study law. He explained that in order to do so, I needed to have an undergraduate degree, which would take four years. But he told me that Suffolk offered a combined degree program, and if I did well, my fourth year of undergraduate work would become my first year of legal study. I assured him I would do well.

I left Suffolk and dropped by the Boston Conservatory, where Max now taught full time, to tell him about my new plans. It was a familiar story to him. But I swore to him that this time would be different, and when I left him, I went to a bookstore to look at the college entrance examination preparatory handbook. When I got to the math section, I laid the book back on the shelf. I knew that I could not even begin to pass that! I left the store feeling very dirty in my new suit.

I walked the streets listlessly for days, finding comfort only at the pizza shop. When Theo was not at school or working, I would teach him how to speak English, and he would teach me to speak Greek. Pretty soon I had his accent and mannerisms down so well that I was unable to stop mimicking him. Some nights I would meet him for a beer after he got off work. One evening he took me to Athens After Dark, a Greek nightclub, featuring live singers and dancers. I watched their slow, mournful dances and was impressed. I knew then that I would be a famous Greek singer and that the reason I had never been successful in anything else I'd tried was that I'd been waiting for my fate to find me. I would become the most famous non-Greek Greek singer who ever lived.

I gave up all thought of working, spending my time looking at posters of famous Greek singers in a Greek gift shop. I borrowed Theo's tape recorder and listened to his tapes over and over again until I had learned all the songs by heart. I began to go to the Greek nightclub every night, from opening to closing time, and got to know the regulars, who smiled and greeted me with *"Yásu! Marco!"* One evening Ari Andropolous, a well-known singer, performed. I introduced myself to him later and asked him to teach me the song he'd just sung. Instead, he sold me his current album. I became totally obsessed with the whole aura of Greek life and music.

Theo and I became friendly with our downstairs neighbors, the student nurses. When I met them, I spoke to them in broken English, and they believed that I was from Greece. I acted the role of poor little Greek waif to the hilt, and Theo never gave me away; he liked black humor. For myself, I was too ashamed to tell them the truth: that I was a twenty-six-year-old American without a job, home, or family or all the other things Americans had. I needed to hide in my "Greekness."

So each night I'd return to Athens After Dark and beg the owner to let me go onstage to sing, and each night he would refuse me. "You're not Greek," he used to say. "My customers won't accept it." Finally he relented. The night of my debut I rented a tuxedo, went to the club and waited backstage from eight to two in the morning. I never went on. But the owner promised to make it up to me the next night. I asked the musicians if I could come early the next day and rehearse my song with them. They agreed, and when the owner asked the bouzouki player if I was any good, he nodded his head vigorously and said, *"Ne! Íne oréos."* I was sure I would sing that night. I invited my nurse friends to come and got them front row seats. Dressed in my tux, I stood by the door and watched. The house was full. I was to go on after the belly dancer. When she was done, I appeared on stage to the cheers of *"Yásu* Marco!" The band struck up and I began to sing. But the music was not in my key. I said, *"Signomi, Parakaló!* [Excuse me!]," in my best Greek. The band began again. I closed my eyes and sang my heart out. When I finished, I was given a standing ovation, and I was thrown flowers. I floated offstage. Those I knew and those I didn't came backstage to greet me and to say how well I'd performed. I was on my way. The next morning I went downstairs to see the nurses, who gathered around me and said they had had a wonderful time.

I had begun to feel especially close to one of them. Her name was Clarisse, and I was drawn to her maturity and stability. I asked her to bike over to the Charles River with me. Once there I spoke to her in clear English and told her how much I liked her. We kissed to seal the mutual feeling. When we got back to the house, I confessed to the other three girls about my being an American. They reacted first with shock, then with confusion and anger, and finally they began to laugh. It had been a good joke.

I was happy with Clarisse: happy that I could be myself and happy that I was feeling strong enough to give something of myself to Catharine, who had stumbled back into my life. In that June of 1974 she needed a friend more than ever. Her boyfriend had just run out on her, her father was dying, and she was talking of suicide. Clarisse and I tried to talk to her and to make her see how much she had to live for. I was proud that I could do this; my relationship with Clarisse was helping me mature. I had even taken a job as a restaurant manager—a first step to getting my feet back on the ground. After a couple of weeks I decided that I had accepted too much of Theo's hospitality and that it was time for me to get a place of my own. I asked Clarisse for a loan to cover the first and last month's rents and promised that I would pay her back in installments. She agreed to lend me the money. A week later I was fired. Too ashamed to tell Clarisse the truth, I panicked and took off.

With the money I still had I took a room in a Bay Village house, rented out by a woman about my age named Carol. She had been an associate professor of history at a local college and had been fired for her political views when the administration changed. She was convinced she was being watched and followed; I thought she was being paranoid. I never questioned her intelligence, however, and we had many good conversations about our dreams and professional aspirations. She was kind and thoughtful and tried to draw me out, but I never said anything to her about my past because I still feared people would hate or reject me if they knew the truth about me. Instead, I told her my stock Daisy Buchanan's story about my mother's being a stockbroker and my father's being a trial lawyer.

Actually, I told this to so many people that I had come to believe it, too. It was extremely hard to pull off, for I had to lie and make up stories constantly. But I managed to succeed in this by not letting anyone get too close to me. Inevitably the past dwelt on me, but I told myself that in time the memories would just go away. True, maybe it was in the downtown area of Boston, around the Combat Zone, with its pimps, hookers, drunks, and wheelers and dealers, that I should have felt most comfortable. And in many ways I did; these were people I had been forced to grow up with. But I wanted something better for my life. After all, couldn't I play Mozart's Clarinet Concerto (although rather badly), and hadn't I dreamed of becoming a composer (and a trial lawyer and a business executive)? I was sure that my abilities and aspirations alone would see me through. What did other people know about life anyway? What had *they* been through? Their parents had succored and nurtured them, educated them, had even bought them cars and fancy wardrobes. I had been thrown to the wolves at seven, yet I had survived. What did they know about *anything?* Still, I knew I was jealous, angry, envious, and I hated myself for it.

The quaint old house we lived in had once been occupied by Edgar Allan Poe; it was on a small street with gas lamps and brick sidewalks, in a small neighborhood where the artisans who built Beacon Hill had built their own homes. Best of all, it was a five-minute walk to the Greek nightclub. I was still obsessed with my Greek singing, and I went to the club every night. By now I knew most of the regulars and had a fair understanding of the language. My life revolved around forging my new career.

Then one July night I met Stravos Pappalardo, a famous Greek stage actor, who was now embarking on a singing career. He heard me sing and asked me to come to Greece with him. He would be my agent and introduce me to the right people. I was elated. My hard work and tenacity had paid off. Then a few days later, Pappalardo split to Canada. I later learned that he was wanted in Greece on pornographic charges.

My room in Bay Village continued to delight me. It was the first home of my own I had ever really had. I never wanted to leave. But my August rent was due, and I had little money. Whereas I had heretofore blamed myself for all that had gone on before in my life, I was now starting to blame society. I thought that since society had always considered me a criminal, then that was what I would be. I would commit a crime. The crime would be premeditated, and I would feel sweet retribution. I felt that society at least owed me shelter from the crazy world it had thrown me into.

I had never committed a robbery before, but I guessed I needed a gun. I was not given to violent behavior, and I didn't want anyone to get hurt. I wanted to be a sort of gentleman bandit. All I wanted was money to pay my rent. But the idea of a gun threw my plan askew. I had no idea where to get one and scrubbed the idea of a robbery until I saw an ad in a magazine for exact replicas of various kinds of guns. These were real in every way except that they could not be fired. I sent away for an army .45 caliber. I wished with all my heart that I could just work and live a normal life, but working in close proximity to outside people just made me too agitated.

While waiting for my "nongun," I conceived a plan to hit the last restaurant I had worked at, the place I had worked at when I was seeing Clarisse, and a place where I thought I had been rudely let go.

After about a week I received my model gun. When I lifted it out of the box, I was impressed with its weight and played with it as a little boy plays with his toy six-shooter. I still had some time before my rent was due, so I turned my plan over and over in my mind. I felt a sense of both exhilaration and apprehension. I really did not want to do this. Yet I supposed I had committed myself to it, and now I tried to get myself psyched up. One thing I had in my favor was the element of surprise; I also still had a key to the front door, and I knew there was no alarm system. I reckoned that I had a fifty-fifty chance of success and that at this point I didn't really care if I got caught. Jail was better than the streets in winter.

I agonized over it as I waited for the last days of the month to go by so that I would be forced into doing it. I knew that what I was doing was wrong, but I no longer had a fear of the law or any perspective about its function. I waited until the last moment to do the robbery and finally decided I didn't have the courage to do it alone, even though in my mind I had it worked out like clockwork: I would let myself into the restaurant before the manager came to work. I would hide in a room near the office. I would not touch anything; I would be a ghost. When he arrived and went into the office, I would put a nylon stocking over my head, step out and ask him politely for the money, and then lock him into a room. I would walk casually out the back door, into the alley, and act like a derelict until I got to my rented car.

Still, I could not do it alone. I went down to the Combat Zone and asked around if anyone was interested in a score. Since I'd been locked up with guys like these all my life, I knew who would be cool and who wouldn't be. As I moved about, mixing it up with the other guys, I gathered confidence and felt a surge of power in me. I decided that I had planned my first crime so well that it must be true: I *was* the criminal everyone said I was. I felt a strange freedom from all the years of caring about wanting to be a decent and productive citizen. I felt as though I were finally being honest with myself: I was a criminal, and that is why I had failed so miserably at being straight. I began to fantasize about becoming a master criminal, pulling off elaborate bank robberies and driving a car like James Bond's. As I continued to walk the Combat Zone, I spotted a guy who looked as if he had "score" in his eyes. He did and agreed to go with me.

That evening I rented a car, and the next morning we went in and pulled the caper off exactly as planned. We drove to my apartment and split the money. It wasn't a lot, but it was more than I had ever had. I felt pretty proud of myself, as if I had accomplished something. Everyone had always been telling me that the only way to offset all the prison years was for me to get a few accomplishments under my belt, and good or bad, now I had one; it was a play I wrote, directed, starred in, and reviewed. But when the initial elation wore off, I felt a sadness I'd never known. I felt dirty and tainted as if I had lost my virginity to an old whore. I felt I had plummeted from innocence into the depths of depravity. It was an unsettling feeling, and the rewards of the robbery could not even begin to pay the interest. But I succeeded in pushing these thoughts aside. I was able to pay the rent, and I had a home.

With some of the money I bought a stereo system and some furniture for my bare room, which until now had contained only a futon and a dresser. When Carol asked where I had gotten the money, I said from my parents, whom she believed to be well-off or at least to be reasonably so. In my mind I convinced myself that this was true, that my folks had given money to their wandering but beloved son.

With my new stereo, I stayed in my room all day, listening to tapes of Greek songs and planning my career as a famous Greek singer. Every night I went to the club at eight and bought drinks for the Greek regulars there who I thought were my friends. Only later did I realize they were laughing behind my back; I was the court jester.

Although I should have had enough money to see me through the next couple of months, by late September it was nearly gone. One day I made a pot of coffee and absent-mindedly placed it on the Formica countertop, where it created a bubble. Because of this, I was asked to move. I sold my stereo and rented an apartment in a converted hotel. It was quite nice, and I was actually glad to be living alone. But I knew I would not have enough money to pay the next month's rent, so I tried to get a job. But now, whenever I thought of a job and all the bad associations I carried with me of my previous employment, I became physically sick and was unable to go out for interviews. Again, rent was coming due, and it was turning cold. I needed to get the money together, but fortunately, guilt and shame prevented me from thinking of committing another robbery.

Then I remembered having read about a woman who had rented a Cape Cod summer home the year before. She had proceeded to rent out the place to many different people and to abscond with the receipts. This gave me the idea of doing the very same thing with my apartment. I went to an office supplies store and purchased some standard lease forms and placed an ad for the apartment in the local paper.

Once more I put myself above morality. The people to whom I would sublet were professionals who had everything. After what I had been through, their temporary inconvenience would be nothing more than that; maybe I even thought I was doing them the favor of giving them a street education. Maybe they wouldn't be so snotty and sure of themselves after that. For me it was strictly a matter of survival. I knew that I was not well and that I was incapable of holding down a job. I had to take care of myself because I couldn't take care of myself. Gone were the lofty thoughts of singing careers and legal careers; gone were the dreams of composing and of making a happy family life. All that mattered was the street mentality: just to get by. Those people I would rip off would be all right. They had friends; they had families; they were outside people; they knew how to live. I had tried so hard to be like them; I'd tried so fuckin' hard. But despite all my studying outside people, despite my intense efforts at self-analysis, my chiding, deriding, and positive thinking, their secrets eluded me. My only thought was to survive until I got better.

My scam was cracked right away when a woman who answered my ad went to the building management office next door to check out the legality of the sublet provision. I had a sixth sense about her, so when I saw her go into the realty office, I left the apartment and didn't bother to go back. Some master criminal, I thought. I called Theo, who was now living with two Japanese men he knew from Boston University. I told him I needed a place to stay for a while. He told me one of his roommates had just moved out, and he was sure that I could take his place. What luck! That evening I moved in with Theo and his friends, Tadashi Yamano and Yoriyoshi Nakamura.

We got along almost immediately. The apartment, interestingly enough, was just a stone's throw from Berklee. Although I no longer had plans to go there, it was nice to know that it was so close by. Our place had large picture windows that allowed a good view of Boston, a wood-beamed ceiling, a fireplace, and all the modern conveniences; it definitely looked like my image of a bachelor's pad.

As I got to know Mr. Yamano and Mr. Nakamura, I became more and more interested in their language and culture. I gave up my Greekness and got into being Japanese. I liked the Japanese. I found them to be polite, clean, and considerate. If they had one great drawback at all, it seemed they were too formal and stiff. Maybe for this reason they liked my looseness and childlike friendliness so much. They must have found me comical; I could always make them laugh. Mr. Yamano and I enjoyed listening to classical music together; Mr. Nakamura taught me to play shogi, Japanese chess, and I taught him how to play Western-style chess. For some reason I always beat him at shogi, and he beat me at Western chess; I guess we both were diplomats of sorts. Some evenings we attended Japanese film festivals. I especially liked the samurai films. Unlike American movies with their cheap and frivolous use of violence, the violence in Japanese culture was almost artful. It was never done for effect but always had a complex purpose behind it and was beautiful, never ugly. I began to like the Japanese more and more.

In order to make rent money, I devised a new scam. I took

$50 I had, and under an assumed name I opened a checking account. I went around to various stores and, paying by check, bought things which I then sold in exchange for cash at half price in the Greek community. I saved what I made and paid my share of the rent when Mr. Yamano went back to Japan to get married. My room was upstairs and had a sliding glass door. My furniture was simple, and I hung an eight- by eleven-inch picture of Catharine on the wall. Settled in now, I had begun to see her every so often.

I lived only in the reality of the moment. That usually meant going out to the discos with Theo every night. Once in a while we would go to the Greek nightclub, but the place no longer held the same magic for me. I really did not like the disco scene either, but I liked going out with Theo and our playing the roles of Greek shipping magnates' sons; the silly college girls we met enjoyed hearing our "stories," and it seemed like harmless fun. I wasn't especially interested in picking up girls, but Theo was. Most of the time we didn't succeed, but that was fine by me; I wanted only to get plastered and pass out. In my heart of hearts I wanted to find a woman to love and to love me, but the prospect seemed as remote as could be. Role playing helped repress my dismal failure in life thus far and the painful thoughts of Angela and Marie. Renewed attempts at settling into the role of husband and father had proved bankrupt. I also knew that my state of mind at this time was so twisted and warped that if I were with Marie, some of my craziness could fuck up her head. It was impossible for me to understand how someone could love and care for me or want to help me. I felt more confused than ever.

Perhaps for this reason I began to see Catharine more often. I was not in love with her, nor she with me, but we fell into a very special, easygoing sexual relationship. I should not have let this happen. She was only eighteen, and I was twenty-six, but more important, her emotional problems dwarfed mine. She was also severely dyslectic and could not retain written information. She had failed her school tests and her employment tests, and these failures literally shook her self-confidence. She had always been fastidious about her grooming and personal appearance. Now she began to shower and change her clothing three times a day and to wear sanitary napkins whether or not she needed to. When she began to talk about having her sweat glands surgically removed, I knew something was wrong. I also knew that there was only so much—and so little—that I could do for her and that she needed to get professional help. I should have tried to contact her family, but I was afraid. I knew they weren't wild about my age and joblessness. Finally, though, I did call her mother and explained that I thought Catharine needed help. Soon after, she began seeing a succession of fancy psychiatrists and spending time at the library reading up on her problems, just as I had in my own search for answers. Since I understood what she was doing, I encouraged her to keep at it, but that was all. I wanted her to get well and find a nice guy for herself. And I knew that for myself I needed someone my age, someone I could talk to.

One evening soon after Thanksgiving, Theo, Mr. Nakamura, a Japanese girl named Hiroko, and I were having a little party in my room, and the sake was flowing. Intoxicated, I began to sing the various Japanese songs I'd learned when Mr. Nakamura asked me if I'd like to meet another Japanese girl. I said sure. He went to get her, but they never came back upstairs. I heard them talking downstairs. I felt left out and went to sleep. The next morning the girl, Mieko, called me and said that she had found out that she was supposed to meet me, and she apologized for Mr. Nakamura's impropriety. We arranged to meet each other that evening. I met her at her dormitory; she was studying English at Northeastern University. I was feeling a bit giddy from the two whiskey sours I'd had to fortify myself for our date, and by the time I arrived to pick her up I was feeling pretty loose. Mieko turned out to be as cute as a button. She was tiny and intelligent and had beautiful, bright eyes. We went to see a production of *The Little Prince* at a local church. We sat in the front row. I was feeling fidgety and got up to go to the bathroom while the play was in progress. I roamed around and found myself backstage. I put my head through the curtains and must have had a silly look on my face, for when Mieko saw me, she laughed out loud. I was kicked out of the theater and waited outside for her. When she came out and saw me, she began to laugh again, an honest, infectious laugh. She had a wonderful sense of humor.

We started seeing each other regularly, and Mr. Nakamura started acting hostile to me. I found out from Mieko that he was in love with her and had asked her to marry him. She had turned him down. He was furious. His father was a wealthy importer-exporter in Kyoto, where Mieko was also from, and he was used to having his way. It enraged him to lose her to an American. But Mieko herself did not care for Japanese men and their possessive treatment of their women. As I got to know her, I found that she was as solid as a rock, wise, and very together.

But Mr. Nakamura and I were increasingly at odds. One day he grabbed me and with an air of cryptic importance said, "Do you know how to take care of yourself in the woods? Can you survive in the woods?" I just looked at him and felt glad he didn't have a sword; I was sure that I would have joined my ancestors. I told him that I didn't really know how to survive in the woods, but if I ever were to find myself in such a situation, I would learn quickly; I was a survivor. Our relationship continued to deteriorate, as he walked around muttering loudly to himself in Japanese, "I'm samurai; you're stupid."

By Christmas 1975, Mieko and I were a pair. Her dorm was closing for inter-session, and Mieko had to find a place to live during those two weeks. We decided to take a place together. I went home and packed the few pieces of casual wear I had, probably no more than two changes of clothes. It didn't matter to me that that was all I had; I often wore the same clothing for many days at a time, and I rarely took showers. These were signs of my continuing depression, but I didn't recognize them.

When I arrived at our rooming house, Mieko surprised me. She had bought me new underwear, socks, pajamas, and a toothbrush. This last was especially welcome because I had never taken care of my teeth; I had blocks about even such simple but important things as having regular dental care. One reason was that because I couldn't maintain steady work, I never qualified for any medical coverage. Whenever I would become sick, I would go to a hospital emergency room and get treated under an assumed name and address.

Mieko and I spent a blissful two weeks together. She told me about her family and how loving, kind, and supportive they had always been while she was growing up. She told me that her father was a civil servant and that her mother taught reading at an elementary school; she had a married brother who was a pilot and a younger sister, Chie, who was planning to be a nurse. Mieko explained that while her home was modern, her mother and father still slept on tatami mats on the floor; the thought made her giggle. As I listened, her eyes twinkled with such purity and innocence that I felt drawn into her being. She told me that she had had a good education, but she had twice attempted suicide after failing her entrance examinations for the prestigious Tokyo University. This threw me; were all women suicidal, or did I just attract them?

I told Mieko that while my family lived in Massachusetts, I was estranged beyond repair from them and that I felt I had no family. I talked about my life and told her that I didn't think that she should get involved with me because I was not a good person. She said in her spare English that it didn't matter to her because she felt there was something good and special about me. Hearing her say this made me feel overjoyed that someone who was so fine and good as she could actually say these things about me. When it was time for Mieko to go back to school, we decided we would get an apartment together in the spring.

Throughout this time I was afraid even to attempt to get a job; what was the sense, I thought, since I'd only alienate others again and lose it? I was still living off my fall checking account scam, buying vacuum cleaners, radios, and whatever else I could sell quickly. I knew checks were bouncing all over the place, but I kept ahead of them until I made an error in judgment and went back to one of the stores where I'd written a bad check and I was almost caught; good thing I could run fast. I ran into the train station and caught a train that let me off near the Charles River, where I went into a wooded area and cried and begged God please to help me, please to make me well. I dropped my check scam and spent the next several days locked in my room.

As winter turned to spring I resolved to try harder and began looking for work again. But going out on job interviews became increasingly hard and painful because I was so self-conscious of the fact that I was now twenty-seven years old and that in the two years I'd been out of prison I had not accomplished anything except to leave a trail of failures. I couldn't figure it out. For years I had tried to blame my problems on everybody else, but I realized now that unless I accepted responsibility for my own life, I would be powerless to change my circumstances.

I hoped that this new line of reasoning would change everything, but it didn't. I took a job as assistant manager of a small pizza shop. I tried to be sociable with my co-workers but couldn't get on with them; I think they sensed I didn't like myself very much. In the evening, when we closed up, I had to put the day's receipts into a paper bag and hide them. Two weeks into my job I was accused of stealing the previous day's receipts. I hadn't done it. The owner said he didn't believe me and fired me. I left and was walking down the street with my head hung low when it occurred to me that he'd probably stolen them himself and had set me up in order to fire me. I told Mieko about it that evening. It didn't matter to her, she said; she was sure I would eventually succeed.

When she finished school in June, she bought a used car, and we went apartment hunting. We found a one-bedroom apartment in a nice housing complex. Mieko paid for everything. Feeling better now, feeling that I was becoming almost like an outside person, living in a nice apartment with nice middle-class professionals and all, I tried another job. I was hired as an assistant manager at a Jack-in-the-Box restaurant. It was a national chain with advancement opportunities. I was determined to stick it out and rise up through the ranks to become a regional manager in charge of several stores. I lasted one month, fired for incompetence.

This time Mieko did not hide her disappointment in me. She let me make love to her that night, and in the morning she felt better. I did not. I was starting to think that perhaps all I was able to offer a woman was my childlike dependence and bedroom prowess. I began to think of myself as nothing better than a gigolo who did little more than sit around all day until the woman who footed the bills came home and I could service her.

We had been living at the apartment complex for only three months when we decided to move to a Beacon Street brownstone. If I had once thought that living in the fashionable Back Bay would transform me into a successful adult, I knew better now. I was definitely a street person. I loved the activity of city life. I took a job in a deli across the street from the Prudential Center. I worked the graveyard shift, six days a week. It was difficult for the owner of the deli to find reliable men to work these hours, and he usually had to employ alcoholics, transients, and psychopathic types since they were the only ones who would work late-night hours. I fitted right in, so that it worked out fairly well. At my other jobs I would sometimes hear employees talk among themselves about their families and about the years they had been on the job; their talk only reminded me of how transient and alone I really was. But at the new deli I didn't hear any of this kind of talk, so I felt much more comfortable. The only drawback was the schedule. Because of my hours, Mieko and I didn't see much of each other. In October she told me that she felt we should split up for a while. I agreed. She went to live with a friend in Harvard Square, and I moved to a men's rooming house on Commonwealth Avenue. It was there that I really began to weird out.

I knew that I had failed with Mieko, yet of all the women I

had known, she was the only one I had wanted to make it for. If any girl had ever really loved me for my real self, it had been Mieko. Yet I had failed. During the day, when I wasn't working, I stayed in my room and paced the floor. I was feeling hate, bitterness, and rage. It frightened me because I had always succeeded in repressing those kinds of feelings. And whereas I had once thought of myself as a fairly physically attractive person, when I looked into the mirror now, I began to see a face deathly old beyond its years, my eyes looking back at me like extinct stars. When I saw this, I became even more anxious; I would sit on my bed and wring my hands together or run to the bathroom on the hour as if I were trying to extrude it all. My stomach and muscles ached constantly; I felt as though I'd been picked up off the ground and dropped from the roof. I had no idea what was going on. I began to drink to steady myself; the drink was far preferable to the anxiety that consumed me. I still had my make-believe gun, and sometimes I lay on the bed and fondled it for half the day. I imagined it a machine gun and myself going up to the State House, where I would begin shooting everyone in sight until at last I was gunned down. In a way I wanted to commit suicide. I believed that the state and its workers had been responsible for my wanting to destroy myself and that I would therefore take with me as many of them as I could.

Thankfully I knew that such imaginings were stupid and pointless. It had been three weeks since Mieko and I had split. I decided that I had to get out of my room and spend my days doing something that would benefit me in the future. During the summer I had determined that my biggest problem was my lack of education and that math was my biggest obstacle to getting one. I went to the Massachusetts Rehabilitation Commission and asked if it would pay for a course in mathematics. It agreed, and in September 1975 I had been put into a basic fractions class with students more than ten years my junior. I didn't care. But when Mieko and I broke up, and I weirded out, I had stopped attending. Now I applied myself diligently and passed the course in December with an A. My teacher commented on my report card that I "could well blossom in a class with better minds." He also told me he thought I could skip the second course in algebra and go straight into trigonometry. I skipped down the street like a child who had decided to be a mathematician. I realized why I was so different from other people: I was eccentric, and weren't all mathematicians?

I called Mieko. I was working; I had completed, with honors, a course in math; I had maintained a home for three months, and I felt as if I were finally growing up and getting better. I welcomed in 1976 with an unaccustomed sense of accomplishment. The next semester I started trigonometry. In two weeks I knew it was too difficult, and rather than seek extra help or tell anyone, I bolted. I dropped out, citing financial difficulties. Soon after, I began to weird out again.

This time it was much worse. I began to go through the same behavior patterns as the last time, but whenever I was outdoors, on my way to or from my job, I started to feel trapped by the buildings on the streets, as if they were closing in on me. The sound of police, fire, or ambulance sirens would set me off, and I would run down the street in terror to the nearest liquor store, where I would buy a half pint of Scotch and guzzle it down. The liquor burned and stung as it made its way through me, but it relaxed me and knocked me out so that I could sleep. When I awoke, the anxiety attacks started all over. Sometimes, when I walked along the streets, I could not feel my feet on the ground. Sometimes I lost all sense of a third dimension so that the sky seemed like a huge piece of paper that I could reach up to and crumple with my hand, or that the world was a tiny spinning ball, whirling and whirling, under my feet. Other times, as I walked down the street, I would see people slaughtered, drawn and quartered, and hung on hooks. I could hear their horrifying screams piercing my being. I had always been able to control these hallucinations while at work; the customers kept me busy and out of my own head. But then they started to plague me at work. I began to see my body, dead and blue, in the refrigerator case. I could not slice meat without imagining that it was my heart that I was slicing. My hand would shake so that it would take me half an hour to slice the four pieces of meat needed for a sandwich order. I had to yell at myself that it wasn't my heart I was slicing and to calm down.

I was barely keeping my job. I was just barely *getting* to my job. Whenever I would pass a policeman on my way to or from work, I would imagine him putting his gun to my head, and I could feel the hard power of the bullet rip through my brain. I could barely withstand the short subway ride that took me back and forth between my room and place of work. When the train entered the tunnel, I imagined that it was coursing through the arteries of my own heart. I would turn my face away from the other commuters and command myself to stop it, Stop It, STOP IT, MARK!

After a time it did. Memories of these torturous images had left me exhausted. I would lie stuporlike on my bed and watch television. That March I saw a news report that made me sit up and take notice. State employees were lobbying to have juvenile institutions reopened. I hadn't been aware that any of them had been shut down. But I learned that during the administration of former Massachusetts Governor Francis Sargent, his director of youth service, Jerome Miller, had virtually cleaned out reformatories such as Lyman School, which had been closed since 1972, and the IJG, favoring the more progressive method of community-based treatment. Experience had taught Miller that isolating wayward youths in such sterile environments had resulted in the same sort of shock syndrome that I had experienced. Youths were ill-equipped to make meaningful and lasting transitions back into society, and more often than not, they quickly reverted to crime and a return to the institution. His argument that community-based treatment was not only more humane but less expensive to taxpayers had fallen on deaf ears, and when Michael Dukakis defeated Sargent in the 1974 gubernatorial race,

Miller lost his job. Now members of the union representing Division of Youth Service employees—civil service workers who had lost their cushy jobs when the institutions closed—were lobbying to have them reopened.

It had been a long time since 1966, when I had been released from the clutches of the division, but I had remembered its lessons well and felt sure that I was qualified to address the issue of why juvenile institutions did not work. I phoned the television station to ask if it would offer me time to give an opposing view. The editorial director agreed to give me air time, pending approval of my message. I worked on it for days and, when I was satisfied, sent it in to the station. The following week the station called and scheduled a tape date. Mieko came along with me for moral support. When we arrived, I was taken to a studio and placed in front of a camera. I rehearsed my message, reading it off the teleprompter. When everything was set, I began:

> The abolition of the present juvenile institutions in Massachusetts is a very sound move in my estimation. These types of institutions do not work and adversely affect the children committed to them. The effect is usually regressive rather than rehabilitative. Isolating children in a germ-free environment accomplishes little. An alternative program such as a community-based treatment center is a far superior and realistic approach in dealing with the serious problems confronting these children. How do I know? After spending ten years of my life growing up in these institutions, I know. . . .

When I finished, the production staff congratulated me. They told me that I had been excellent on camera, that I had good presence, and that they were amazed that my eyes had not strayed as I read from the Teleprompter. They all agreed that I should seriously consider a career in film acting. The wheels in my head began to click; that was it! I was an actor, and that explained why I was always taking on different identities. But I had been down the road of dreams and fantasies so many times that I gave it up as just another harebrained scheme. Sometime after that, though, I picked up a copy of Mary Renault's novel *The Persian Boy*. It was such a good story that I finished reading it in one day. About a week later I saw on the cover of a dance magazine a photograph of a good-looking man followed by the caption "In Search of the Persian Boy." I bought a copy and read that the book was going to be made into a movie and that the producers were looking to cast the film with unknowns. I wrote the producers and sent them the videotape of my editorial, even offering to work for free in order to learn the craft. After sending it, I forgot about it.

In April, for my twenty-eighth birthday, Mieko gave a party for me. It was wonderful. She had spent hours preparing sushi, sour rice, tempura, miso soup, and other Japanese delicacies for me. Theo came, as well as Mr. Yamano, who had recently returned from Japan. Mieko had also invited a couple of her friends from Harvard, where she was now studying English. At first I felt a little intimidated talking to Harvard students, but soon I realized there wasn't anything to feel intimidated about. They were just regular people.

At one point in the evening Mieko's roommate, Mary Alice, and I sat down at the kitchen table, and somehow our conversation got around to poetry. I said that I liked poetry but that I had not read much at all. She produced a volume containing some of her favorites and began to read aloud to me. I did not always understand their specific poetic allusions and literary references, but there was one poem among them I understood only too well, even though it was dated 1586. No words I had ever heard expressed so eloquently how I had been feeling most of my life. The poem was "Tichborne's Elegy," and it was subtitled "A Lament on the Eve of His Execution":

> My prime of youth is but a frost of cares;
> My feast of joy is but a dish of pain;

My crop of corn is but a field of tares;
And all my good is but vain hope of gain;
The day is past, and yet I saw no sun,
And now I live, and now my life is done!

My tale was heard and yet it was not told,
My fruit is fallen and yet my leaves are green,
My youth is spent and yet I am not old,
I saw the world and yet I was not seen;
My thread is cut and yet it is not spun,
And now I live, and now my life is done.

I sought my death and found it in my womb,
I looked for life and saw it was a shade,
I trod the earth and knew it was my tomb,
And now I die, and now I was but made;
My glass is full, and now my glass is run,
And now I live, and now my life is done.

The poem catapulted me through a full range of emotions; I felt it summed up all that I felt and was yet unable to express. I realized that although I was not going to be executed the next morning it might not be long before I executed myself. Tichborne's "Elegy" made me resolve, however stubbornly or futilely, that I would not be defeated and that I would try again. I determined that the only thing that stood between me and outside people was finances and that I would get money any way I could and to hell with morality. I started to put every cent away that I could from my wages, but I soon realized that I would never get into a position of financial strength by saving from my job.

After work one afternoon the following month, I stopped in my neighborhood bar for a beer. At the bar was a guy named Willie. He was talking to a friend about cars and how car rings worked. I sat down to listen. He told us that the stolen car business in Massachusetts was so big that a fellow could actually go to a dealer of hot cars and order the model and year he wanted at a fraction of the retail price and that all the serial and identifying numbers could be changed. Willie mentioned that he really wanted to get his hands on a new Porsche Targa. When I heard this, an idea popped into my head. I asked Willie how much he would pay for a new Porsche. He told me $2,500 if the car was new. This seemed to me like a lot of money and a good springboard to my financial independence. Since I had sold cars, I knew how to go about getting one. First I knew that if I went to a dealer, I could ask for a demonstration ride and more than likely be encouraged to take one out, especially if I casually hinted to the salesman that I was interested in a competitor's car. I also knew that the salesman would size up my appearance and would probably want to go out on the ride with me. I decided I needed an accomplice.

I was friendly with a girl from England who was living in the neighborhood, and I knew she was hard pressed for funds because she was attending a local college. I asked her to accompany me to the car dealer, assuring her that all she had to do was to look expensive and ride in the car, and then I would give her a cut of the money I got. She agreed. We went up to a dealer near Boston University. Perhaps the salesman would think we were rich students. This was fun! I wasn't the least bit frightened because the actual crime would not take place inside the dealer's; it would take place only when I took the car out on the road and didn't return it after a reasonable time. My only real concern was whether or not the salesman would allow us to take it out alone. We went into the showroom and began looking with casual interest at some of the cars on the floor. A salesman approached us and offered us assistance. We tried to act cool and said we would call him when we wanted help. A bit later we motioned to him, and when he came over, I let her do the talking; I figured her English accent might have a wealthy sound to it and impress him. She asked him if we might be able to take a Targa for a test drive. He brought us a set of keys and helped us into the car—with its $20,000 price tag—and we were off.

About a mile down Commonwealth Avenue I let her out. I then drove the car over to the Prudential Center, parked it in the underground lot, and went to the bar to find Willie. I told him that I had a Porsche for him. Because he didn't believe me, I took him to see it. When we got back to the bar, he gave me all kinds of excuses for why he couldn't buy it. He said that if the car had been taken from New Hampshire or elsewhere, there wouldn't be a problem. Since it was from Massachusetts, it was no deal. I told him he was nothing but a big talker and to go to hell.

Now I was stuck with a $20,000 Porsche that I didn't know what to do with. I went to my room, undressed, and got ready for work. The next evening I moved the car to another parking lot where I thought it would be safe until I figured out how to get rid of it. I left it in the lot and forgot about it for a couple of weeks. When I went back to the parking lot, I was surprised to see that the Porsche was still there. I decided to make believe it was mine for a while. I took it out on evenings I was off from work. One evening I stopped to have a couple of drinks and parked the car in the public alley behind a bar. I decided that night to abandon it somewhere near the dealer the next day. But I got pretty drunk, and when I got back into the car, I passed out. I was awakened by a cop who pulled me out of the front seat. I was placed in the back of a paddy wagon.

I spent the night in the drunk tank. The next morning I called Mieko, who immediately came to see me and promised that she would hire me a lawyer. I couldn't believe she could be so steadfast and so caring for me. Here was a girl who, it seemed, had traveled halfway around the world just to look after me. She was kinder to me than my own family had ever been. I vowed that if I got off this rap, I would devote myself to rebuilding our relationship and that I would eventually marry her.

Later that day I was taken to Charles Street Jail. I was charged with auto theft. I could not believe that I was back in jail. I was desperately afraid of being sent back to prison for the rest of my life. I heard another inmate talk about an habitual criminal act, some new Massachusetts law that basically provided that if a prisoner had a long history of past crimes, he could be given a life sentence no matter how minor was the crime he was now awaiting trial for. I imagined that I could certainly be a candidate for a life sentence, and I was sure that because I had been a State Boy, I would die an old man in a cell.

I decided that I had to try to get help and that I had to tell someone my story. I knew many ex-cons with records far worse than my own who had been able to plea-bargain their way out of sentences. I had never gotten off even once, and what had I really done? I wrote a letter to Mieko enclosing a letter to a well-known underground Boston newspaper called *The Real Paper*. In it, I described what it was like to be in Charles Street Jail and how I was afraid I would spend the rest of my life in prison. Mieko brought the letter to the paper, where a reporter named Mark Zanger edited it into a short article that was run at the end of June. I was really surprised that I had something published.

While I was in Charles Street Jail, I also remembered that I was still waiting to hear from the producers of *The Persian Boy*. I thought that if I heard from them before my court date that they were interested in me for the film, I might be able to get off. I made a call from the prison, charging it to Mieko's number with her permission. I was able to find out that my videotape had been sent to Hollywood and the initial reports were favorable; I would hear soon, I was told. I didn't mention Charles Street.

A week later I was taken to Boston Municipal Court. Mieko had gotten me a lawyer who was well known around the courthouse, a fact that made me recall something I once heard in the Petersburg Reformatory: If you can't get a good lawyer, at least get one who knows the judge. My lawyer was easily pushing seventy, so I was sure that he knew all the judges. I managed to get my charge reduced to receiving stolen goods and to get off with a year's probation. Almost. Then I was informed there was a warrant out for my arrest in Cambridge on that long-ago armed robbery charge. Apparently someone had testified that they had seen me leaving the restaurant. I began planning my stay at Walpole. I was taken in handcuffs from the docket as Mieko looked on, teary-eyed.

When I arrived at Cambridge Jail, I was put in a cell until I could be arraigned and bail could be set. I was sure that I was going to Walpole State Prison, and I began to think about how best I could serve out the twenty or so years I was sure I would draw. I grieved at losing Mieko but told myself she was better off without me anyway. I was given a court-appointed attorney who asked me if I had committed the crime. I said I hadn't. When my time came, I stood before the judge and listened to the bailiff read the charge. My attorney requested a low bail since I was indigent. The DA surprised me by responding that he had no objections; the judge called my lawyer and the DA to the bench to confer, and I was let out on personal recognizance.

Back on the street again I could hardly believe my good fortune. I called Mieko, and we celebrated. That night I told her I had made a decision: I was going to move to New York. I wanted to get away forever from the state of Massachusetts, where I had been in nothing but trouble all my life. Mieko told me she supported me totally. She decided to go with me because she hoped to find better employment opportunities there than in Boston.

I went home and tried unsuccessfully to get my job back. I had two or three weeks before I was due to appear in court, so I still had time to get some money together for the trip. I found a job as a cook in a Cambridge restaurant. As I worked and saved, I turned over in my mind the many reasons for wanting to get out of Boston. Although I was frightened of moving to a strange town, there were many more compelling reasons inducing me to go. I was afraid I would go to prison for life. And even with my one-year probation for receiving stolen goods, I just couldn't go through the process of reporting to a probation officer again, of being checked up on all the time. I wanted to pursue an acting career, and the tentative interest of the producers of *The Persian Boy* in me seemed reason enough to go. Finally I decided that I wanted to start work on a book about my experiences because I felt I needed someone to defend me legally, and I knew I also needed psychiatric help. I reasoned that if a lawyer and a psychiatrist read my story, then perhaps they would take an interest in my case.

I went to meet Mark Zanger at *The Real Paper*. He had a scraggly beard and wise, trustworthy eyes that gave him the look of a rabbi. He encouraged me to work on the book, saying that he felt it was a story that people should know.

In the early part of July 1976, with a few bucks in my pocket, I headed for New York City. I was fortunate to find an inexpensive room quickly, and with so many restaurants and delis in New York I had no trouble finding a job. When I had settled in a bit, I called Persian Boy Productions. I was promised word soon, and a few days later I received a letter asking me for some still photographs. I jumped for joy. I called Mieko to tell her that I had everything set up. She said she would be down at the end of the month.

I went to work as a deliman. Whereas in Boston I had been pretty fast with my hands making sandwiches, I was slow by New York standards, but the management liked me enough to let me try to work up my speed. I was clearing about $200 a week, and because I was paying only $50 a week in rent, I was able to save some money. Then the producers of *The Persian Boy* movie contacted me to say that they were at least a year away from getting the money together to start production but that they were still interested in me and would be back in touch when they were ready. Further encouraged, I decided to take acting lessons, although I felt that I could go right before the cameras and act without difficulty since I had no fears about standing in front of many people and performing; I felt that most of my life I had been performing in some way or another.

Mieko arrived at the end of July and found us an apartment on Second Avenue between East Fiftieth and Fifty-first streets. I had been in New York for more than a month and found I really liked the city. I liked the pace and the action and the anonymity of city life. Mieko found a job as a secretary with a Japanese bank in downtown Manhattan. We purchased some furniture and settled into our cozy little home. I felt better than I had ever felt in my life. I began investigating acting schools and found that lessons were expensive. I began to save as much as possible in order to pay for the best school I could find. I bought copies of *Backstage* and *Variety*, the trade publications of the theater and the film industries, and read them from cover to cover. I considered myself fortunate that although I had never had an acting lesson and had not undergone the hardships of the aspiring actor, I already had producers interested in me.

I began work on the book I wanted to write, hoping I could use my story as a prototype of what happens to very young kids who are sent to prison so that perhaps children's prisons would be closed. As I began to write, I realized that nothing was more important than getting the story out. I wrote three pages and an outline and took them to a publisher whose offices were located a few blocks from my apartment. An editor looked at them and said that the story was important, but before he could offer me a contract, the story would have to be worked out more fully and include some supporting documentation. I felt encouraged now. In late August I sent to Massachusetts for my records.

Meanwhile, I wanted to get on with the business of acting. I was having trouble saving money fast enough to get started. I decided to approach some acting teachers with the letter from the movie producers and to show them as well the first few pages of my book in progress in hopes that I could barter free lessons for work and promise of payment later. I was fortunate in finding Madaleine Klein, who agreed to help me. That September I began attending classes three evenings a week at her theater on West Thirteenth Street. I found that I was not a very good student. I was impatient to get onstage and begin acting right away; I did not care for the theater games and exercises required of us. I dropped out but stayed on as the weekend theater manager, in charge of the box office, seating arrangements, ushering, and making the coffee served at intermission. This allowed me to pick up a few extra dollars every week.

Each day, when I did not have to work or go to the theater, I worked on the story. It was really starting to get to me. It was as though I had opened up Pandora's box. Trying to piece together twenty years of names, dates, and memories played havoc with my senses until it all swirled painfully through my head. On some days I would resist working on it or want to stop and forget about the project. Yet I also found that I was constantly thinking about it to the exclusion of all else. I was hopelessly drawn into finishing it.

At work I was so wrapped up in bringing back and piecing together those memories that I was not doing well and often made mistakes, like filling an order wrong or forgetting to fill an order. Finally the management said that it would have to let me go but would allow me to stay on the few remaining weeks to December so that I could qualify for unemployment compensation.

After my time was up, I started to receive my $115-a-week unemployment insurance. It freed me now to work exclusively on the story. But it was a mistake for me to have so much time on my hands. As I got more into the task of sorting out the chronology of events, I became depressed since I had to keep reliving those years over and over in my mind. I would write and write, twenty or more pages a day for weeks on end. When it became too painful—the Bridgewater years especially so—I would lie on the couch and drink to shut it all out for another few days. As soon as I recovered, I would read what I had written only to realize that much of the chronology was wrong and that my writing was amateurish; this would throw me into another depression and start the cycle again. Yet I continued to keep trying, and with each new effort the manuscript got just a little better.

226

I started spending time in the local bars on Second Avenue and away from Mieko. In the bars I would tell my story to anyone who would listen. Those who did hear it thought it was quite a story; they encouraged me to keep at it.

On weekends, after I'd finished working at the theater, I would head for a bar down the street called the Bells of Hell. There I found other aspiring writers such as myself, and I would hang out drinking black and tans until closing time. Oftentimes I would sleep at the theater; I wasn't contributing any money toward our living expenses, spending what little I had on drink. Finally, in February of 1977, Mieko asked me to move out. I did. I had been hoping that she would understand what it was I was trying to do, what an enormous task I had taken on, and that she would stay with me until I was able to complete it. Even though I was still married to Angela, whom I had not seen in more than three years, I continued to hope that when I was fiscally responsible and mentally well again, Mieko and I would marry.

Around this time I learned about the Irish writer Brendan Behan. I picked up a copy of his prison autobiography, *Borstal Boy*, and discovered that among other things, he had been in a juvenile prison. He also had loved to drink and loved to sing. I began thinking of myself as Brendan Behan. I'd been looking for an identity my whole life, and surely this was it. A drunken Irish writer! I could get into that. Wasn't I Irish, too? Certain now that I was a drunken Irish writer, I stopped working on my story; it was no longer necessary to write since I knew what I was. I began to spend most of my time in the Bells of Hell and switched my drink to Irish whiskey.

Shortly after discovering my real self, I came across an advertisement in *The New York Times Magazine* for the Second Annual Paddy's Irish Whiskey Poetry Contest. It invited everyone to write in a poem that alluded to either Murphy's or Paddy's Irish whiskey. Each month one winner would be chosen until twelve months later a final winner would be picked. The winning poet would receive a case of Irish whiskey, and I decided that if I were truly to be recognized as an Irish writer, I had better enter this contest. One Sunday afternoon in early spring I went to a small park with a waterfall and started to write. I called it "Murphy's Elegy":

> "Excuse me, Sir! I've only just a moment to spare.
> But, What give ye such mirth and cheer, this
> drizzly, dreary, marnin' Sir." Said the ruddy
> faced constable quite up on my ear. Espying as
> he did with covetous stare, half a bottle at my
> hand quite near.
>
> "Why! 'tis Murphy's spirit. Come ta haunt me agi'n
> I fear; this seer with a warmin' sear. Lyin' here,
> in this hand-blown crypt." Motionin', as I did,
> to the bottle near.
>
> Now! The constable, with 'only just a moment to
> spare,' calls for a glass and an empty chair.
> "Aye! He's been seen everywhere; and a fine
> fellow he is, too. Comin' back to us as a good
> whiskey, Sir."

Satisfied that I could do no more with it, I signed myself "Mark Devlin, Road's Scholar," and sent it off. I thought that if I could win the contest, I would have had one real accomplishment in my life and that I would die a happy man. A few months later I received a certificate naming me an "Honorary Irish Poet." Although I had wanted to win, I had my certificate, and a title and felt a true sense of accomplishment.

I was now eager to get back to writing my story, but I felt I really did need my records to help me piece things together, and my earlier letter of request to the Division of Youth Service had gone unanswered. Now I wrote again. The response was that my records had already been sent. I asked for another copy, which I was then told would be mailed out right away. Two months later, when I had not received the package, I decided to call my mother to help me obtain them. I had not spoken to her in several years, and she was surprised but pleased to hear my voice. She told me that Angela had been in the state hospital for a long time and that Marie was living with my sister Patrice, now married and herself the mother of two. This was bittersweet news: Marie was eight years old now, and I guessed that she would not recognize me. I felt bad that I had missed her growing up and hoped she didn't feel I had abandoned her. In any event my mother agreed to go up to the Division of Youth Service for me and to get my records.

It was already the middle of the summer, and Mieko came by to see me. She had to start making some decisions: she was lonely in New York, and, additionally, her parents were asking her to go home. I loved Mieko, but I encouraged her to return. I didn't think there was any future with me, not for a few years anyway. We spent some wonderful times together in those last weeks remaining to us, and when I went to see her off, I kissed her passionately. She told me that she still loved me and wanted me to come to Japan and marry her. We hugged and cried, and when I let go of her, I knew I would never see her again. As the tears came harder, I knew I couldn't tell her that I was afraid of flying and that when I tried to imagine my plane landing in Japan, I feared that the country was so small that as I stepped onto the ground, I would fall off the world.

Talking to my mother again, and hearing about Marie had started me thinking about my own family. I had turned twenty-nine that previous spring; I thought it was time for me to go home, too. I would get a bus to Boston, where I would live and work on my story. I had been in New York only a little more than a year, yet so much had happened that it seemed longer. On the bus home I thanked whoever it was that had sent Mieko to me and hoped someday, somehow, we would find a way to be together again. But right now getting the story down on paper was the only thing that mattered to me. I wondered if I could ever do it.

When I arrived in Boston, it was late October and turning cold. I didn't have much money and needed to find a job right away. I took one selling encyclopedias door to door, something I had tried before. In the meantime, a co-worker named Phillip offered to let me crash at the brownstone apartment he shared with his girl friend and Golden Retriever, Georgie. I began to work on the book again.

My mother had succeeded in obtaining my records. I took them home and pored over them. I had to read them several times before I could begin the difficult process of piecing together the state's position and weighing it against my own feelings and memories of things. To make sure of the chronology of events, I tried typing up page after page of official reports and cross-reference them to my own memories, and as in some complex puzzle, I shuffled the papers around to try to begin to understand how the story all unfolded. The parts that hurt me the most were those records that stated my father beat me as an infant; I wanted to find him and beat him bloody. Yet oddly enough, I also felt compassion for him. I knew how unhappy childhood experiences could influence one's adult behavior; perhaps something in his upbringing made him do these things to me. I was trying to find a way to erase the past and to forgive my parents; it was very difficult. I was torn between hate and an understanding of their problems for a long while. As I began to get some distance from the records, I noticed that the records from John Augustus Hall were missing. I knew they existed; I had seen them when I had gone back to visit Mr. Costello in 1971. I asked my mother to call the Division of Youth Service to see where they might be. She was told that she had received all existing records.

That evening, as I lay in my bed, I went over and over in my mind the report made by the superintendent of Lyman School in the fall of 1961 after my second escape attempt. For me this was the most confusing and bewildering and, ultimately, most damning report of all; it was the one that got me sent to the IJG:

Mark Devlin is now thirteen years and six months of age, has a reported I.Q. of 112, and has been in our custody for five-and-one-half years during which time he has received total consideration from facilities under Youth Service Board. Yet the total result of our efforts in his behalf, whether academically, socially, morally, or religiously, have amounted to practically nothing. One of the greatest obstacles in our treatment of this youngster was the fact that he was so abused, misused and unloved during the first seven years of his life that it now appears impossible for us to reach him. Our social history indicates that the boy on many occasions was beaten unmercifully by his father. Since early childhood to the present time he has been enuretic. He has been involved in homosexual activities; he has suffered from severe nightmares; and he is completely incapable of respecting any adult, or any form of legal authority.

I do not believe there is anyone who is capable of placing themselves in a position to evaluate this boy's feelings. He has probably lived a full lifetime in his first thirteen years, and they have probably made him an old man at least socially, if not physically. The one thing that apparently is very clear in Mark's philosophy, which is, "Everyone around me and everything will receive exactly what I received from my father." The only pertinent comment I can add to this assessment is that, unfortunately, one can almost detect a sadistic smile of satisfaction when Mark is making life miserable for those around him.

During the time that Mark has been a resident at Lyman School he has made practically no progress. He has been abusive of smaller boys; stabbing them with a knife or fork; has been involved in homosexual activity; was banned from

Catholic Confession for his behavior; has been repeatedly thrown out of the academic classroom for refusing to do any work, for instigating small riots. When discipline is applied, Mark reacts violently. He is a fantastic story teller who enjoys anything that has to do with blood and death. Vulgar four-letter words sprout out of this boy's mouth like water out of a faucet. I once wrote to his mother and indicated to her that this boy is the most vulgar young man I have met in my ten years with Youth Service Board.

I think I have disillusioned myself that Mark is susceptible to treatment and kindness. We have not reached this young man, and I seriously doubt if anyone can reach him. Mark has run away twice during his most recent return to Lyman School, and it is part of his motivation that he honestly believes if he is irritating and troublesome enough, the Youth Service Board will release him to his home. In spite of his age I am afraid he has the potential to become a dangerous criminal, and am therefore requesting his transfer to the Institute for Juvenile Guidance.

When I read this report my eyes stung with tears. During my stay at Lyman School the superintendent had always treated me well and civilly. And to know that he had written such a harsh report hurt me. But now while I lay in bed, my hurt turned to anger as I realized that in effect, his report meant that the state had decided to give up on me at age thirteen.

Initially, too, the report had made me doubt myself, doubt my memory of things. All the while I had been writing a story that I thought was true, but I wondered if I was in fact the sadistic criminal he suggested I was. Now I tried to recall the incidents he wrote about. As I did, I became hopeful again and decided that he had taken random events and grouped them together to form a profile of me as a "potentially dangerous person" to support his recommendation of sending me away, in spite of my young age, to a maximum security prison populated by hardened criminals. I thought that no, he was the sadistic one.

His report called me "abusive of smaller boys." I was probably the smallest boy there; maybe I had gotten into a fistfight. Certainly that is common enough of small children. He went on to say that I'd bitten other boys. True enough. Sometimes those of us who were too small to be included in organized recreational games were left to create our own form of play, and one of these was biting contests, held to see who could bite the hardest. I remember biting a boy so hard that he ran to the master. I was also charged with "stabbing [boys] with a knife or fork." Obviously we weren't permitted to carry knives and forks around, so the incident he was referring to must have involved a game we played in the dining hall. One boy would try to sneak his hand up to another boy's tray to snatch away his dessert. The object was to prevent this by "repulsing" the attacker with a waiting fork. Once I managed to catch a boy, and he yelled in pain, drawing the attention of the master. It was a crazy game, but then one had to remember the kind of place we were in. If children are said to channel aggressive behavior into paramilitary game playing like King of the Mountain, one has to consider that we didn't have water guns or expensive cap pistols at our disposal.

The superintendent's report also suggested that I instigated "small riots," as if I were some thirteen-year-old guerrilla leader, stalking around the institution, forming strike groups. Could he have been thinking of the incident where I threw my pencil at Mr. Renner and stood up to him while the boys cheered? Small riot, indeed. He accused me of using coarse and vulgar language. These were the lessons of my masters; they were my only means of self-defense. It was true; my bedtime stories were of blood and death. Constantly. I was frightened, constantly frightened, especially while at Lyman, with its close proximity to woods where I thought monsters lurked. I was, after all, only a child.

I continued to work on the story and got in touch with Mark Zanger, whom I had not seen or talked to since I'd left Boston in 1976. I showed him what I had—almost 500 pages—and he agreed to come by once or twice a week to help edit it down. I quit my job in order to devote all my time to writing. To support myself I enrolled under assumed names in several book clubs and resold the free books I received as a new subscriber. My needs were simple, and I got by on a couple of dollars a day. I could always scrounge a meal or a couple of bucks from my old friends in the Greek community, and sometimes I would ask Mark for money, and he never refused me. If I was short on rent money, Phillip told me I could pay him at some future date.

In February 1978 a terrible blizzard swept Boston. It snowed for three days and nights, and when it was over, we were trapped in our house because the snow was waist deep. During the day Phillip and his girl friend and I read or watched TV or talked. During one of those conversations I talked to them about my book. Phillip asked me if I had ever been diagnosed as a hyperactive child. He said that his son from a previous marriage was hyperactive and that he had a book on the subject that might offer insight into my childhood behavior patterns. The book was Paul Wender's *The Hyperactive Child*. That evening I began to read it, and what I discovered stunned me.

Hyperactivity, according to Wender, is a chemical deficiency in the brain that results, among other things, in impulsivity, attention difficulties, distractibility, immaturity, perceptual and learning difficulties, and sudden and dramatic mood changes. While all children have these characteristics, what distinguishes the hyperactive child is the intensity, the persistence, and the patterning of these symptoms.

Wender's book explained that from the beginning, hyperactive children exhibit feeding problems and suffer from colic; that they are destructive, but not intentionally so; that they incessantly are in motion, fidgeting, drumming their fingers, shuffling their feet. They act on spur-of-the-moment impulses, tend to wander away from home, and are relatively fearless and, as a result of their daring, constantly end up with cuts and bruises. The hyperactive child also demonstrates an uneven intellectual development, which often produces difficulties in school adjustment. Parents and teachers describe hyperactive children as stubborn, unpredictable, disobedient, sassy, and not caring; punishment just rolls off their backs. Consequently, in the home the hyperactive child's siblings are favored because they are "good" children and he is "bad." Severe and harsh discipline can produce additional problems because the child may feel resentful but has only limited ways of fighting back. He may risk further punishment, dig in his heels, and be negative, ornery, or stubborn, and he may attempt to strike back by doing annoying or hurtful things in other areas. Finally Wender went on to note that studies have indicated that when animals have received powerful punishments—such as electric shock—they are apt to show erratic and neurotic behavior. And so Wender concluded by cautioning that punishments that may prove effective in preventing offensive hyperactive behavior in the short run may permanently produce even more disturbing behavior than that which was prevented.

As I read through the book, I thought he was talking about me. It was as if I were reading my own records, my own life story. I felt that I had found the final piece of a strangely shaped puzzle. I thought that now I could become like outside people, able to work and love and live a normal life. But there was a hitch to my new-found sense of well-being. Wender said that he believed that children eventually outgrow hyperactivity but that it was hard to know what might have happened to someone who had been diagnosed as hyperactive in the early fifties and then subjected to hard punishment. This threw me; the words *grows out of it* echoed around and around in my head. When I next saw Mark, I told him about my discovery but added that I thought I was still hyperactive. He told me that he was skeptical about the whole thing and that he didn't see my problems as being anything nearly so simple as hyperactivity.

235

I was disheartened now and fell into despair. How could I ever hope to change my life if I couldn't find out what it was that had made me such a mess in the first place? I was sure that I must suffer from some kind of chemical imbalance. I was sure of it. What else could explain the reason for my mixed-up chaotic existence? I wanted to pursue this line of reasoning, but my lack of medical, emotional, and intellectual resources made it impossible. I decided that I would always be a fuck-up, and therefore I must get out my story in hopes that it might at least prevent others from ending up as I had. And so through it all I kept writing.

I missed and needed Mieko so much. She had promised to write from Japan as soon as she arrived. Finally I got a letter from her. She told me how happy she was to be back home, and she gave me her address and telephone number. Each Sunday evening, when the rates were low, I would go to the Boston telephone directory and pick out a doctor's name and office phone. I would then call his home number to make sure there was no one there, and then I would call Japan, charging it to the doctor's office number. Mieko and I would talk for a half hour or more. We would tell each other about the week's events and sign off with words of love.

In April Mieko sent me a card and a kimono-style jacket for my thirtieth birthday. I was starting to feel old and decided that I had to get the book finished. But I knew that if I were ever to get it done, I would need a quiet place in which to work and to be free of financial worries. With about two-thirds of the story completed I brought the manuscript to a Boston publisher's officer, where an editor looked at it and agreed it was an important story, but he also felt that I showed no talent as a writer. At first I tried not to let his reaction discourage me, but it did. I stopped writing and started drinking again. In the summer of 1978 Phillip asked me to move out because I was not paying the rent. I wanted to say, "Help me, Phillip; I can't help myself." I thought that if he knew I had no other place to stay, he might change his mind.

But I was too ashamed to say anything, and I just didn't care anymore.

That evening I slept on top of a cardboard box under a clump of bushes very near Phillip's house. During the day I sat in the Boston Garden and watched the ducks. I just sat there hour after hour; I was so tired from my life. I no longer wondered what my problems were; all I thought about was scraping together the money to buy the few beers that would get me drunk enough to go sleep under the bushes. The bushes were in a pretty dangerous section of town, but I didn't care if I lived or died.

I was starting to look pretty grungy: My hair was long and unkempt; I was unshaven; my clothes were dirty and smelled of urine from the nights I wet my cardboard bed. Each morning I would crawl from my place in the woods and travel to McDonald's, where I used the bathroom to try to clean up as best I could. If I had extra change, I would buy a coffee. I was sure I looked worse than I wanted to believe I did; I could tell by the way others looked at me. At first I was embarrassed, but I quickly enough got used to it. I justified my life-style to myself thinking that I deserved not to care anymore; the world seemed so dark and desperate. Yet during it all I still wanted to finish my story. I kept in touch with Mark but never let on to him what was going on. I was afraid he would reject me, and I didn't want to lose him as I'd lost everyone else. I didn't call Catharine either, although I had called her again when I had first returned to Boston. But I thought her life was already complicated enough, and I also did not want a woman to see me this way. Somehow, after a time, when I was sick of being a bum, the old indomitable spirit pushed through, and I decided to find a job.

I managed to get my clothes cleaned and my face shaved. I walked into a deli and was hired on the spot. I knew the deli business, and I was a hard worker, yet every day, when I came to work, I would be fighting a hangover that would kill ten men. Although the deli owners were paying me well, I still got drunk each night after work and slept under the bushes. Sometimes I would wet myself and would have to sneak into work through the back door where I changed into my dry cook's whites. Mostly I was glad to have a job simply because it gave me a place to go each day rather than walk aimlessly around or sit in the Boston Garden all day. I wanted to get a room, but for some reason the idea frightened me. But I held my job for a couple of months and did so well that one Saturday night the owners asked me to manage the store. I was instructed to put the night's receipts into a bag and hide it. When I closed up that night, I counted out $800 and hid the satchel, as they had asked.

It was about 3:00 A.M. when the last of the Saturday crew departed, and I turned on the jukebox and sat down for a well-deserved rest; it had been a busy night. Since the restaurant would be closed on Sunday, I planned to sleep on the floor and get a good night's sleep. I went into the kitchen looking for a nightcap. I found almost a full gallon of burgundy. I drank the whole thing and two days later found myself in New York with Saturday's receipts, or what was left of them. I was sick. How could I have done such a thing? I had never wanted to commit another crime, and especially I didn't want to do this to the men who had hired me and had trusted me. I had also heard they were dangerous. I decided that I could not go back to Boston and that I would get a job and pay them back.

I took a room in a hotel on West Fifty-first Street between Eighth and Ninth avenues and found a job in a nearby deli. I worked an eight-hour six-day shift and took home about $250 a week. I joined a health club, and each night after work I went to the spa to exercise and take a whirlpool bath. I cut my drinking down to one can of beer before bedtime. In the evenings, after I came back from the spa, I read. And so after a while I was feeling healthy and reasonably happy again. I called Mieko in Japan and Catharine in Boston to let them know where I was.

Around the first part of November my bad ear became infected again. I went to Manhattan Eye and Ear Hospital to have it checked. The doctors told me I would need an operation. My

238

first instinct was to cry. I had no insurance and no money to pay for an operation. I called Mieko in Japan and told her about my problem, and in spite of my protests, she sent me $1,000. I had saved $600 of my own, but the total gave me only half of what I would need for the operation. I began each week to bank the absolute maximum I could. I had been saving money to return to the owners of the restaurant in Boston; now they would have to wait.

I allowed myself no unnecessary expenses, with one exception. January 1 was Catharine's twenty-third birthday. A few weeks before, I had sent her a card and a $20 bill and had scribbled her a note that I would call her soon to wish her a happy birthday. When the operator placed the call, Catharine's brother answered. The operator asked to speak with Catharine, but her brother replied that Catharine was dead. She had committed suicide.

I knew she had tried to kill herself at Thanksgiving and had phoned her mother to ask her to get Catharine some help. But her mother had told me to mind my own business and to leave her daughter alone. Now Catharine's brother told me that the family held me responsible and that detectives were investigating her death. I fell to the floor and lay there, shaking, for a long time. I cried for Catharine, but I knew I had had nothing to do with her death; if anything, I had helped keep her alive longer. But I had the outstanding default warrant on me in Cambridge, and I feared that before long, I would be found. This snapped me back into reality. I had to get out of Dodge again, and fast. The next morning I went to the bank and withdrew my savings.

My first thought, as it had been once before, was to run to California and to become an actor. Then I decided I would go to Mexico to write a novel, or maybe I would join the French foreign legion. Indecisive, I tried to do both: I went to the Mexican Consulate and got a six-month visa, and I sent to France for an application to join the legion. In the meantime, I shuttled back and forth to Boston. In Boston I sat and drank and contemplated committing suicide over Catharine's grave; I thought that would prove to her family that I'd had nothing to do with her suicide and show them how much I'd cared for her. In the end I didn't have the guts to do it. Each day a kaleidoscope of thoughts and feelings crowded my mind. I kept imagining myself in the legion, in Mexico, in California. My head spun like a calliope playing the same song again and again. That winter and spring I drank myself into oblivion in Boston, now back in New York, then in Boston again, and in New York once more. Finally, as summer came, the shock of Catharine's death at last receded, and I resolved to succeed in her memory. I returned to Boston, got myself cleaned up, took a job and found a room with a nice family.

Living in a real home in a good suburb did wonders for my head. I even rented a clarinet and started to study again. On my days off work I swam in a nearby lake and befriended a couple of college girls who resided in the neighborhood. I even began to put away some money each week to pay back my former employers. I had stopped drinking and by October felt I had obtained at least the semblance of control over my life.

While at work one day I looked up from the counter to see my former bosses, the ones whose receipts I'd stolen, coming toward me. I ran out the back door as fast as I could. I was running so fast that my pants unbuttoned and fell down to my ankles. After getting them up, I dived into the bushes and hid until it was dark. I realized that I would have to get out of my room and that I would again be without a job. As soon as I thought the coast was clear, I made it to a telephone and called one of the girls I'd met at the lake, and she agreed to let me stay with her until I could get settled again.

I decided that the Massachusetts Rehabilitation Commission was the best place to begin, and again it agreed to consider me for client status. But my ear began to act up once more, this time more seriously than ever. My counselor agreed to make an appointment for me at the ear clinic of a local hospital and told me that the commission would supplement whatever I could contribute toward the cost of my operation and hospital stay. I was grateful for the help but depressed about my whole situation just the same. I was now thirty-one and I didn't even have the basic necessities of life. It also seemed that if it wasn't one thing that was wrong in my life, it was another. Nevertheless, I was operated on in November; for the moment, at least, one problem was licked.

On December 7, 1979, to celebrate my hospital release, I borrowed the car belonging to the girl I was staying with, went drinking, blacked out, and hit a tree. I awoke in the emergency room. My kneecap was shattered, my ribs were cracked, and most of my teeth were gone. I was told that I had been lucky; I had been pronounced dead at the scene. But I knew I was just too damn stubborn to die.

I was operated on that afternoon, and in the evening my whole family, my father included, came to see me; they had heard about the accident on the morning news. My father looked well. I had not seen him in ten or twelve years, and I was glad to hear that he had not taken a drink in a few years. My sister Cheryl also came; she was married now, and invited me to stay with her in her home north of Boston while I convalesced. While I was there, she and her husband were very kind to me. On weekends my father stayed over as he always did. Cheryl and my mother were still estranged, and Cheryl seemed to truly like having our father around.

It was really strange to be in such close proximity to a man for whom I'd felt only contempt and loathing for so long. He and I would get into fits of talking which would go on for hours. I would ask him questions about his family; I thought if I could understand him better and find some reason to justify his beatings of me and his abandoning of the family, then perhaps I could find a way to forgive him. We talked about all the things I imagined fathers and sons discussing: women, the Second World War, and, in our case our greatest common bond, our alcoholism. He told me he had many regrets, and I could understand only too well how drinking could drive men to do things they were ashamed of. In March 1980 my cast was removed, and I had to go through the painful process of breaking the adhesions that prevented me from bending my leg even a little bit. With my convalescence over I returned to Boston, and before long I was in trouble again.

I was without a job or a home. My first night back in town I walked the streets until morning. I realized I had better do something because I might be picked up by the police if they found me wandering the streets at night. I didn't know what to do and called Mark, who gave me some cash. That day I sat in the Boston Garden and watched the ducks until darkness fell, still wondering how I could keep off the streets. Then it occurred to me that the porno theaters in the Combat Zone stayed open all night and that I could go there.

I looked for the theater with the cheapest admission price I could find—$2.50. My first night I couldn't sleep at all because I was so frightened by the strange-looking characters sitting around me—drunks and fags, harmless enough maybe, but they kept approaching me. I would give them dirty looks, and they would retreat. The theater was also small, and a foul odor pervaded it. The seats were broken, and the films being shown disgusted me. But I was off the streets, and I was taking care of myself.

I left the theater as soon as it was light. I purchased a newspaper, thumbed the help wanted section, and found a job as a prep cook in a Harvard Square restaurant for $40 a day cash. Each night after work I went to a local bar, where I sat alone and drank expensive pints of black and tans, reserving just enough money to buy myself into the theater when the bar closed.

Sometimes I would spend all my money and flop down for the night in an unlocked car. I got myself a good-size nylon bag and a couple of inexpensive changes of clothing, some pencils, legal pads, and a battery-operated pencil sharpener. I thought I was going to try writing again. Each morning I came from the theater and went to work. Each morning I arrived with a hangover that could have killed five men, yet I worked harder than anyone. I was functioning on anxiety. Although I could have certainly saved the money to get a room for myself, I had a terrible block about doing so. Instead, I grabbed four or so hours of sleep a night at the theater, spread out across four seats, often being awakened by the armrests sticking into my ribs and by the moans and groans of the actors on the screen. I told myself that I loved this life, or at least I tried to pretend that I did. When I lost my job after only a few days, I decided that whereas once I had been sad not to have a place to go, now I was glad to be free of regular hours and obligations, and I knew that I always had a home at the theater.

But the fact is that I knew it was no life. The theater was cold, and I would often wet my bed of seats. When the theater closed at 5:00 A.M., I would be kicked out and have to sit in the dark, cold and shivering and shaking, until the underground station opened at 6:00. I would resolve that morning to get off the streets for good, but by nighttime I had had enough to drink to make me forget that resolution. I was also now getting sick to my stomach from drinking so much and would throw it all up with such force that the pressure would cause my nose to bleed and give me painful stomach cramps, which would last for days. I didn't know if I was right side up or upside down. If it were not for the cool of the evening defining my body heat, I would not have known where I was. One night I remember banging my head repeatedly against a hard wall. When I awoke, I was lying in a pool of my own urine, and my clothes were completely torn and shredded. I had been drinking steadily for five or more years. I finally knew it was time to get help; I was trying to kill myself. In the spring of 1980 I called a detoxification center outside Boston and made arrangements to check myself in.

I decided to take a taxi to the center because I didn't want to risk not making the bus connections I would need to make if I were to get there before two to claim my bed. I directed the driver to Trapelo Road, although I was hesitant to tell him that I wanted him to drop me at the detox center. But I had no other choice. He looked at me through the rear-view mirror and told me he had watched his father drink himself to death at the age of forty-five. I closed my eyes and leaned back into the seat. I knew I was doing the right thing.

The car made its way through the twisting road and turned onto the drive of a lovely wooded estate. The first building I saw was a large Tudor cottage. I was impressed. It seemed innocuous enough. But the driver passed right by it, the car ascending a steep grade before coming to a stop in front of a huge brick building from the Victorian period. I blinked. It looked like an institution. I wanted to tell the driver that I was only sightseeing and to turn around. But my hangover did not allow me to.

I paid the driver, stepped inside the main entrance, and presented myself at the nurses' station. I gave them the assumed name I had used when I had phoned that morning. I was shown into an office and took a seat across from a man seated at a large desk. He asked me how I felt, and when I said I was fine, he sighed and began to ask me for my medical history and Social Security number. I gave him fictitious information. When he finished filling out my admittance form, he told me that I would be treated over the next five days and then released. The rest would be up to me. He went on to say that he was glad I had decided to come and that he himself hadn't had a drink in the eight years since he had lost the sight in his left eye after drinking a bottle of skin bracer, the thought of which made me flinch. He left the room, and I stared out the window, past the lush green foliage of the grounds to the city in the distance. For the first time in I didn't know how long I felt calm, almost passive.

A nurse entered and asked me if this was my first time in a detox. I answered that it was, and she proceeded to give me a routine physical examination. When she was done, she gave me a pair of pajamas that didn't match and a bathrobe. I would wear these for the rest of my stay. My street clothes would be locked away with whatever money I had on me—$20, all I had in the world; they didn't want me getting itchy feet, she said.

After living on the streets for the last couple of months, averaging only a few hours of sleep a night, I was exhausted and looked forward to being cared for for the next few days. I was given a shot of multivitamins and taken to my bed in a small eight-bed dormitory. Unlike most of the dorms I'd seen, this one had brightly colored bedspreads and nice curtains on the windows. I felt relieved. Although this was a state institution, it seemed as though my fears that it would be sterile and cheerless were unwarranted. I lay down on the bed. Tears streaked my face. I thought of my father, my years at the IJG, the street years as an alcoholic and derelict. This time I swore I would stop drinking and make myself strong again. I drifted off into a sound sleep.

When I awoke, a man was sitting on a bed on the far side of the room. He introduced himself as Ted and with considerable effort made his way over to the bed next to me. He was shaking and mumbling bits and pieces of sentences. I couldn't understand a thing he said, but after a while his conversation became more lucid. I asked him what had made him decide to come in. He explained, "I was just beat." He had tried and failed to beat drinking twice in the past two weeks. The last time he had lasted three days at the center and was determined to stick it out this time. I wished him luck.

When an attendant called us for dinner, I got up and headed down the corridor. From a distance I could see a group of ten or so men of varying ages. I felt my body tighten. I felt that I was back in prison again, the new kid in the cellblock, and that I had to try to give them the impression I was tough and not to be messed with. As I drew closer, I realized that none of them was much interested in checking me out and that I wasn't back in prison but in detox. The food line was comprised of broken-looking men whose bodies shook like jackhammers. I took up my place on the line.

I found a seat in the small dining room. The food, although institutional, was hot and not half-bad. I looked around me. There was little conversation; it seemed that it was more than enough for the men simply to move the food from their plates to their mouths. After the meal I wasn't sure what to do; in all my years of institutions my every move had been planned and watched. But here we weren't restricted in any way and were permitted to move freely about the building. I got up from the table, cleaned my dish, and sat back down for coffee and a smoke. A young man about my age sat down and started to talk. Like me, he had made the decision to come because he was sick and threw up everything he took in. His hands were shaking so violently he could barely hold the glass of juice he was drinking. I began to think that maybe I wasn't as bad off as I'd thought.

When I returned to my room, the nurse entered and took my pulse. Withdrawal was starting to set in, and my pulse was therefore faster than it had been when I entered. She told me I would be receiving my medication shortly. What medication? I asked. Librium, she said. I remembered Angela and became panicked. I protested that I didn't need any drugs, that I didn't want to substitute one habit for another. The nurse and I began to argue; fortunately, before anything could be decided, I was called downstairs to attend my first AA meeting.

I went into the meeting room and took a seat. I felt cynical about what I knew was about to happen: A group of complacent strangers would troop in and begin to tell their life stories. What did happen surprised me. Three men and a woman entered. They were well dressed and healthy-looking. Each story was told from the heart, with animation and incredible honesty. I felt ashamed. I had always thought of drunks as men like my father. But here were good and decent people—outside people—who were just as afraid of life as I was. Listening to them, I understood that like them, I drank to relieve my anxiety, an anxiety borne of some twenty-four years of being bounced around like a Ping-Pong ball. When the meeting adjourned at eight-thirty, I returned to my room and decided I would speak my piece when my turn came at the next meeting.

The night nurse came in to check my vital signs and told me that I would have to begin taking my Librium the following day. I became depressed and agitated all over again. I grabbed the sides of the bed and pressed them tightly. I got up and roamed the halls and finally settled down to watch a movie in the TV room. I looked right past the screen. I got up and paced, trying to shrug off the withdrawal symptoms, which now returned with even more severity. I felt afraid. I headed down to the chow room to pour myself some juice to calm me down. A couple of men were in there playing cards and drinking coffee. I took a seat next to a guy who told me his name was George. He asked me if this was my first experience in detox. I answered it was. The other men snickered, and George said it wouldn't be the last. He himself had been in thirty-eight times previously, and one of the other men reported that this was his fifty-sixth time. I felt like a rookie.

For the next couple of hours I roamed the halls again before I finally returned to the TV room. It was empty except for one young man who couldn't have been more than twenty. We started to talk. His name was Peter. He told me he had started drinking at the age of twelve and had survived five pancreas attacks and that his pancreas had disintegrated. He looked seriously ill indeed. His color was pallid, his reflexes were shot, and he could barely steady himself. He told me he knew if he drank again, he would be dead. He had been to many hospitals and many detox centers and had only one more day left in this one. I asked him, "What will you do?"

"I don't know," he replied, and turned away.

The next morning after breakfast I went back to the TV room to look for Peter. I was told he had left before breakfast. I bowed my head. The nurse entered a few moments later, pulling a medicine cart behind her. She started to make her way around the room, giving each of us our prescribed doses. When she handed me mine, I refused to take it. She told me that if I didn't swallow the little green and white pill right then and there, I would have to leave the hospital. I didn't argue. I got up and went to the nurses' station to sign for my belongings. I would get an administrative discharge: I had refused medication and therefore had refused treatment.

I called a cab. When we reached the highway off the grounds,

I told the driver I had just left detox. He told me he had gotten out only a few weeks before.

As soon as I arrived back in Boston, I went straight to a liquor store and headed for the Boston Garden.

Epilogue

I REMAINED ON THE STREETS for the next three years. I had transcended the need for food and shelter. I lived only in the reality or unreality of the moment. The Gardens were now my home and my asylum. I was now pretty much detached from the world around me and from trying to integrate myself into society. Whereas outside people were preoccupied with the conscious world of building their futures, I was preoccupied with the subconscious world of the past and trying to destroy it. Between alternating thoughts of wanting to keep trying and of hanging myself, with manuscript in hand, I tried to puzzle it all out.

I realized that I still had a State Boy mentality and was locked into Bridgewater. I felt like an overly dependent child who didn't deserve whatever good that he got and who deserved all the bad that came his way. Scrounging around the streets had been most debilitating, yet it was so deeply ingrained in me that I didn't know what to do about it. Rather than deal with these new insights, I allowed myself to dwell at the edge of madness, always wanting to step over the edge but frightened at the prospect. Maybe this is what the state meant in the records, about my imagination, nightmares, my screaming in the night. Was I somehow inclined toward insanity and to a tormented life? Had I merely been fighting insanity all my life? Was my stubbornness the refusal to give in to some demon that was trying to push me into suicide?

I turned these kinds of questions over and over in my mind until I was riddled with such a desperate anxiety that I felt too exhausted to feel anything at all and too weak to give a fuck about my imaginings anymore.

As I wandered around, there were moments when each step seemed a whole lifetime. I was no longer confused about past events; my confusion was centered in my present and future. Knowing what had happened did not erase any of the problems I had in day to day living. I knew I needed psychiatric therapy and felt that I was ready for it. I lasted three sessions. The doctor at the free state clinic who saw me told me he suspected temporal lobe epilepsy, a rare form of epilepsy in which the brain falls into seizures so mild and temporary that the victim isn't even aware of them. Usually the victim thinks only that something has interfered with his concentration. I did go to a library and read up on the affliction but decided that since I remembered everything I was thinking, this couldn't be what was wrong with me. I didn't go to any more sessions.

Another reason that I did not go back to the state clinic was my intense hatred of the state and its institutions. I didn't really know to what degree the state was responsible for my present condition, but I did feel that it owed me the education it had denied me and that without one I would always feel degraded and be unable to take care of myself. I approached the American Civil Liberties Union with the idea of suing the state. The lawyer with whom I spoke believed that the statute of limitations had run out. Like the young man in Colorado who had sued his parents for being detrimental parents and had won, I suggested that maybe I could sue the state for being bad parents. He said that I might try pursuing this with a private lawyer since the ACLU handled only cases that would affect national laws. I tried to argue that if I sued Massachusetts and won, then perhaps other states would have to be accountable for their preadolescent and teen-age prisoners. Nonetheless, the lawyer continued to stress that he thought the statute had run out and that he was not really interested in pursuing it any further. I thought, How could a statute run out on a person's life, especially in a country where education made the difference between success and failure? Finally I gave up my idea that the state had to be made accountable for its crimes. I judged Massachusetts "delinquent by reason of indifference."

Meanwhile, I trudged the streets and in the evenings went to a men's shelter. My greatest fear of all had become a reality: I had joined my father and all the thousands of other broken men. At the shelter I saw men I knew would probably not recover. At least I was still young and reasonably healthy; these men could not survive a week on the streets, and I had survived a lifetime of it. During this time two things kept me from going completely under: Mark Zanger and the stubbornness that had first sent me away and continued to get me by. I finally got control of the drinking, and so, clear-headed for the first time in years, I armed myself with pencils and paper and sat in fast-food restaurants from morning till night and rewrote my entire manuscript. And now it is done.

It is no longer a crime to be a Stubborn Child in the Commonwealth of Massachusetts. The law changed in 1974 when the classifications of Stubborn Child, Runaway, Truant, and Habitual School Offender were stricken from the Delinquent Child statutes. Today these categories of children fall under the statutory protection of C.H.I.N.S.—Children in Need of Services, a civil law administered by the State Department of Social Services. It provides for home, foster, or group care, and offers a variety of services such as therapy and counseling. It maintains no lock-up facilities. On the other hand, adolescents who commit crimes continue to fall under the legal jurisdiction of the Department of Youth Service, which still maintains a detention center at Roslindale for youths awaiting trials. The Lyman School for Boys remains closed, as it and the state's three other training schools have been since the early 1970s. The Institute for Juvenile Guidance at Bridgewater ceased operating in 1970. From what information I have been able to gather, there are no longer any facilities in Massachussetts for the warehousing of adolescents.

Angela is sometimes well and sometimes not. I have had no contact with her for a number of years. It's best, I think. My daughter is fine as far as I know, as are my siblings, who are all married and have children of their own. My father has been sober for more than six years. I have heard that Bill, who is long divorced from my mother, is alone and physically sick because of all the years of booze and he is deteriorating rapidly. I am still in touch with Max Dinova. After suffering a mild heart attack recently, he is up and about again. Mieko is happily married and has a young son, as I learned from her roommate, Mary Alice, who is also well. I imagine that Catharine's family still thinks I am responsible for her suicide; I hope they don't, for not a day goes by that I do not grieve for her or have dreams about her that torment me.

A special word about my mother. During the years I lived on the streets, she and I re-established ties. I told her about this book as it evolved. She believed in my project and gave me emotional and financial support for most of that time, often when she herself could not afford it. I often exasperated her beyond endurance, yet she was there for me, every day, and her help and caring were incalculable. After she and Bill split up she took up with a man who had been her first love in high school but with whom she had been forced to break up because of religious differences. Today she holds an important position with a good company and is a highly respected member of the community. I wish her all the happiness she is due.

As for the other characters in the story, I am not in touch with them and am unaware of their lives today.

As for me, I try to see the world as a bowl of fruit and a vase of flowers. Much of my self-destructive impulses have left me. And although I do not have a sense of well-being, I can imagine having it. I still have a curiosity and reverence for life which I will never compromise, even though there were those who tried to compromise it for me. With the exception of my mother, I am still estranged from my family, although I do try to remember the good times when we all were together and untainted by the savagery of our circumstances. I forgive them, although it is difficult to feel genuine love for them. But I tell myself that they are still, as we all are, Children of the Universe, and that is where my love—the only love I am capable of—lies.

Sometime during these past few years I became convinced that one did not necessarily "outgrow" hyperactivity. I wrote a letter to Dr. Wender and suggested the same. He wrote back and said that in the years since *The Hyperactive Child* had first been published, he had revised his original assessment and now agreed that children did not necessarily outgrow hyperactivity and that in fact, it could continue into adult life. In the year 1981 or 1982 I had the occasion actually to sit and talk with him and with one of his colleagues. We met at a mental health center in Rhode Island. We spoke for a very short time, but I came away with the impression that he was not convinced that I was hyperactive. On the bus back to Boston I thought about our conversation of what does or does not constitute a hyperactive child or adult, and in my gut I was certain I knew exactly what I was talking about. I questioned what, even with his vast study and knowledge, he really knew and suspected that he was like a celibate priest trying to explain intercourse to me.

As far as I can tell, I am still hyperactive and definitely still a Stubborn Child.